Rudow's Guide to
Fishing the Chesapeake

Tidewater Publishers
A Division of Schiffer Publishing, Ltd.

4880 Lower Valley Road, Atglen, Pennsylvania 19310

RUDOW'S GUIDE TO

Fishing
the
Chesapeake

Lenny Rudow

Tidewater Publishers

A Division of Schiffer Publishing, Ltd.
4880 Lower Valley Road, Atglen, PA 19310

All maps created with PC Planner + [©C-MAP 2000–2004]

Library of Congress Cataloging-in-Publication Data

Rudow, Lenny.
    Rudow's guide to fishing the Chesapeake / Lenny Rudow.— 1st ed.
        p. cm.
    ISBN-13: 978-0-87033-568-6
    1. Fishing—Chesapeake Bay (Md. and Va.) 2. Fishing—Chesapeake Bay (Md. and Va.)—Guidebooks. 3. Chesapeake Bay (Md. and Va.)—Guidebooks. I. Title.
    SH464.C47R83 2005
    799.1'09163'47—dc22
                                        2005013442

Schiffer Books are available at special discounts for bulk purchases for sales promotions or premiums. Special editions, including personalized covers, corporate imprints, and excerpts can be created in large quantities for special needs. For more information contact the publisher:

Published by Schiffer Publishing Ltd.
4880 Lower Valley Road
Atglen, PA 19310
Phone: (610) 593-1777; Fax: (610) 593-2002
E-mail: Info@schifferbooks.com

For the largest selection of fine reference books on this and related subjects, please visit our web site at **www.schifferbooks.com**
We are always looking for people to write

books on new and related subjects. If you have an idea for a book please contact us at the above address.

This book may be purchased from the publisher.
Include $5.00 for shipping.
Please try your bookstore first.
You may write for a free catalog.

In Europe, Schiffer books are distributed by
Bushwood Books
6 Marksbury Ave.
Kew Gardens
Surrey TW9 4JF England
Phone: 44 (0) 20 8392-8585; Fax: 44 (0) 20 8392-9876
E-mail: info@bushwoodbooks.co.uk
Website: www.bushwoodbooks.co.uk

Manufactured in the United States of America
First edition, 2005

To Dear Ol' Dad, who got me started fishing

CONTENTS

Part II: Tactics and Tackle

Part III: Chesapeake Bay and Tributary Sportfish

INTRODUCTION

Do you want to catch more fish? Of course—and if you fish in the Chesapeake Bay or its tributaries, this book is the best tool you'll find to help meet that goal. The bay offers you one of the world's most diverse sportfishing opportunities, and we'll cover it all on these pages. We'll cast for trophy stripers on the Susquehanna Flats, jig for sea trout in the shadow of the Bay Bridges, and fight cobia in the briny waters of Virginia where the Chesapeake mixes with the Atlantic Ocean. We'll become better fishermen as we try to get into the heads of our quarry; exploit daily tidal cycles; and use marine electronics, computers, and time-tested techniques to accomplish our common goal: catching more fish. And while we're at it, let's catch bigger ones too, okay?

In the first part of *Rudow's Guide to Fishing the Chesapeake,* we divide the Chesapeake into three regions and detail over 550 hot spots—some well known, some nameless secrets. All channel markers and buoys that mark good spots are identified, and hot spot names and identifying numbers are labeled on the charts, so you'll know exactly where to go. Every tributary is examined in detail from its headwaters to its junction with the Bay. Special sections on launch ramps and hot spots for shore bound anglers are also included for each area. The second part details the main techniques and tactics you need to know to effectively fish the Bay. And in the third part we'll take an in-depth look at each specific Chesapeake Bay sportfish.

Fishing on the Bay since I was old enough to walk, writing hundreds of how-to/where-to articles on fishing for books and magazines, and working on the Chesapeake's waters have given me a good deal of insight into the Bay's fisheries. Of course no one man can be an expert at everything, and there are many gaps in my personal knowledge. Whenever I encountered one during the writing of this book, I leaned (sometimes hard!) on friends of mine who are charter boat captains, guides, or local angling experts. In researching this book I examined my own detailed catch logs going back over a decade, over 400 fishing reports from the media, Internet databases, Maryland and Virginia records and reports, and spoke with several dozen professional captains, mates, and local experts. My goal was to acquire every tidbit of fishing information possible to make this book more comprehensive than any other fishing resource available for any body of water. But without question, it was jawboning with inveterate fishermen that provided the most detailed information. Several captains were kind enough to share their own hard-won knowledge with me to make this book as valuable as possible to you sport anglers. Many thanks to them all. Most importantly, I want to thank those that I've fished with and learned from on a first-hand basis: Captains Ed Darwin, Sonny Forrest, Mike Murphy, Ted Ohler, Ritchie Gaines, the captains of Shiebles Fishing Center, and Harrison's. Special thanks also go out to John Page Williams of the Chesapeake Bay Foundation, Bud Hien of Fishbone's Bait and Tackle and Joe Bruce of The Fisherman's Edge. Other anglers who provided hot spots and tips include David, Steven, and Bill Rudow; Rocky Calia; Jack Saum; Brian Lowery; Matt Boomer; John Unkart; and Scott Hyers. Now— ready to become a better Bay angler? Great, let's go!

How to Use the Regional Guide

As the Bay is addressed in separate sections (upper, middle, and lower) and each section is divided into subsections (Western Shore rivers, Eastern Shore rivers, and main-stem Bay) so are the charts. Each particular hot spot is followed by a designation developed from the section and subsections' initials. For example, consider a spot mentioned in the Patuxent River. It will be identified by "M" for middle Bay, then "R" for river, then a "W" for Western Shore, then a number particular to that hot spot. Thus, if there was a dip along the channel edge that is named "The Dip," and if it were the ninth hot spot specified in the middle bay Western Shore rivers section, it would appear as follows in the text: The Dip (MRW9). The corresponding chart showing this hot spot would be labeled with MRW9, and an arrow pointing to the specific hot spot. When charted buoys or channel markers are used to identify hot spots, the marker number may be used in place of this numeric designation.

You'll notice that on the charts, numeric designations for specific hot spots do not always seem to be organized in an orderly fashion. Hot Spot number 10 could be nearest to hot spot number 20, for example. Because the Bay is shaped so erratically, with tributaries, bars, and channels going in every possible direction, it was impossible to arrange the numbers corresponding to each hot spot in a way that they appear to be well-organized. Care has been taken, however, to arrange them as logically as possible.

You should also note that charts in this book do not include some information that would be found on National Oceanic and Atmospheric Administration (NOAA) charts. Bottom type, light ranges, and latitude/longitudes are not present, for example. This information has been omitted for clarity's sake to make the charts readable. In many areas depth soundings are also not present and on all of the charts, certain depth soundings had to be eliminated to make hotspot marks legible. The best way to use these charts is to have a full detail chart book at hand as you're planning a trip to a particular section of the bay, so you can match up the charts in the book with the full-size chart. ADC's Chesapeake Bay Chartbook (www.adcmap.com, 800/ADC-MAPS) is good and it's the one most commonly found in stores throughout the area, but for even better detail get Maptech's Region 4 Chart Kit, Chesapeake and Delaware Bays (www.maptech.com, 888/839-5551). And remember, the charts included in this book are not intended to be used for navigation. Many thanks to C-Map/USA for allowing the reproduction of their charts in this book.

Part 1:
Chesapeake Bay
Regional Guide

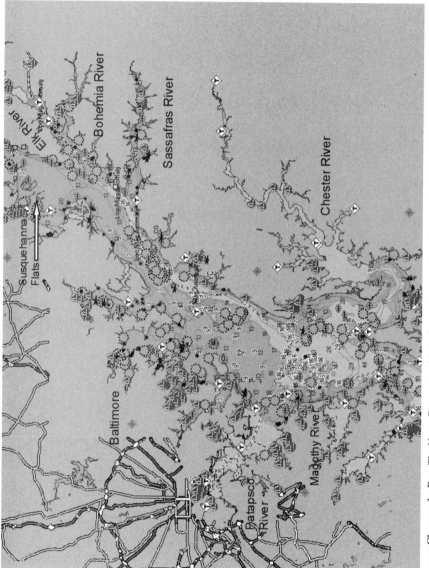

Upper Chesapeake Bay. The Upper Bay starts with the Susquehanna and runs down to the Chesapeake Bay Bridges.

THE UPPER CHESAPEAKE BAY

Where can you cast spinnerbaits for largemouth bass, drift eels for striped bass, and cast spoons to breaking bluefish, all in the same day? The upper Chesapeake provides all these opportunities—and many more. In some areas the northern Bay is like a lake, and in others, seems to be an ocean. In both cases, it merits the attention of a wide variety of anglers, through practically every month of the year.

The Western Shore Rivers

Thousands of years ago the entire Chesapeake Bay was a single river, the one that we call Susquehanna. This river continues to be the single most important freshwater contributor to the 160-mile long watershed up to this very day. Throughout this book you'll note references to the "old riverbed channel" that snakes its way down the Bay, providing deepest waters and often the best structures in any given area. Back when the Susquehanna flowed through this channel, the rest of the Bay was merely its floodplain. When the glaciers receded and the last ice age ended about 12,000 years ago, the plains were submerged as water levels rose worldwide. The Chesapeake as we know it today was created.

Through the Susquehanna an astonishing average of 22 billion gallons of water flows every day. That accounts for about half of the total amount of freshwater entering the Bay. And as the river flows, draining land from as far away as the state of New York, it carries silt and sediments loosened from the earth and brought to the river by rainfall, smaller tributaries, and all varieties of runoff. The Susquehanna carries these sediments until the river's banks open wide, near the town of Havre de Grace, Maryland. Here, where the water can spread out over a much larger area, the current slows and many of the sediments settle to the bottom. The area in which they settle, where a huge delta has been created by centuries of deposits, is called the Susquehanna Flats (URW1). This is one of the best areas in the world for an angler to try his hand at ultralight fishing for very large, heavy, pre-spawn cow stripers.

Fortunately, the powers that be have been wise enough to make the entire flats area catch-and-release fishing only, when it comes to striped bass. Since

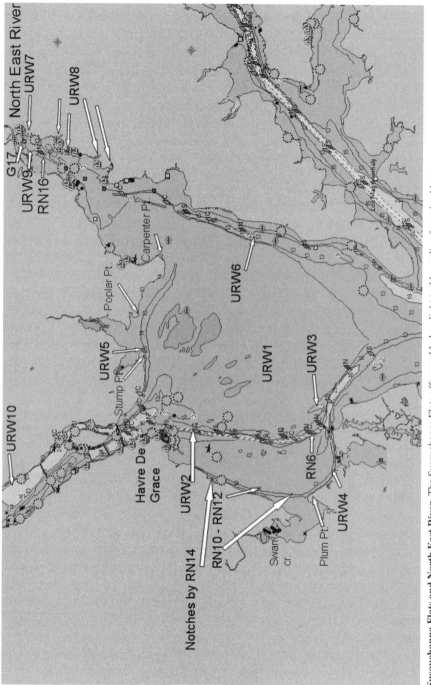

Susquehanna Flats and North East River. The Susquehanna Flats offer world-class light tackle angling for striped bass.

a huge proportion of the stripers that spawn in the Bay do so in the Susque-hanna, and since many of the fish caught here are pre-spawn females laden with roe, it is imperative to follow the least harmful fishing practices. In fact, I personally do not fish the flats any more. It's possible to hook up with large post-spawn fish elsewhere. But I also feel that everyone should get a shot at the experience, and certainly wouldn't deny any angler his or her fair chance. Follow good, safe, catch-and-release methods carefully, and you should do minimal harm to the fish. So go for it—judiciously.

Before detailing the flats and the best fishing spots in it, any angler who plans on fishing here must be aware of the risk that fishing could be shut down due to muddy water—sometimes for weeks at a time. When there's a heavy rain, sooner or later the Corps of Engineers will open the floodgates at Conowingo Dam. During a wet spring when flows are high and the water is muddy, this will bring fishing at the flats to a screaming halt. In fact, during some springs the entire number of fishable days on the flats can be counted on one hand. Before planning a trip here, you should call an area tackle shop, a local resident, or log onto the DNR's web site and find out how the conditions are. One other caution: the dates during which the catch-and-re-lease trophy season are open on the flats changes from year to year. April and May are usually the best months to try fishing here, but before planning a trip, consult the current regulations. Fortunately, the Maryland DNR does a great job of keeping its web site up-to-date, and you can usually get reli-able information on regulations and water conditions by logging on to www.dnr.md.state.us.

Fishing the flats is not like working the open Bay and takes a particular type of boat. You'll want shallow draft to access the holes that aren't close to the channel, and a light enough displacement that an electric motor can con-trol it (more on this later). In most cases, this means aluminum jon boats and flats style boats work best in this area. Another option is to run a small poly-ethylene boat. They usually require a hair more draft than aluminum, as they weigh slightly more, but I like poly boats because they are inexpensive, virtu-ally indestructible, and completely unsinkable. In my world, cheap and safe are two very important traits. Whichever material you deem best for your uses you'll want to stay between 14' and 18' LOA, and a draft of no more than a foot and a half; less is better.

The majority of the flats are unfishable no matter what your boat is or how the conditions are, simply because they're so shallow you can't access them. This limits most of the fishing to the channel edges and a few holes located along the outer edges of the flats. Starting at Havre de Grace, where the launch ramp and marinas are located, the main channel runs north-south and is well marked (URW2). You can locate fish by drifting with the wind or current, and casting along the edges. You'll want to toss your lure into the shallow water that will be between one and three feet, depending on the tide. Then retrieve it by bouncing it along the bottom, down the channel edge.

Savvy anglers will carry a small anchor with just 25' or 30' of rode on their boat, so they can quickly and easily drop it and hold position when they find a productive section of the edge. Unless the wind's blowing, a 5 lb mushroom anchor will do the trick for most small, shallow draft boats. Some anglers simply use a half of a cinder block, though cinder blocks tend to scratch up both aluminum and fiberglass boats.

Leadheads with plastic tails, dressed bucktails, and diving plugs are very effective lures for this type of angling, but many people will also cast topwater lures on the flats. They won't catch as many fish, but the adrenaline rush generated by a 40" striper slugging a topwater lure is extreme. Note that savvy anglers replace the treble hooks on their plugs with single barbless hooks, to keep from harming the pre-spawn stripers. Regardless of what you're casting, fish will usually strike as the lure transitions from the top edge of the channel into four or five foot deep water. In colder weather or when strong fronts move through, the strikes will tend to come in deeper water, usually on lures fished tight to the bottom.

Of course, the current and wind almost never cooperate to give you an ideal drift down the channel. And you don't want to drop anchor and hold a position until you've located a concentration of fish. So, you need some way of controlling your drift as you work along the channel edges; an electric motor is the best way to go here. Use it to adjust your drift every minute or two, and keep your boat in the deep water. Bow mounts are best for this purpose, but transom mounts will work fine as long as you keep the stern into the wind.

Many anglers will start their day here by fishing down the main channel, which is a good starting point until it gets crowded. As you near the red nun buoy number six, the channel takes a dogleg to the east (URW3). There's a point of mud bottom that has a finger of deep water running up next to it. Fish this area by anchoring your boat on the tip of the point, and casting up into the deep water finger. Fan-cast along both sides and the middle, then pull anchor, ease 20 or 30 yards up the finger, anchor again and make another series of fan casts. Move up again and continue this process until you run out of deep water. In the top of this finger, you'll often locate some good fish.

From this point you can go in one of two directions: head west into the secondary channel (URW4) or south along the shoreline of Aberdeen Proving Grounds. More fish are caught in the secondary channel, but it's also going to be crowded on a weekend of good weather and clean water. That makes the Western Shore line appealing at times. The drill is pretty simple: ease your boat in as close as possible to the shore, cast towards it, and retrieve. Casting spinnerbaits up to this shore line will produce some largemouth bass, as well as stripers.

Fishing the secondary channel on the western edge of the flats probably accounts for the lion's share of the stripers caught on the flats. Many anglers like to anchor on one side of the channel, then cast cut herring baits across it. This is an effective method, but I wouldn't recommend it as using cut bait will result in harming more fish than using lures will, almost without exception. Even when circle hooks are used, the fish will sometimes swallow cut bait and end up gut-hooked.

From the split in the channel up to Plum Point, the western channel runs right along shore. Casting to the shoreline itself will produce fish, but more often largemouth bass than stripers. The stretch from Plum Point running north across the mouth of Swan Creek, however, is an awesome area for stripers. You can cast up into the mouth of Swan Creek or to the east, up onto the flats. If you have a shallow draft boat, try nosing into the creek itself and cast to the eastern side of Swan Creek Point. Just don't hang out too long if the tide is dropping—you might end up stuck in the mud. The stretch of this channel from the red nun #10 to #12 is all worth casting to, but pay more attention to the notches on the western side of the channel, just north of #14.

The northeastern shore line of the flats also has a natural channel (URW5) that does hold fish but is harder to get in and out of. Your best bet is to access it from the western edge. Do so at slow speed, with a close eye on the depth finder. This area is not well marked and the sticks that locals have pushed into the mud in some spots can be more confusing than helpful. If you choose to try and fish here, it's best to enter it on a rising tide and leave before the water does. Fish this area the same way, by keeping your boat in deeper water, casting across the channel, and bouncing your lure back down the drop. All three points along this channel—Stump, Poplar, and Carpenters—are good targets to cast at, although you'll have to move out of the channel to reach Carpenter's (there's usually enough water here to do so without running aground).

There's also a channel running along the far eastern side of the flats, up into the North East River. (URW6) This channel is much wider than the others and is well marked. However, you'll have to run a while to get here because you'll need to go down the main channel to the west until you're south of the flats, then turn to the east and run back up along the other side. Some locals may know how to safely get from the channel to the north to the eastern channel, and on the charts it looks like there's enough water to get through, but it's something you'll have to feel out slowly once or twice with your own boat to make this run successfully. Once there, the tactics are the same: keep your boat in deep water, send your lure into shallow water, and retrieve back over the edge. Note that as you get deeper and deeper into the North East River the stripers will become fewer, while largemouth bass become more and more plentiful.

If trophy stripers aren't your game or if you're fishing this area during a different time of year, it does offer several other opportunities. The pier pilings in the North East River hold crappie and bass year round. Most anglers use an electric motor to hop from marina to marina, and cast their lures as close as possible to pilings and bulkheads. There are two areas of the North East that bass anglers must not overlook. The first is the triple cuts, a series of three small cove-like cuts at the head of the river (URW7). The points at the mouths of these cuts are full of debris—and bass. Try casting to each point, up inside of the cuts, and to the pilings and debris lining the shores. The second area of the North East that deserves special attention from bassers are the four small coves along the shore line, running south of the triple cuts, at URW8. Again, cast to the pilings, bulkheads, and riprap around the shorelines of these coves. The third cove to the south gets a special nod and is worth some extra attention.

Since there's not much water flow and very low salinity in the North East River, it freezes relatively quickly. That means that in the winter fishing gets shut down, right? Wrong! Cut through the ice, set out tip-ups baited with bullhead minnow or jig tiny ice jigs, and you often can catch a pile of perch and crappie with a surprise pickerel or bass mixed in. That's right—you can even go ice fishing on the Chesapeake some years, or at least on some Chesapeake tributaries. When the ice gets good and thick, check out the section of deep water at the head of the river, between the red nun #16 and green #17 channel markers at URW9. Unless it's been a particularly frigid winter, don't stray upriver into the headwaters where the shore line closes in because increased water flow here can make the ice thinner than it is in open water.

Going through the ice requires some special equipment: an auger or a spud (a chisel mounted on the end of a handle, for chipping through the ice), a spoon for straining ice chips out of your hole, and a long length of rope. The most important item is the rope, which one angler can use to help another get back out if they fall through the ice. Most anglers consider three inches of solid ice absolutely minimal, with four providing an appropriate safety margin.

During the summer months, when you'll see bass anglers shooting up and down the river in their glitterboats, another readily available fish you can target is catfish. No one area seems to hold the most cats. Just place a cut bait anywhere in the main channel, or in the channel of the river's headwaters, and let it sit on the bottom.

The marinas and pilings at Port Deposit (URW10) just upriver from Havre de Grace are a favored crappie and perch spot of many locals, particularly for late fall and early winter fishing when perch run strong here. As with the North East River, bass can also be found among the piles, and in this area you may also encounter smallmouth bass. Another fish you'll find in good numbers in this section of the Susquehanna is catfish. Both bullhead and channel cats can be caught year-round, by casting cut bait and allowing it to sit dead on the bottom. However, once you go upriver of Havre de Grace use special care—rocks, submerged pilings, and other propeller-eating obstructions are all over the place.

About five miles upstream from the mouth of the Susquehanna, Deer Creek feeds the river's southwestern shore. It's not really considered a part of the Chesapeake but is noteworthy because it's one of the few remaining places in Maryland to find a strong early spring shad run. These fish are protected and fishing is catch-and-release only. To minimize harm to the fish I don't partake in this fishery at this time, but everyone should check it out at least once, just to see the swarms of shad moving upriver to spawn if not to catch them. It's the closest thing to watching salmon run upstream that you can find in the mid-Atlantic region, and it is a stirring sight. As with the Susquehanna, conditions here vary greatly depending on water flow, weather and rainfall amounts. Again, the DNR web site is a good place to go to check on conditions.

The next two river heading down the Western Shore are the Bush River and the Gunpowder River. Both of these rivers offer largemouth bass, pickerel, and catfish, along with limited perch runs late in the winter and into spring. In some years, the Gunpowder even provides a limited shad run. However, these two rivers will not be discussed in this guide. They are bordered in part by Aberdeen Proving Grounds, and several areas in this vicinity have unexploded ordinance, restricted access, and ever-changing navigational restrictions. It used to be a non-issue, but since 9/11 things have changed. Since these rules can and often do change unexpectedly, I don't want to provide information that could cause an angler to violate a law, even if by accident. If you want to fish and learn one of these two rivers, I suggest doing so with a knowledgeable guide only.

Dundee, Seneca, and Saltpeter Creeks that lie between the Gunpowder and Middle Rivers are easier to deal with. They also offer somewhat limited opportunities, as they are small, easily accessed (there's a public ramp on Dundee Creek, which sees a lot of action) and at times overcrowded. They will, however, be of great interest to largemouth bass and white perch anglers. Pickerel, yellow perch, sunfish, and smallish stripers can also be taken from these creeks. Neither has water much deeper than 10' and most of the water is 3–4' feet, but in a way this is a blessing—some springs these creeks produce excellent weed beds.

Look for weedbeds just about anywhere in Saltpeter and Dundee. In Seneca you won't find as many, because slightly deeper water goes right up to the banks. (This can change from year to year, depending on water clarity and the amount of runoff entering the Bay.) Common tactics here for the panfish include casting and retrieving small minnow just over the weeds, or cast and retrieving small spinnerbaits like Beatle-Spins, Mepps, and Roadrunners. To target pickerel, use the Roadrunner and add a live bullhead minnow to the hook.

Bass anglers will also want to focus on the weedbeds, although there is some other bass-attracting structure, particularly in Saltpeter and Seneca. In

Saltpeter, look for the duck blind and half-exposed pilings near the cut that connects to Seneca Creek. The cut itself also attracts fish, particularly on a moving tide. On a falling tide pay the most attention to the outside of the cut; on an incoming focus on the inside of the cut. In Seneca Creek, look for bass around the marina pilings and the southwest point at the creek's mouth. This edge supports a nice drop-off and gets hit by a stronger current than most of the surrounding territory.

Two more rivers—and I promise, the only others—that won't be addressed in this guide are the next two to the south, the Middle River and the Back River. To be blunt, they stink. Literally. Centuries of abuse due to their close proximity to Baltimore's industrial areas have turned these two rivers into tainted water. There are constantly health warnings placed on what little life is caught from these rivers, suggesting unacceptably high levels of mercury and other chemicals exist in the fish and in the water. There are safer, more productive waters to fish around here, so let's move on to them.

During the past decade or so, the river that Baltimore overlooks directly, the Patapsco, has improved greatly and today it's in much better shape than some others in the area. This is sometimes credited to the shift from industry to tourism in Baltimore's inner harbor region. In any case, the Patapsco does support a quality fishery, although there are still health warnings issued on eating some types of fish (mostly catfish and eels) from the inner harbor itself.

Light tackle striper angling from mid-spring through late fall is the most important fishery here. Trolling along the channel edges also produces some keeper fish, but the majority of anglers found in the Patapsco will be casting to the plentiful structure found along its shores. The river terminates in two branches, which split at Ft McHenry. (Note: all waters inside of Ft McHenry are slow-speed zones, with a 6-mph speed limit). The Northwestern Branch runs up to the Inner Harbor and the Middle Branch runs to its south. Anglers should plan on which to fish according to the season; early in the year and through the fall the northern branch holds more fish, and late in the fall and into the winter, the southern branch seems to support more fish.

If you're casting jigs, plugs, or spoons for stripers from spring through fall, start off just outside the inner harbor (which ends at Federal Hill), and work the southern side of the branch. You will note countless broken off pilings that stick just above the water at high tide, large unloading piers, and modern marinas. All of this structure holds fish. One of the best spots is the series of broken down piers and pilings just downriver of Harborview Marina, marked by URW11. Don't just cast blindly far into the rubble or you'll never get your lure back out, but instead look for the pockets of open water that curl back into the mess. Cast as deep as possible into them, then retrieve quickly enough that your lure never sinks more than a couple of feet. Often it's helpful to switch to light leadheads in the ½ oz range for fishing in this jungle of broken

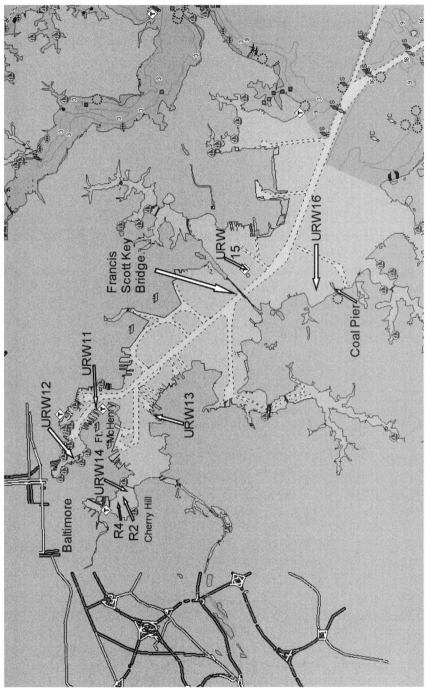

Patapsco River. The Patapsco River is a surprisingly productive tributary.

down piers. Floating lures and shallow divers will also do the trick. Don't even think about bouncing over the bottom, because you'll snag instantly.

Another hot spot in this zone is the water discharge at the sugar refinery (just follow your nose—and the huge sign that says "Domino Sugar," near URW12). Fishing here can be tough because the smell from the raw sugar often being unloaded from barges and ships can be overpowering, but fish do like to congregate where the discharge pipe flows into the harbor.

The large unloading piers and the commercial docks at Locust Point also hold fish, but fishing in this area can be dangerous. If you cast in these waters, be sure to steer clear of the ships, tugboats, and barges coming in and out of port. Also keep an eye peeled for orange boats in the 26' size range that are USCG patrol boats protecting the port. When you see them near a particular ship or unloading pier, move on to a different spot.

Up near Ft McHenry itself the drop-off becomes much less significant, as does the number of fish you'll find. Once you've reached the fort, shoot across the branch and fish your way up the northern shoreline.

In the Middle Branch, there is a lot more featureless, fishless water. The piers of South Locust Point look like they should hold some fish, but catches never seem to meet expectations. Look southwest from these piers, however, and you can see the top half of an old ferry boat sticking up out of the water (URW13). The boat sits in about 12' of water, and is a great habitat; try casting near the stern of the port side of the wreck for the best action.

To get to the next hot spot heading up the Middle Branch, you'll have to run up the channel and under the bridge at Cherry Hill (URW14). Stay in the channel when running up here, because outside of it the bottom is littered with wrecks, submerged pilings, and other rubble. Slow at the bridge and take a shot at casting to the upcurrent sides of the pilings. Then work your way up the channel, in line with the red #2 and red #4 markers. The channel maintains at least 10' or 12' at all times and is surrounded by 5' to 7' feet of water, and stripers will school right along this edge. December through March is a great time to find them in this area, as long as it doesn't freeze over. In fact, this is one of the best places to cast for stripers during the winter months, ranking right up there with warm water discharges. Although the average size of the stripers caught here in the winter is 22" to 26", plenty of 30" fish get snagged here, too.

Heading south from Ft McHenry, there isn't much casting action until you reach the Francis Scott Key Bridge. Most of the shore on the northern side is taken by Seagirt and Dundalk Marine Terminals that handle heavy commercial ship traffic. The south side looks better, but I've never done well along this shore, nor has anyone I know of or spoke with during the research phase of this book. However, trolling the channel edges along this stretch does produce keeper-sized stripers from mid-summer through the end of the regular striper season, with dressed bucktails trolled near the bottom being the favored tactic.

The bridge pilings of the Francis Scott Key Bridge do often hold stripers, and white perch also like to congregate here. However, the real fish-attractor in this vicinity is Ft Carroll, the small island just south of the bridge. Ft Carroll was built under the direction of Robert E. Lee prior to the Civil War, and today sits idle in the middle of the river. But lucky for us, it attracts fish. At most times of the year casting bottom rigs baited with grass shrimp, blood worms, or clam snouts near the island will get you your fill of white perch. From summer through fall you can pull stripers in the 16"–24" range by casting lures up to the broken down pier on the eastern side of the island at URW15, and in the fall for some reason snapper bluefish like to congregate in this area, too. This is also the northernmost spot on the Western Shore you're likely to catch seatrout; they'll make a showing here about one year in five.

Look to the southwest from Ft Carroll, and you'll see a string of huge smokestacks coming from a large building. This is the power plant at Hawkins Point and is one of the best upper Bay places to catch wintertime stripers. Added bonus: the launch ramp at Ft Armistead Park, just off Exit 1 on the Baltimore Beltway, has a roomy ramp with plenty of parking, and is less than a mile's run to the fishing.

The power plant discharges a constant supply of warm water, and when the surrounding waters may be in the low 30s, you can usually find a plume of water 10 to 20 degrees warmer. URW16 marks the basic area but it is sometimes tricky to find because it shifts with the wind and current. Here's the drill: From the boat ramp run directly at the center of the long coal unloading pier that shoots out from the plant. When you're about a half mile from the pier, slow to idle and fire up your depth finder, assuming it has a temperature gauge on it. (If not, you'll need to bring a thermometer). Don't look for a specific temperature, but look for a spike in the reading as you putt around. Now circle around in ever larger circles until you find the temperature change. Found it? Good—now you'll need to determine the area it covers. This will change throughout the day, as shifting wind and currents work to push the warm water plume around. The best method is to mark the spot with a float marker, then continue circling from that point until you've established what direction the plume goes in, and how much territory it covers. On calm, windless days expect to find a large circular plume, and on windy days look for a long, thin oval of warm water. On rare occasions the plume will intersect with some of the coal pier's pilings, and create a condition that the fish absolutely love.

You can also locate warm water at the mouth of the trench on shore, right up next to the power plant. Usually this is where anglers find white and yellow perch, catfish and small stripers. They can be targeted by casting grass shrimp or minnow on bottom rigs or shad darts suspended under bobbers, right up into the trench. However, be cautious about fishing here. Since 9/11 the rules related to coming this close to the power plant have changed several times, and as of this writing, anglers are NOT allowed to pull up right to the trench. (In the past, they have posted signs on shore here stating the minimum distance you must keep.)

Be aware that on blustery days when the wind and tide are opposed, the plume can also more or less disappear, as it gets pulled in opposite directions. One other caution—this area is exposed to a south/southeast wind, and fishing here in freezing conditions on a windy day can be both uncomfortable and dangerous.

The quality of the fishing at the warm water discharge will relate directly to the surrounding water temperatures. During mild winters, the power plant may be more or less dead. During harsh winters, when the Patapsco runs cold, fish really pile up in here. Work jigs, bucktail/minnow combinations, sinking Rat-L-Traps, and similar plugs along the bottom in the warm water, and you should be able to locate stripers up to and sometimes over 30". Most of the fish that winter here seem to run in the 16" to 26" class, but I do know of at least two fish over 40" taken from the plume by an angler, as this book was being written.

The last Western Shore river of the upper Chesapeake is the Magothy. The Magothy is not known for great fishing, and truth be told, there isn't much going on inside the river mouth during most of the summer and fall most seasons. However, you can consistently find some stripers casting to pier pilings, Magothy Narrows, and the river's points. (Pay special attention to those inside of the green #3 and red #4 markers). And the north side of Dobbins Island seems to be a nursery area for many species; at times you'll catch dozens of four-inch croaker, stripers, and perch there. But the best opportunity the Magothy has to offer is for late fall, winter, and early spring pickerel angling. In fact, it's probably the number one pickerel river on the Western Shore of the Bay.

The best pickerel spots in the Magothy are mostly upriver of Ulmstead Point in the backs of the creeks and coves. Generally speaking, the farther upriver you go, the more pickerel you'll find. In years of drought, the pickerel will only be found far up the river, and in years of heavy rainfall they'll spread out and work their way downriver, all the way to Gibson Island. To find them, start as far up the river as is practical (up near or even past the Magothy Bridge Rd bridge is a good starting point) and work your way in and out of the coves, casting standard pickerel fare wherever you find weedbeds, piers, or fallen trees. Remember: weeds equal pickerel. Locate a good patch of weeds and you'll often be able to hook into a dozen pickerel in the same spot.

Yellow perch can also be caught in the Magothy during the colder months, but current regulations do not allow the harvest of yellow perch from the Magothy, Severn, South or West Rivers. If you feel the need to catch and release them, or if the laws change in the future, try casting live minnow suspended under a bobber to the piers and riprap along the creek edges.

The Eastern Shore Rivers

The Elk River, the northernmost river on the Eastern Shore of the Chesapeake, has been transformed from its original form by the construction of the C&D Canal. This canal connects the Chesapeake and Delaware bays, and tremendous volumes of water flow through it on every tidal cycle. In fact, it's not unusual to hit a three knot current in the Elk. It's also common to be passed by freighters, tugs and barges, and plentiful pleasure boat traffic. This being the case, it is not the most picturesque river on the Bay to fish. If, however, you like catfish, it may be the best river on the Bay.

It should be noted up front that in all of these areas of these northern Eastern Shore rivers, which usually have low salinity levels and support as many freshwater fish as brackish or salt species, you'll experience an intermingling of striped bass and largemouth bass. Except for far up the creeks and rivers (and occasionally even then) anywhere that you catch largemouth bass you may also catch stripers. The more runoff any given year has the more dominant the largemouth will be, and in years of drought the stripers will take charge.

The upper section of the Elk, near Elkton, Maryland, has several holes and channels that are often inundated with the good eating, hard fighting, always under-rated catfish. The creeks that feed the Elk (URE1) are also productive areas for perch anglers in the spring and fall, and for bass and crappie anglers in the summer months. As with most of the winding creeks that feed rivers along the Eastern Shore, the inside of the bends is where you'll find deep holes. Yellow perch move into these holes as early as mid-January and will hold there until they make their spawning run in March. Bullhead minnow on bottom rigs is the easiest way to catch these fish, although small jigs will also prove effective at times.

The deep hole by the red nun buoy #8 is a prime catfish spot. Put cut herring or a similarly stinky bait on the bottom, and you'll likely hook up in no time. Same goes for the area to the southeast of Welsh Point (URE2) where the C&D canal splits off from the Elk River's headwaters. More good catfish waters can be found in the mouth of the Bohemia, and in the section of the Elk from the Bohemia south to Turkey Point. Through this stretch, the channel is surrounded by a good amount of 10' to 20' deep water. All of it will produce cats. (Go to small hooks and dime-sized baits, and you'll catch plenty of eels in this zone, too.) Pay particular attention to the downcurrent area of Arnold Point (URE3). Both sides of this point get slammed by a strong current, and both will be productive. Set up on the downcurrent side of the point when you start fishing, and look for the swirls and eddies formed by the moving water.

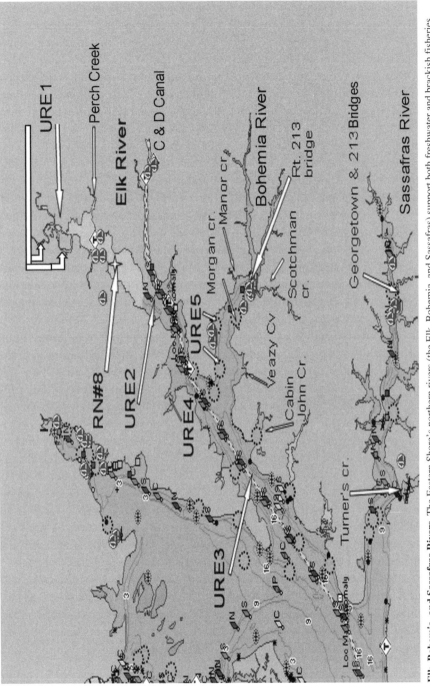

Elk, Bohemia, and Sassafras Rivers. The Eastern Shore's northern rivers (the Elk, Bohemia, and Sassafras) support both freshwater and brackish fisheries.

Bass anglers, however, will want to pitch their baits to the weedy sections of the Elk in and south of Perch Creek, before working their way up into the headwater creeks. These creek holes also hold largemouth bass much of the year. Cast and retrieve right up to the shoreline, with spinnerbaits or minnow suspended under bobbers, and you've got a good shot at them.

Bass can be found in even better numbers near the large wooden structures lining the edges of the main shipping channel that leads into the canal. Crappie are available here too, though they bite in strict accordance with the tide. Many days, it seems like you can only catch them during a half-hour window of the tide, usually when it falls slack.

Another good area to hunt bass is in Piney Creek Cove. The northern creek (URE4) is a good place to start at, and casting spinnerbaits to the weedbeds in the cove is also a good bet. If it doesn't pan out, don't hesitate to head for the Bohemia River. The Bohemia has several marinas along its northern side, providing pier pilings and wrecks along the shore at URE5 that bass love to hide in. Bass anglers: concentrate on these pilings. They provide the best bassy structure in this area of the Bay and are usually even more productive than the weedbeds. Note that the weedbeds tend to be more productive on a full flood tide, whereas the pilings often remain productive throughout the tidal cycle.

The same is true for crappie—but the opposite is true of pickerel. You'll find lots of pickerel in the weedbeds here, pretty much year-round. Structure like pier pilings, however, really doesn't seem to interest these fish very much. To focus on pickerel, stick with the shallow areas (Veazey Cove, Morgan Creek, Manor Creek, and Cabin John Creek just south of the Bohemia) that have weeds coming to within a foot of the waters' surface. These weeds will be thickest in spring, and by mid-May it will be impossible to fish some areas because they have grown so thick. There is a die-off, however, usually by the time June ends, and large holes will appear in the weedbeds. Pickerel will hide in the surrounding weeds, ready to pounce on anything that swims into the open water. When the weedbeds start to die off completely with the arrival of cold weather pickerel fishing will improve, and when only small pockets of weeds are left around the cove edges in November and December, pickerel fishing will be at its best.

The upper river is also a productive area, as the river channel here is much deeper than one would think. To catch bass stick with the shallows to either side of the channel, and in Manor and Scotchman's Creeks. Or, cruise up beyond the Rt 213 bridge. Both branches of the creek support weedbeds and well-defined channels surrounded by marsh and shallows. As with the Elk's headwaters, these creeks are good places to find perch during the winter months. There aren't as many significant bends with deep holes, but the channels remain relatively constant throughout. This can make locating the fish a bit harder. The best way to fish here is to drift down the creek, using an electric motor to keep the boat in the deep water, until you locate concentrations of fish.

The Sassafras will hold white and yellow perch but it doesn't see as strong a yellow perch run as most other Eastern Shore rivers. Nor does it hold an exceptional crappie fishery. Good thing there are plenty of bass and pickerel in this river. As with the Bohemia, the best fishing for bass is under the piers and pilings, and for pickerel, over weedbeds. There are also some trees laying in the water along the Sassafras's shorelines that are another good bet for largemouth.

Turner's Creek is known for excellent bass fishing, and white perch move in here as early as May and will stay for much of the season. Grass shrimp on bottom rigs, or suspended under a bobber, will do the trick. For bass, hit the usual suspects—weedbeds and pilings—but also pay close attention to the creek's mouth. Both the eastern point and the two western points have good drop-offs that run close to shore, and all of these points hold fish.

Farther upriver near Georgetown there are several large marinas, as well as a bridge and several duck blinds. The north shoreline just downriver from the bridge has the highest concentration of piers and is a good area to fish for bass. Upriver of the bridge there are fewer piers but generally speaking, they are more productive. There are also about a dozen smaller creeks feeding into the Sassafras. They do hold bass, and interestingly, they are also full of sunfish—redears and shellcrackers, as they're called locally.

For the Chesapeake's more commonly sought after brackish and saltwater species, the Chester is the first significant river along the Eastern Shore. Here, you can catch just about everything from blues to the occasional black drum. And if you go far up river, bass are in attendance, too.

The Chester winds along for over 30 miles of fishable water. From Chestertown to its source (Unicorn Lake—an outstanding pond to catch pickerel in!) the water is more or less fresh, and will be of interest mostly to bass, perch, and crappie anglers. One exception—from mid-February through mid-March, the Chester will support a decent yellow and white perch run. The yellows come first, usually during the last weeks of February, followed closely by the whites. These fish can be targeted pretty much anywhere in the channel on this stretch of the river. But as with tidal creeks, you'll do best by paying close attention to the inside of bends. The sharp bend just north of Foreman Branch at URE6 is a significant staging area—a place where the perch bunch up before making their spawning run. The next bend upriver (URE7) just beyond Deep Landing is another place the fish will stack up prior to the spawn.

Bass anglers will also find a lot of action in this stretch of the river. Crumpton is a good starting point, as it has a large bridge, deep channel, marsh and weedbeds, all in close proximity. Once downriver from Deep Landing, the channel cuts pretty close to shore and there isn't a lot of good bass territory until you reach the creek mouth of Foreman Branch. Here, as

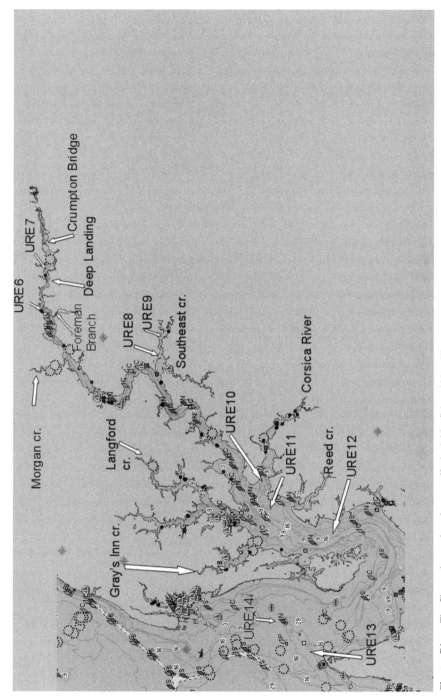

Chester River. The Chester is one river that can offer both bluefish and bluegills.

well as at the mouth of Morgan Creek and all through Southeast Creek, you'll find bucketmouths feeding on a dropping tide. On the incoming, try casting up into the shallow bowls (URE8 and URE9) that have good weed growth and some fallen tree cover. You'll also catch crappie and pickerel in these areas, if you toss the appropriate baits and lures. As with the other tidal bass rivers, anywhere you find pier pilings or wrecks can also prove productive.

The stretch from Southeast Creek to the mouth of the Corsica is an area that can be more fresh or more salt depending on the given year. Some seasons you'll find bass and pickerel in this area, other years stripers will rule this territory. In both, this stretch will also support decent numbers of channel cats.

The Corsica River is more or less a tributary to the Chester and is not really a river in its own right. In fact, it's not much larger and has no more freshwater flow than Southeast Creek. It does, however, have deeper water and is a famous perch area. White perch move into the mouth of the river, and many anglers like to fish just off of the Russian embassy property on the northern point of the river mouth (URE10). Grass shrimp on bottom rigs is the way to go here, although you can also take fish on small jigs and lures. Whites move in here late in the fall, usually November or December, and use it as a temporary staging area before moving farther upriver to the deep holes, in preparation for spawning. The mouth of Reed Creek, just to the south of the Corsica, will also hold some fish. These creeks, as well as Langford and Grays' Inn Creeks, also attract stripers.

Small boat anglers looking for protected waters in this area will want to look for the can marked "LC," off Nichols' Point. The drop along this edge (URE11) provides the northernmost spot in the Chester that's productive for chummers looking to catch striped bass. In some years, bluefish and croaker will also venture this far up the river. About four miles downriver, there's another tremendous edge where the depths drop from 12' to 15' all the way down to 50' and 60' (URE12). This is all good jigging territory for stripers, from the time the summer rock season opens through the fall. (In the spring, this area is off-limits to striper anglers, as are other tributaries). The deep water continues down the river from this area all the way to Love Point. This entire area can hold stripers, catfish, and most years croaker as well, but it's really not a prime fishing area because of boat traffic. Hundreds if not thousands of pleasure boats cruise to Kent Island, and all of those going to or coming from the upper Bay go through the narrows and come out via this section of the Chester. On a summer Saturday much of this stretch is washing-machine rough regardless of the wind conditions, simply from all the boat wakes.

At the mouth of the Chester, there is a light pole on a rockpile. Perch and small stripers will often collect around these rocks, but don't expect to find any lunkers here. Oddly, both stripers and blues can often be found breaking water late in the fall in the shallows between the light and Love Point at

URE13. Most of the time they will be sub-legal, but I have seen 20" stripers come from just three feet of water here.

To the east of the light, there's a red nun #2 marker, right on the edge of a hole, with a lump to its north (URE14). This is a great chumming spot for stripers and blues from the time the fish school, on through to the end of the season. In past years, large bluefish used to school around the lump here, and it was possible to catch 4–10 lb fish all day from this tiny little pimple. That seemed to peter out with the return of the stripers, but when we have another year of drought and if decent bluefish come up the Bay again, this will be a place you'll want to check out.

A note about the fallen trees you'll find on the banks of the northeastern Bay tributaries: for some reason, the bulk of these awesome looking spots will be vacant. But don't give up on working them. For every dozen or so great looking spots, one will pan out. And once you find a particular tree that holds fish, take note of it. On return trips, that very same tree will almost always produce, while the great-looking ones around it remain barren. I can't say what the reason for this phenomenon is, but I've experienced it time and time again on Bay tributaries holding freshwater species—they will orient to the same specific tree, while surrounding ones that look great to the human eye are ignored. You'll notice, however, that I don't mention specific trees in this book. This is because tree cover changes from year to year. A particularly great tree may lie in the same place in the same way for a season or two, but then it usually either deteriorates, is washed free into a different position by a storm, or is pushed up onto the shore by a tidal surge. You'll have to play a numbers game on your first couple of trips to an area on one of these rivers each season, and learn which trees hold the fish. Hopefully, once you find them, the trees will remain in place for a few trips to come.

Upper Bay, Main Stem

Many people believe that the farther south you go on the Bay, the better the fishing is. As a general rule of thumb, this is often true when it comes to species that like saltier water, such as bluefish, seatrout, and flounder. But when it comes to stripers, during much of the season the Upper Chesapeake holds an edge over the southern Bay's waters.

Turkey Point (UM1), the spit of land dividing the Susquehanna Flats and the Elk River (the entrance to the C&D Canal) is a great area to fish for stripers during the spring, summer, and fall. Same goes for catfish. In fact, if you toss out cut bait near the green can marked "ER" to the west of the channel, you often will be inundated with channel cats in the 1–10 lb range. Stripers can also be taken here, but bait fishing for them is sometimes impossible because the cats won't give the stripers a chance to get to your offering. Grass shrimp on bottom rigs will also produce a healthy crop of white perch in this area. The drop-offs from 10' to 20' at Grove Pt and Howell Pt (UM2, UM3) are productive spots for soaking baits.

When the stripers are in town and seasonal regulations apply, trollers will find fish along the channel edges from the Elk River to Pooles Island. Outside of the channel, in most areas this far up the Bay the water shallows up quickly. There are a couple of spots, however, where pockets of deeper water also allows for bait fisherman to take a shot at catching these fish. Deep water comes very close to Howell Pt (UM3), and the water to the south and west of Shad Battery Shoal (UM4) drops into the 30s in several places. These drops are also a good place to catch white perch and catfish on cut baits.

In the fall, this entire area is prime for eeling. (It may be productive for them in the spring, too, but at the time of this writing, it's against the regulations.) The lumps around Shad Battery Shoal at (UM5), Worton Pt (UM6), and Pooles Island (UM7) are famous for boatload catches of striped bass using this effective if slimy method. Remember that when eeling, the stripers will be very tide-sensitive. When you locate a productive lump while eeling and the bite shuts off, follow the tide up or down the Bay. All of the bumps in this area hold fish; the tricky part is figuring out when those fish will bite. By going in the same direction as the tide is flowing when your bite shuts down, you can overtake that critical period of tide during which the fish feed and experience that good bite all over again. Keep this in mind when planning a trip to this zone of the Bay, and map out your strategy accordingly.

Here's an example of a good eeling pattern, using three excellent groups of bumps in this zone. If the tide is incoming in the morning, start out eeling at the bumps between the green #7 buoy (at the southeast tip of Pooles) and the green #33 channel marker to the east. The ridges and bumps here will rise up to 10' or 12', and are surrounded by 20' of water—prime eeling territory. When the bite ends, run north to bumps and edges to the west of the red #40 channel marker (look for the 10' to 20' shelf). You should get in a 15 to 25 minute bite here, too. Then pull up stakes and hit the edges of the hill at the red #44 marker, north of Worton Point. Continue working your way north, to keep up with the peak stage of the tide. If the tide is an outgoing, run the opposite route.

Trollers can also fish these bumps, with the traditional bottom-bouncing method. Because the edges of these bumps are so sharp, however, this usually leads to a lot of snags and lost tackle. It also should be mentioned that in most years, Pooles Island is about as far up the Bay as you're likely to find salt-loving species like bluefish.

The next spot of interest in the main-stem upper Bay is the water around Hart-Miller Island. Hart-Miller used to be a pair of small islands, but several decades ago they were encircled by a riprap wall, and filled with dredge spoil. Yup, you're right—miles of riprap means fish. White perch and stripers can

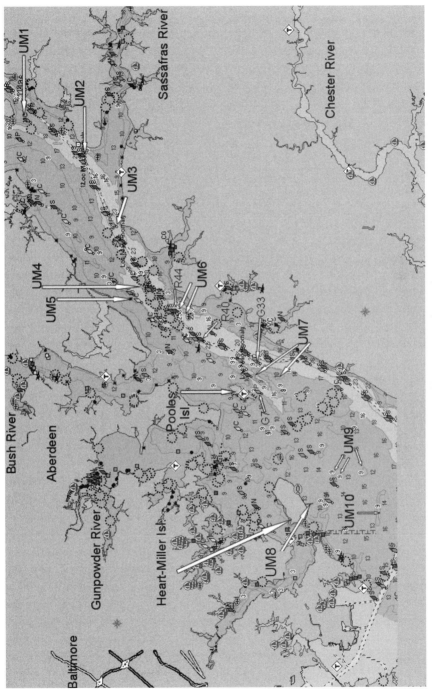

Northern, Upper Bay, Main Stem. The Northern Main-stem Upper Chesapeake is striper territory.

be found all along the riprap walls, by casting light tackle up to the rocks. The old unloading pier located on the southeastern side of the island (UM8) holds a lot of fish, as does the small pier jutting out from the rocks, just to the north of the unloading pier. There are also several spillways located around the island. These were used to drain off water mixed in with the dredge spoil, and for many years they were a reliable place to find fish. For some reason, stripers in the 16" to 26" class loved feeding around the spillway outlets on moonlit nights. But since new dredge material is no longer deposited here, these spillways aren't always in operation. Still, if you're casting to the riprap and you see flow from one of them, by all means hit it hard.

The northwestern side of the island has a beach that is used by thousands of boaters for swimming and sunbathing during the summer months, so anglers will want to stay out of this area. Also avoid the cut on the southern side of the island. It looks passable on the chart and on the water, but I've run aground going through this cut on a high tide and have seen others stuck in it as well.

In the open Bay to the south and east of Hart-Miller, there are four shoals that merit your attention. All will hold white perch, channel cats, stripers, and, during years of high salinity, bluefish. Chumming, eeling, and fishing cut bait will all work on these shoals, and casting grass shrimp or bloodworms on bottom rigs is best for perch. In the fall, stripers can be taken from these shoals in large numbers by bottom-bouncing bucktails. The northernmost shoal is Tea Table (some call it Tea Kettle) Shoal (UM9). When it comes to catching keeper stripers in the fall the best edge along this shoal is the westernmost, where the bottom drops from 12' and goes to 20'. The second shoal of note is Man O' War Shoal (UM10) that is shallow enough to ground on if you're in an inboard-powered boat. This shoal is exceptionally easy to locate since it has a lighthouse, on the western edge. Although plenty of stripers come from Man O' War, I've always found it more reliable as a white perch spot. Anchor in 15' or 16' of water on the south side of the shoal on an incoming tide or the north side on an outgoing tide, cast back to the shallow section, and slowly creep a bottom rig baited with grass shrimp back down the edge—you should be able to quickly load up on these panfish.

A couple of miles to the southwest of Man O' War is Seven Foot Knoll (UM11). The rocks here come all the way out of the water and used to have a screw-pile lighthouse marking them. The lighthouse was taken down decades ago, however, and is currently a part of the Living Classrooms Foundation in downtown Baltimore. It was replaced with a large lighted pole, and locals now call this spot Seven Foot Pole. Like Man O' War, this is usually a better bet for white perch than for large gamefish. In some years I've seen perch so thick around these rocks that bare gold hooks needed no bait to catch fish. And in some other years, the rocks have been surrounded by stripers in the 10" to 15" range. (The southern side of the rocks always seems to be the most productive area, for some reason). Every few years, however, larger fish make a showing here. Sometimes they can be pulled from right around the rocks with lures, and sometimes chumming along the eastern edge of the shoal, where there's a fast drop to 18' (UM12), does the trick. All anglers must be aware that the main shipping channel runs close by Seven Foot Knoll, and some quirk of geography causes ship wakes to build taller than usual when they hit the shoal. Whenever you see a ship go by as you fish here, keep a close eye out for its wake.

Six Foot Knoll lies just southeast of Seven Foot Knoll, and this is the shoal that seems to hold large fish more consistently than the others. Chumming is particularly effective here during the late summer and fall season. Set up on the eastern side, where the water drops from 8' to 20' (UM13). If you can drop anchor and position your boat so it stays in the 16' to 18' range near the bottom of this slope, you should be in good shape. Bottom-bouncing bucktails also proves effective here, for fall stripers. The far eastern edge has a pretty good drop, but its harder to get a Danforth-style anchor to stick here. If you plan to fish these shoals, it's a good idea to take along a grappling anchor, too, and use it when your Danforth bounces over the shell bottom without catching.

The Western Shore side of the upper main-stem Bay holds a few surprisingly good hot spots. The first is Bodkin Point. Sure, there's good perch, croaker, and spot fishing off Bodkin Point, along the edge where the green can #1 is located. But the real secret lies in close to shore. There used to be a lighthouse here, many years ago. It's gone now, but there are several clusters of rocks that are just covered by the water at low tide, the last remnants of that building at UM14. And they hold excellent numbers of stripers, usually from late September through November or even December. Don't plan on fishing here with a large boat. In fact, a foot and a half of draft is all that's safe, and even then, you risk dinging up your prop. The best way to fish here is to launch a 14' or 16' jon boat or skiff in Bodkin Creek, and come out into the Bay only when conditions are near-perfect and winds are under 10 mph. Because the rocks are located close to shore, a west wind won't create large waves here and makes for the calmest seas.

To locate the rocks, exit Bodkin Creek and follow the channel to the green #5 marker. At this point, you're already outside of the rocks. Turn hard to starboard and putt slowly towards the outermost part of Bodkin Point. You won't travel more than 30 to 40 yards before you start seeing the bottom jump up from four or five feet to one or two feet on the depth finder—you've found the rocks. You can fish here in one of two ways. Either locate the rocks, drop a grappling anchor on a short leash and fan-cast light lures (anything over half an ounce is doomed to get snagged), or troll unweighted lures or very small bucktails slowly back and forth over the rocks.

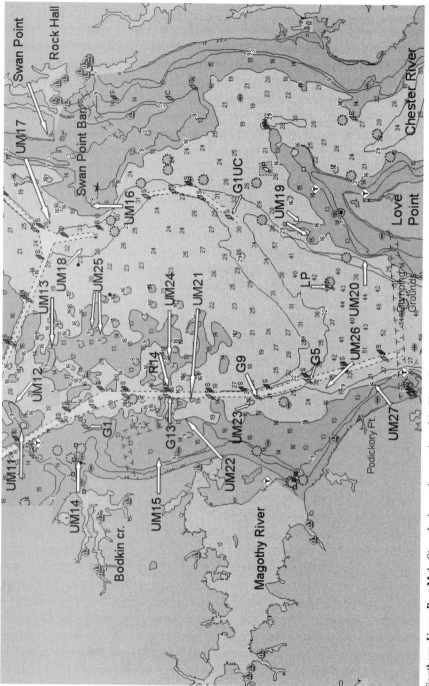

Southern, Upper Bay, Main Stem. In the southern section of the Upper Bay, saltier species make their presence known.

The next point of interest along the Western Shore is Snake Rip Bar, an oyster bar located about three miles to the south of Bodkin Point (UM15). The bottom here drops rapidly from 8' to 15' and is covered in oyster shells. Some old timers tell me that this was once a good area for croaker in the spring and stripers in the fall, but I've found it more reliable as a white perch spot. To find it, simply head south from Bodkin Point until you spot the spider buoy a couple miles offshore. Turn and head on a 240-degree course, until the bottom comes up.

The eastern side of the main-stem upper Bay holds some of the better known striper territory, some of the best rockfishing spots in the Bay. The first is Rock Hall, where one of the northernmost charter fleets on the Chesapeake runs from. During the full moon, when crabs molt and stripers move into the shallows to feed on them, try trolling through the forest of crab traps just west of Swan Point Bar, at UM16. Stay in the 10' to 14' zone, especially during high tide. When the tide falls, or during a waning moon, you can often troll up stripers along the edge to the west where it drops from 14' to 25', then into the 30s.

On the charts you can see where Swan Point Channel joins with Tolchester Channel and the Brewerton Extension, about three miles west of Rock Hall. This area is known as the Triple Buoys and along the edge at UM17, as many stripers have been caught in this spot as any in the Bay. In the spring trophy season trolling from the Triple Buoys to Love Point and back is a favored tactic. Drop anchor in the deep water to the southwest of the Triple Buoys (near UM18) and chumming over the mud for trophies is also effective. In the summer and fall when the fish school, stripers are often so thick in this area that you can literally watch them swim up to your boat and eat your chum the moment it hits the water. One caution: some years, 16" fish inundate the Triple Buoys, and you may have to weed through 40 to 50 fish to find a single keeper. (When this happens use oversized baits or the head of a menhaden, dropped down to the bottom, to keep the little guys off your hook). Fall chummers may also encounter blues here, although the last few years the high flow of freshwater has kept most of the bluefish farther south.

The stretch from the Triple Buoys down to the green #1UC can is all good bottom for chumming over the mud. The breaks from 30' to 40' are usually the best spots for spring trophies, and the 28' to 34' zone is usually better for summer and fall fish. One unique feature to this area is its ability to hold good sized fish during the dog days of summer, when the fishing slows. Many years, good catches of 18" to 30" fish come here even as most of the hot spots on the Bay don't produce, and when your usual haunts leave you wishing for greener pastures, this is a good area to try. Trolling here in the summer and fall does not seem to keep pace with chumming.

The next area heading south is Love Point, another amazingly reliable place to go for stripers. The past few years we've also seen good runs of croaker near Love Point in May and June, and in some years seatrout will travel this far up the Bay.

Each and every spring, my first several trophy trips take place at Love Point—I have that much faith in this spot. More often than not, it pays off, too. The area surrounding the LP buoy, located two miles west of the point and three miles north of the Bay Bridge, is the best starting point. The muddy bottom here lies 43' to 45' feet below. Trollers will want to pass the LP buoy and continue heading down to the bridge area, or troll all the way from the triple buoys down to the bridge. But chummers should make ever-widening circles around the LP buoy until they start seeing large pockets of baitfish on their depth finder, as well as some scattered arches down deep. You may locate more of them up to two miles north of the buoy, a mile east or west, and a mile or so to the south; anywhere in this zone is usually good. You'll want to anchor in 36' to 45' of water, and follow standard spring chumming techniques.

While some croaker will come from the muddy bottom, many more will be caught up closer to the point itself, on the other side of the old riverbed channel. The Love Handles at UM19 jut out from Love Point, providing some nice hard bottom that drops off into 30' deep water. Drifting bloodworms is the best bet for croaker, and chumming here is also effective for schoolie stripers once they congregate for the summer and fall. In years of drought, you'll also catch plenty of bluefish here.

Jump one and a quarter miles south of the Love Handles and you'll see a spot where the shallow water protrudes out close to the channel, creating a very steep, sharp drop-off marked by UM20. This is another good fall chumming spot for stripers. During the late spring you can anchor with your boat in 28' to 32' of water and be in close proximity of the deeper waters of the Dumping Grounds, which gives you a shot at both late trophies and early schoolies. The last two weeks of June, give this edge a shot. The Dumping Grounds themselves can be fished much as any other mud bottom. Troll or chum over it for spring stripers, but don't expect much in the way of fall chumming or bottom fishing here.

To the northwest of Love Point is Belvidere Shoals, another fantastic area that cannot be overlooked by any serious upper Bay angler. It covers a lot of territory, as the shoals run along the eastern and western side of Craighill Channel from Six Foot Knoll clear down to the mouth of the Magothy. We'll take a look at some of the best bumps in here, but always remember that any one edge, shoal, or drop on Belvidere is worth trying, and could hold fish during any given year. The shoals hold mostly white perch and stripers, but in dry years plenty of bluefish visit these waters, too. During years of heavy rainfall catfish will invade the shoals, and sometimes spot, croaker, and weakfish also make a showing at Belvidere.

The bumps of Belvidere cover both the western and eastern sides of Craighill Channel, with the majority of the territory being on the eastern side.

There are a couple of spots on the western edge of the channel, however, that must not be overlooked. The first is Billy's Lump, UM21, that rises to 16' in the middle, drops off into the 45' channel on the eastern side, and to 24' on the western side. This is a small lump, no more than 20 yards across and 30 or 40 yards long. But if you bounce eels along its edges late in the season, you'd better hold on tight—many 30" to 40" fall fish have been taken here. This bump also supports large numbers of perch, spot, and some years croaker, during the warmer months. To locate Billy's Lump, go to green #13 channel marker, and zigzag along the channel edge until you find the lump, about midway between #13 and #15. It's so close to the channel edge that anchoring over Billy's Lump to chum would be foolhardy, so plan to either eel, drift fish, or troll here.

Just west of Billy's Lump is a series of bumps that come up to 12' or 14' and are surrounded by 16' to 20' of water, at UM22. These bumps often hold perch, and bottom bouncers may want to swing across them as they troll a north-south pattern. This spot runs hot and cold. Perhaps one year out of four or five it will hold some decent stripers, but most years it's better as a panfish spot.

Head south, however, to the green #9 channel marker, and you can locate a bump that holds good numbers of large stripers on a regular basis. This bump, UM23, is about twice the size of Billy's, and it comes right up to the marker and the edge of the channel. (Note: the USCG does move these markers occasionally and they are sometimes moved by ice flows or powerful storms, but since the late '90s, #9 has been right on the edge of the lump—despite what the charts might say. If you come here and do not locate it, zigzag right along the channel edge and you should find it quickly.) This lump is large enough to anchor and chum over, but on crowded summer days you should get there early, as it's maxed-out by three or four boats.

On the eastern side of Craig Hill Channel, the bumps, humps, and ridges are simply too numerous to examine in detail. Any one of these edges can be productive for stripers, perch, spot, and croaker; in rainy years, catfish will be found here; and in dry years, blues usually make a showing. If you're fishing for stripers, bottom-bouncing through this zone can be particularly effective because it allows you to hit lump after lump and edge after edge until you locate the most productive spots.

Although all of these bumps can be good, a couple particular ones stand out. The one directly west of the R#14 channel marker at UM24 is an excellent fall chumming spot, and some years you'll catch a limit of 18" to 28" fish there week after week, through the season. Fish the bottom of the hump on an incoming tide, and the top of it on an outgoing.

The bumps at UM25 seem to also hold fish more regularly than the rest of Belvidere. These bumps are often excellent white perch spots, and if you're fishing here in the late fall, keep your eyes open—for whatever reason, stripers like to break water in this spot. One year, we encountered a school of 28" to 34" fish breaking water. Bottom bouncing and chumming have also proved effective in this area.

South of Belvidere, the last major point of interest to main-stem upper Bay anglers is the water just outside of the mouth of the Magothy. If you were to draw a line from the green channel marker #5 to Podickery Point, you would notice a fairly large area of water that drops down to over 30' but is not a part of Craighill Channel. There's a shelf with a nice drop along here, which goes from 20' down to about 36' at UM26. Some falls, this area is another good chumming spot for striper anglers. It's another on-again, off-again area, and season to season it can go from red hot to dead cold. In some other years, there's also a late May to mid-June run of late spring trophy stripers in this area that lasts one to three weeks. These fish are usually taken by chummers, but trollers also do well along this edge.

Moving in towards Sandy Point the area around UM27 has a rather boring slope and no real stand-out features, but it does experience some interesting and confused current thanks to the point, the Magothy, and the close proximity to the Chesapeake Bay Bridges where currents are exceptionally strong. As a result, this area is worth checking out. Trout particularly seem to like congregating here, usually in mid-fall in 18' to 22' of water. They seem to bunch up along the slope as they move out of the river and get ready to school en mass in deeper water near the bridge. You'll also encounter smallish stripers along this edge, but not usually any big boys; it's best thought of as a trout spot to hit in September or October during years of high salinity when trout move this far up the Bay. They don't orient to a specific item or drop, so it's nearly impossible to home right in on the fish here and stick over them. As a result, slow-trolling feather jigs or bucktails is the most effective way of locating and catching good numbers of fish in this spot.

Shorebound Angling Hot Spots of the Upper Chesapeake

There are days that the shoreline anglers walking along the banks of the upper Chesapeake Bay will catch more fish than the guys in boats. Lucky for you and me, Maryland and its counties usually do a pretty good job at maintaining access to Bay fishing sites. Only those with the very best fishing opportunities are included here. Die-hard shorebound anglers will want to write the DNR or visit their Annapolis office to get (free) copies of *A Fisherman's Guide to Maryland Piers and Boat Ramps* and *Maryland Guide to Freshwater Fishing*. Both show upwards of a hundred public access locations along the Bay and/or its tributaries. Be forewarned, however, that neither of these maps is perfect or completely up-to-date. The places included here are ones I can personally vouch for, spots that have been visited within the last year or two. But in my experience, one out of five places listed in the above-mentioned maps has incorrect directions, or lists some service that is not available at the spot, or has some other surprise in store. Using the Freshwater Fishing map, for example, I once drove over an hour, then arrived at a lake to discover that it had completely silted in and dried up. Usually the results aren't quite this bad, but be prepared for anything.

WESTERN SHORE

• **HAVRE DE GRACE:** At the mouth of the Susquehanna, there is a cluster of public areas that include public piers as well as some shoreline that you can fish directly from. Although the range of species available here is huge—large and smallmouth bass, yellow and white perch, catfish, crappie, sunfish, pickerel, and stripers—most of the fish caught from this area are going to be perch and catfish. For the perch, use small minnow or even crayfish, suspended under a bobber. For catfish, cut herring or menhaden is tough to beat.

The Lapidum area of Susquehanna State Park is a good bet for ambitious anglers. It has plenty of shoreline you can walk, and good numbers of smallmouth bass, red ear sunfish, and largemouth bass within casting distance. The conditions here will vary radically with the water flow—you could find crystal clear water with rocks visible on the bottom, or raging torrents of muddy water. If it's mud city, turn around and go elsewhere. If it's low and clear, however, you're in luck—as long as you remembered to bring a dip net. Then try wading in, flip over rocks, and scoop up the crayfish that come scurrying out. To catch bass, first snap off the crayfish's claws, then put your hook in through the underside of its tail, and out through the back. Suspend it under a bobber, and cast to visible rocks or drop-offs. If you spot a hole that's been scoured out, remove the bobber, put a split shot a few feet above the crayfish, and toss it into the hole.

To catch panfish, follow the same tactics with one difference—use just the tail of the crayfish. Rip off the top half of the body (it will separate easily from the tail) and throw it into the water. Then hook on the tail by inserting the point into the meaty end where it used to connect to the body, and push the point back out through the underside of the tail.

• **HAWKINS POINT:** The boat ramp has a pier that puts stripers, perch, and catfish within reach. Stripers and perch, however, will not be caught in great numbers here—this is really best thought of as a catfish spot. Toss out a piece of cut herring or menhaden, and you'll catch plenty of cats up to 8 or 10 lb. If you care to try night fishing here, also cast a bottom rig with small (#6 or #8) hooks, baited with a tiny piece of grass shrimp, peeler crab or cut fish, and you'll catch all the eels you can handle.

• **FT SMALLWOOD STATE PARK:** At the mouth of the Patapsco River is a better choice if you want a wider range of fish. Although the area surrounding the park is relatively shallow, anglers casting cut bait will hook into snapper blues with some regularity from June on through November. Croaker also make an occasional appearance here, usually in late May or early June. As with elsewhere, they bite better at night. Stripers are caught here in fair numbers, although most are sub-legal. The best shot at taking a good striped bass from the shore here is to cast cut menhaden or herring just before dawn, or as the sun sinks below the horizon, when larger stripers will head into the shallows to feed. Perch are also a possibility. To have the chance of catching striper, perch, or croaker all at the same time, many anglers use bottom rigs baited with bloodworm (all of these species love bloodworms!) and use hooks slightly larger than the norm for panfish, and slightly smaller than the norm for stripers (2/0 is about right).

• SANDY POINT STATE PARK: On the south end of the public beach, there's a jetty that runs 100' or so out into the main-stem Bay. There isn't much room between the south side of the jetty and the Bay bridge, and the channel from the public boat ramp—which sees an extraordinary amount of traffic on summer weekends—is narrow enough that you can almost cast across it. Don't, because your line is sure to be eaten up by the prop of a passing boater. A better trick is to cast just 10' or 15' outside of the rocks, up or down the jetty. Stripers will move in close to these rocks, particularly early and late in the day. You can also catch croaker, spot, perch, and snapper blues by simply casting bait as far out as possible.

Savvy anglers who arrive at this jetty before the crowd should follow a plan split between bait and lure fishing. When you first arrive at the jetty, try a Rat-L-Trap or similar swimming plug that will run three or four feet below the surface. Take 10 or 20 steps out onto the jetty, then cast parallel to the rocks, 10' or 15' out. Retrieving along the rocks is much more effective than casting and retrieving perpendicular to them. If nothing strikes, take another few steps and try again. You'll get in a dozen or so casts before you reach the end of the jetty, and hopefully, will hook up a few times.

Once you reach the end of the jetty, switch gears and put on a bait rig. Again, keep your rig relatively close to the rocks as opposed to throwing it as far as possible into the distance, unless you want to target snapper blues.

Note that on days with a strong north, east, or northeast wind, the water at Sandy Point tends to get riled up. If the winds are 20 mph or stronger, the water will often be too murky to fish here.

EASTERN SHORE

• C&D CANAL: It might not be a part of the Bay itself, but the C&D Canal is worth a mention because it has many public piers lining the shore which can be very productive catfish spots, and at times will also produce stripers and perch. The shoreline of most of the canal (all of it where the public piers are) is lined with riprap. Walking along and casting plugs will produce some fish, but it's hard walking on the riprap and it's nearly impossible to land the fish you hook into. The piers themselves, however, are well designed for bank anglers. They're large, wide, and provide plenty of room even when a dozen anglers show up. They are also far enough out into the canal to avoid some of the snagging caused by the riprap, when casting bait on bottom rigs.

The best bet for action on these piers is to arrive armed with cut herring, and put it on the bottom for channel and bullhead catfish. Bring a lot of lead; the strong currents present in the canal mean you'll need at least three or four ounces to hold bottom. Also bring a long handled landing net. The piers are fairly high up off the water, and you'll lose a lot of fish if you try lifting them up onto the deck.

• **KENT NARROWS:** The very best spot for shoreline striped bass angling on the northern Eastern Shore is probably at Kent Narrows. On the mainland side there is public parking and a pier built over the bulkhead, directly under the new and old bridges. Anywhere along this bulkhead can provide good action.

This is a particularly great spot for catching stripers, because unlike most shoreline spots, many of the fish will be keepers. You also have a reasonable chance of hooking into a really large fish here. Snapper blues, croaker, perch, spot, and (at night under the lights during late summer and fall) seatrout are also available in the Narrows. As with fishing in the canal, you'll need lots of lead to keep your rigs from being swept away by the strong current. There are also a fair number of snags here; bring plenty of extra tackle.

Possibly because of the close proximity to marshlands and shallows, soft and peeler crabs seem particularly effective here. Another great bait in the narrows is live white perch, if you want to catch stripers. You can often catch them on the spot by dropping a bottom rig with small hooks baited with grass shrimp or bloodworm bits, right in front of the bulkhead. Smart striper anglers will come here with a couple of heavy rods and one ultralight. They'll use the ultralight to catch spot or white perch, and as soon as they get a proper size fish for bait, put it on a fishfinder rig (see part II, chapter 12, Standard Bay Rigs) and toss it out into the narrows on one of the heavier rigs. Note, however, that since this area will become crowded on weekends during the summer, it's a bit inconsiderate to run more than three lines at a time.

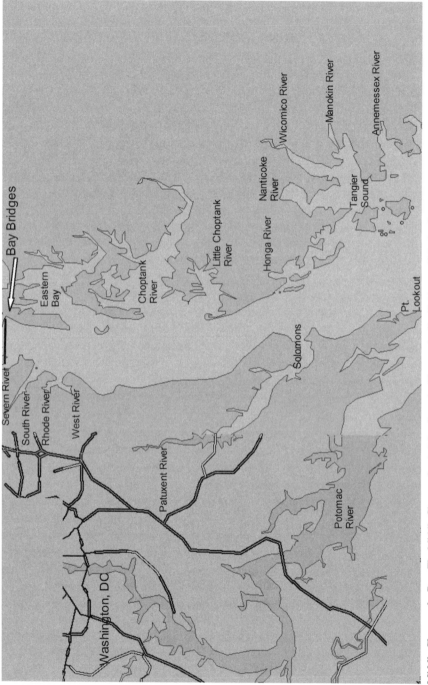

Middle Chesapeake Bay. The Middle Chesapeake stretches from the Chesapeake Bay Bridges to Point Lookout.

THE MIDDLE CHESAPEAKE BAY

Convenient to both the Baltimore and Washington metropolitan areas, the middle Chesapeake is one of the most heavily fished bodies of water on the eastern seaboard. Easy public access is provided by numerous boat ramps and marinas, including Sandy Point State Park—one of the largest and best maintained launching facilities in the mid-Atlantic region. The middle Bay has widely varying salinity levels, which means you'll find a huge variety of species here. You may catch catfish in a particular spot one season then return to the spot a year later and catch a speckled seatrout, even though these two species would never swim in the same waters at the same time. And in the spring, the waters between the Bay Bridges and Point Lookout offer some of the best trophy striper action on the Chesapeake.

Fishing the Bay Bridges

There is no single structure or spot in Maryland waters that attracts the number of anglers that the Chesapeake Bay Bridges do. Does this area hold twice as many fish as any other spot? Doubtful. But there's no doubt that at certain times this will be the hottest place on the Bay to catch stripers, weakfish, or white perch. But to fish here during the peak of the season you've got to be willing to brave the crowds—or make sure you fish in lousy weather. Otherwise, be prepared for lots of competition.

Looking at the bridge purely as structure is a mistake many anglers make. There are two bridges, and north and a south span, each of which provides good structure. But don't forget about the strip of water between them. Since Kent Island and Sandy Point conspire to pinch the Bay in this location, tidal currents are exaggerated. On the eastern side the ancient Susquehanna river bed snakes through, providing access to extremely deep water. Concrete bridge pilings provide cover, and two huge rock piles at the center spans of the south bridge create a reef that jump-starts the food chain. All of these features work together to create productive fishing, so you should try to think of the bridge not as a piece of structure, but as a whole zone that attracts fish. Since those rock piles mentioned earlier provide the fastest action on the most reliable basis, let's start there.

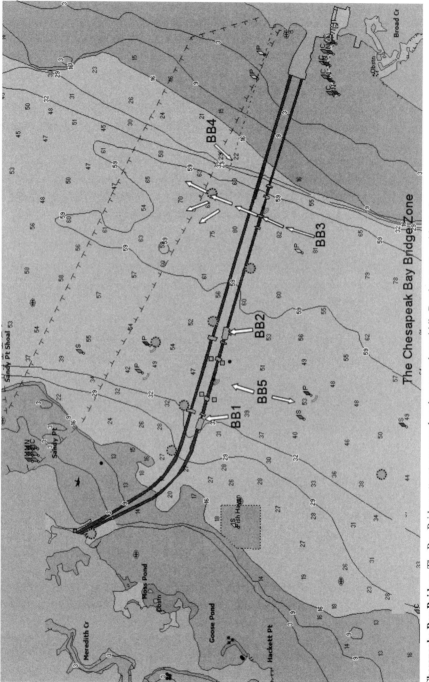

Chesapeake Bay Bridges. The Bay Bridges attract more anglers than any other middle Bay hot spot—with good reason.

The Rock Piles (BB1, BB2) will each at different times take the title for hottest action, but I usually start at the eastern pile. It gets less pressure, simply because the western one is closer to Sandy Point State Park's boat ramp, one of the largest launching facilities on the east coast. Fishing each of them, however, is essentially the same. Start by approaching to within casting distance of the rocks, and putt around them once with a close eye on the fishfinder. Zigzag through the water between the piles and the large concrete piles of the north bridge, too, as these areas often hold fish. Remember—90% of the time if you see marks separated from bottom by more than five feet, you're looking at stripers. Marks that look like caterpillars creeping along the bottom are more likely seatrout. When you've got a feel for which sector holds the most fish, set up to drift through it.

Feather jigging or casting leadhead/plastic combinations are the tactics most commonly used to take stripers (which can be found here almost year-round) from the rock piles. The most effective technique is to cast and retrieve along the rocks, but obviously this does lead to a lot of snags. Tough luck—you play, you pay. But note that when the fish are hanging deep, the most bites often come from the 35' zone where the base of the rocks meets mud and sand bottom. Heavy lures can be worked deep in this zone as you drift along, without too many casualties.

When trout take up residence (usually late September through mid-November) jigging tandem rigs becomes the favored method. During the fall and well into the winter you'll also be able to pull large numbers of white perch off of these rocks. Because of all the snags, the good old top-and-bottom rig bait fishing approach isn't a good move here. You'll have better results casting and retrieving small feathers, shad darts, and twister tails rigged in tandem or above a drop sinker, with enough weight to keep near the bottom.

Never attempt to anchor close to the rock piles. The currents change quickly and radically here, and the bottom is littered with snags. This is probably one of the number-one spots in the middle Chesapeake to lose an anchor. Beside the danger, anchoring here will also aggravate other anglers by blocking their cooperative drift pattern (more on this later).

The many concrete piles of the Bay bridges hold smaller numbers of fish than the rock piles, but they are usually larger—sometimes much larger. If you hope to take a trophy-sized striper off of the bridge, fishing the piles is one of two ways to go about it. (We'll discuss the second way later). But I'll warn you now, it won't be easy. Some charter captains have made fishing the concrete piles their life study, and most will readily admit that even they get stumped by the conditions sometimes. Conditions here—current and wind, in specific—are make-or-break. Too little tide and the fish might not be actively feeding. Too much, and you'll have a tough time holding the boat in position. Now toss a breeze and lots of boat traffic into the mix; you get the picture.

Why is it so important for these conditions to be just right? Because you'll need to hold your boat close enough that your crew can slap the concrete with their lures. The fish are often hugging the piles and the exaggerated currents found here will sweep a two-ounce bucktail out of the strike zone in seconds, so casts five or ten feet off-target simply don't count. Note that I said "your crew." Forget about casting yourself, because the conditions almost always require the captain to bump the boat in and out of gear, to hold it within casting distance for more than one shot.

A few people will tie off to the bridge pilings, but I do not suggest you try it. The winds, currents and sea conditions here can and will change in the blink of an eye, and what seemed like a safe position can become an unsafe one in seconds. Instead, I usually start by positioning my boat on the upcurrent side of the pile I'm fishing, so my anglers can cast about 5' upcurrent of it. Then, the anglers should allow the current to sweep the bucktail past the pile's sides—the closer the better. Often, this is when the strike will come. Since your lure is sinking you won't usually feel the pick-up, but you can detect it by watching your slack line for a sudden change in direction, or an abrupt bump. If you see it, set the hook immediately. Once the bucktail has swept past the concrete, start a retrieve. On the next shot, cast 10' upcurrent, and on the next 15', and so on, so the lure falls past the pile at different depths on each cast. No hits after five or six casts? Move on to the next piling. There are plenty of them, and different ones will hold fish on different days.

What about fishing from the downcurrent position? I've never had much success with this method—and I've never seen baitfish swimming downcurrent in these conditions for more than a second or two, so I don't think this technique will produce the most life-like action for your lures. But, other people do claim success fishing the piles this way. So give it a shot if the desire strikes you.

When it's legal (usually after the fall season kicks in) eeling at the piles can also be effective. Eels need to be weighted and dropped, not casted and retrieved, so if you want to try this method you'll have to position your boat even closer to the piles. For this reason, I've never been a great fan of eeling at the bridge. It's best to try this during periods of slow tides, at the very end of the cycle, when you can get within 10' or 15' of the piles and flick the eel right next to the concrete. Unlike eeling a lump or edge, when you're usually drifting, you want to keep that eel right next to the pile. If the current sweeps it off too quickly, up-size your weight or try to back up to the pile and drop your rig in the calm water right behind it, where it can sink without instantly being pushed away. Again, if you have no bites don't hesitate to move on to the next pile.

The channel (BB3) running along the eastern side of the Bay under the bridge is the second place you're likely to hook into a monster striper. This isn't the main shipping channel, which goes between the towering center spans of the bridge, but is the riverbed from eons ago when the Susquehanna hadn't yet flooded its banks and become the Chesapeake Bay. If you want to target the trophy fish here, you'll need to troll this water during the spring season using standard spring trophy trolling methods (see part II: Tactics and Tackle). Work an east-west zigzag pattern as you move down the channel, from a mile above the bridge to a mile below it. Allow your depth finder to climb to 35' or 40' on the east side before you zig, and to 50' on the west side before you zag. You'll note that the drop is a lot more abrupt on the eastern side. This entire zone can produce some real bruisers, and I'll never forget that this place was where I heard my father curse for the first time ever, when he thumbed the spool and broke off the biggest striper he'd fought on the Bay—right in-between the two bridges.

Though this deep water is most often thought of as striper territory, it should also be considered when jigging for trout in the fall. Large weakfish can be found along these channel edges, usually hugging tightly to the bottom in 40' to 70' of water. It's tough to catch these fish, since you're aiming for a small target far below and your lures will have a long way to drop before hitting bottom in an area of strong current. However, finding these fish can really make your day. On several occasions in the past few years I've located fish in the 5–7 lb range here, while the trout hovering below the schools of breaking fish near the bridges averaged a ½ lb.

Located just north of the bridge on the eastern side of the deepwater channel is the "sewer pipe" (BB4). While it doesn't sound too appetizing, the sewer pipe is worth checking out whenever you're in this area. It's easy to find, since it's marked with a small white and orange float (it looks like a speed limit float marker) and the bottom appears jagged on the fishfinder. In fact, it will jump from 28' to 15' and back down again in no time. I've heard that this is because rocks and riprap were placed near the pipe to protect and anchor it, though I can't profess to know this for sure.

The sewer pipe will hold both stripers and trout, but differs from the bridge proper in that it is possible to safely anchor up and chum here. Just idle upcurrent of the jagged bottom a sufficient distance, and let out enough anchor line to drift back over it. Note, though, that doing this on a weekend will draw you plenty of evil stares from other anglers who had intended on checking out this spot. Don't be surprised if a few drift right through your chum slick.

During the early spring trolling rules the Bay Bridge zone, and during summer and fall fishing the rock piles, pilings, channel edges, and sewer pipe are the usual approaches. But once September hits all bets are off when working birds are spotted. Under these seagulls you'll find stripers and blues chewing on Bay anchovies or menhaden, with seatrout waiting deep below to scavenge the fish parts that fall from above. Find the birds by scanning up and down the bridges and the strip of water between them with a pair of binoculars. When you see them cruise over, but make sure to drop your speed back before you get within a quarter mile of the schools of fish. Often you'll see overanxious anglers drive right into the fray, scaring the fish and sending them deep. Instead, approach at idle speeds and skirt the school, so that you can put your boat in neutral right on its upwind fringes. For blues and stripers, cast jigs, spoons or plugs into the breaking fish and give them a spirited, quick retrieve near the surface. For trout, drop tandem rigs, spoons or other heavy jigging lures down to the bottom.

When you find a flock of birds dipping down to the water's surface but don't see any fish breaking, don't spend a whole lot of time concentrating on the area. Many times you will encounter flocks of birds near the bridge that are feeding on tiny Bay anchovies. Unfortunately, you'll often discover that these gulls are the only creatures feeding on the tiny baitfish, and to locate gamefish you'll have to go elsewhere.

The Shipping Channel at BB5 just to the south of the bridges is another location that often produces fish. There isn't any particular ridge, break or structure to look for here, but if you've fished the Bay Bridge zone without finding much action, it's always a good idea to meander across this area with a close eye on the fishfinder. Schools of stripers and late in the year schools of trout seem to like this spot for some reason.

The Western Shore Rivers

The Severn River is home to Annapolis, and as such, is often clogged with sailboats, scullers, and numerous other pleasure boats. However, it also offers a unique shot at winter fishing in the middle Bay zone. Much like the Magothy, the Severn enjoys a decent yellow perch and pickerel fishery which blossoms in December and continues until ice forms or the weather starts warming up, whichever comes first. During the summer, the Severn also has several areas that are productive for shallow water, light tackle striper fishing. Before describing any of these, we must remind ourselves that the Naval Academy is located along the banks of the Severn, and although the Academy's bulkheads and riprap walls do hold fish, they should be avoided. Since 9/11 these areas have been patrolled by the navy, so it's pretty clear they don't want anglers casting in these waters, at least for the time being. Note also that naval ships often visit this area, and should also be avoided for the same reasons.

Hunting for cold water pickerel and perch on the Severn is best done from a small, shallow draft boat. The majority of the good spots are in tight coves and ponds, and some have inlets that are less than a foot deep. In a couple of cases, to access the water you'll have to step out of the boat and push it over or onto a sand bar, and sometimes, wade fish. For this reason, you should plan on dressing in hip or chest waders that are well insulated.

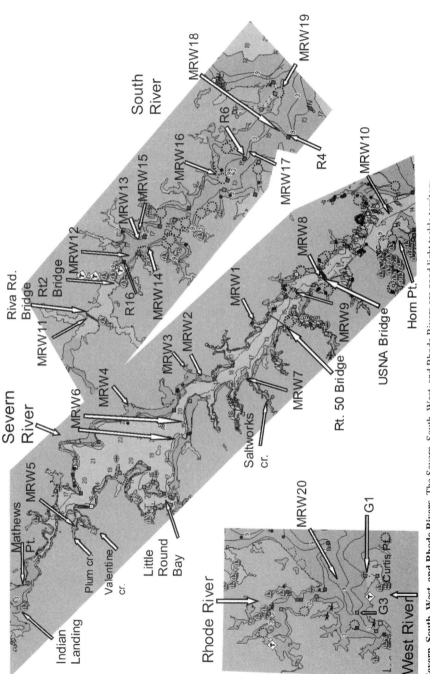

Severn, South, West, and Rhode Rivers. The Severn, South, West, and Rhode Rivers are good light tackle territory.

Several of the coves and ponds on the Severn have relatively deep water, which is not ideal for this kind of fishing. Instead, you're looking for four feet or less water, with weedbeds. Although this is a winter fishery and much of the weeds will have died out, there will usually be remnants of the weedbeds that provide enough cover to attract pickerel and perch. The technique is rather unusual—cast $\frac{1}{4}$ or $\frac{1}{8}$ oz Roadrunners with bullhead minnow on the hook. When a fish takes the bait do not set the hook; pickerel usually grab a baitfish with their needle-like teeth, and hold it for 10 or 20 seconds, waiting for it to die, before they take it all the way into their mouth. Set the hook on the strike, or after a five-count, and you'll miss the fish every time. Instead, simply stop reeling when a fish takes the bait. Remain motionless until you feel the fish turn and start to swim away. This is your cue to strike. If a perch takes the minnow it will usually start swimming immediately, so even though you won't have the wait, you'll still feel the fish swimming away. Note that current regulations at the time of this writing do not allow harvesting yellow perch from the Severn, South, or Magothy Rivers.

The first pond of interest lies on the northern side of the river, just above the Rt 50 bridge. Cool Spring Cove is deep to the right of the cove entrance, but there is a shallower pool behind a sandy spit to the left (MRW1). Poke up inside of this spit, and you should be able to locate some fish. Reys' Pond, two coves upriver on the northern shore, is usually chock-full of pickerel and perch. Also look for the boathouse between Chase Creek and Reys' Pond, as this is also a good place to cast for perch and small stripers (MRW2). Reys' (marked by MRW3) is one of the spots best fished by wading. From the pond entrance, walk along the sand spit to your left and cast into the middle of the pond. Continuing upriver, check out the piers in the small creek at MRW4, too. The pilings and boathouses here often have perch and pickerel hiding beneath them. From here, you'll want to cruise all the way up into the rivers' headwaters, above Mathews' Point. Any of the shorelines and the shallows upriver of Indian Landing can be productive. Unfortunately, this area of the river is also the first to freeze, and some winters it's rare to be able to fish here.

Heading back down the southern shore of the Severn, Plum Creek and Valentine Creek are both good bets for pickerel; pay particular attention to the shallows of Plum Creek at MRW5, and cast alongside all of the piers on shore here. All of the coves off of Little Round Bay (Browns, Maynadier, and Hopkins) are also prime pickerel waters, but stay away from the deeper sections and cast to four or fewer feet of water. Although the rest of the coves running down this shore will be productive at times, they won't have as many pickerel and yellow perch hiding in them as the ones mentioned above. Fish them, but only to fill out the day after fishing these others.

The entrance of Little Round Bay and the waters off Sherwood Forest at MRW6 are noteworthy for another reason: occasionally, seatrout will ball up along these sharp drop offs. You usually won't catch huge fish here, but one of five will usually be of legal size.

All of the creek mouths and points along the Severn, as well as the numerous piers and especially boathouses, are worth checking out for light tackle casting to stripers in the 12" to 24" range. The northern entrance to Saltworks Creek, which has several piers that reach into fairly deep water at MRW7 is a particularly good bet. The Severn is also a good choice for small boat anglers who get locked out of the Bay by strong winds. Trolling the channel edges, which run fairly close to the river banks in most of the Severn, with Rat-L-Traps and small bucktails will produce keeper stripers on a regular basis.

During the warmer months of the year and into the fall, the hottest spot in the Severn is usually the old railroad bridge, which was knocked down years ago but left on the bottom as a fish reef. It worked—white perch and rock often congregate around the chunks of concrete. The bridge chunks are fairly easy to locate in a couple of different areas. The first is on the upriver side of the Naval Academy bridge (the first bridge as you head upriver). As you pass under the bridge you'll notice that you can see a section of the old bridge, which was left standing. Directly in front of it, you can locate the old concrete piles that use to support the bridge (MRW8). They are very recognizable, as they will make quite a significant target on most modern fishfinders. Try jigging or dropping bait on top and bottom rigs to catch perch and stripers around these piles. One word of warning: as you might expect, if you're drift fishing here you will end up hooking bottom quite often.

The second collection of bridge pieces lies in the middle of the river, about half way between the Academy bridge and the Rt 50 bridge at MRW9. To find it, just motor up the middle of the channel with an eye on the fishfinder. These are huge chunks of concrete, and you'll find cliff-like drops from 15 to 22 in several spots. As with the other cluster of bridge parts, plan on losing plenty of tackle here. On the other hand, remember that at times, this spot will provide the best white perch fishing on the Bay.

There's one more place in the Severn that merits your attention, this one in the mouth of the river. Between Horn Point on the southern shore of the river and the green #9, 7, and 5 buoys, there are numerous holes, bumps, and sharp edges (MRW10). This area is tough to fish on the drift or at anchor during the summer, because it sees a lot of boat traffic. But much of the time, slow-trolling and bottom-bouncing small bucktails will produce decent catches of stripers, and in some years, blues and trout, too. Every pleasure boat that comes into or leaves Annapolis cruises right through this area, so forget about it on weekends. But mid-week, off-season and on rainy days, this is a great spot to hit.

The South River lies just to the south of Annapolis. My home is a stone's throw from this river and it is one of my most common stomping grounds.

The one thing I've learned through the years is that this river will run hot and cold, season to season. Some years I've taken flounder, speckled trout, weakfish, stripers, blues, croaker, perch, and spot all in the same day. Other seasons I've come up empty inside the rivers' confines, to the point that I didn't even bother fishing it anymore but went elsewhere. One exception: night fishing under the Rt 2 bridge for stripers is a pretty sure bet, year after year. Cast net a livewell full of peanut bunker along the lightlines, then live-line them with no weight between the hours of 9:00 P.M. and midnight, and I'll bet you get a strike or two or twenty.

During most years, there's good striper fishing at several locations in the river. The farthest upriver spot commonly fished is the Riva Rd bridge, which has fairly deep water on the up-river side. Drift along 40' to 50' from the pilings while casting grubs, jigs or plugs up the bridge. On the north bank, you'll see a pier just 25' or 30' upriver of the bridge at MRW11. Cast to the end of this pier, and between the pier and the bridge, and you'll usually hook into several fish in the 16" to 22" class. Casting to the Rt 2 bridge pilings will also produce stripers, as will casting to the piers along either side of the river. Just down river of the Rt 2 bridge, you'll notice a very deep but small hole on the north side, tight below the red marker #16 (MRW12). Many seasons this hole is deserted, but some years it holds weakfish from late September through November. Other years, I've found blues, stripers and even flounder lurking in here. Don't bet the bank on this spot, but check it out once or twice a season and find out if it's holding fish.

The next point down river I call the Mollie Spot (MRW13) because when she was two years old my daughter Mollie insisted I cast there as we drove past one day. Bingo—the first toss produced a 15" weakfish. Two more followed, and I started fishing there regularly, limiting-out on numerous occasions (night fishing with fresh soft crab is by far the most effective tactic to use here).

Directly across the river from the Mollie Spot is Almshouse creek, which has a productive riprap point and wall, right at the mouth (MRW14). Casting to these rocks will produce stripers up to 26"; however, you'll find that the strikes here come very early and very late in the day during low-light periods, and the spot is usually pretty dead during full sunlight. Same goes for the point at MRW15, to the south of the Mollie Spot. Both the riprap and the pier and boathouse here will produce fish up into the mid-twenty inch range, but generally speaking, only at daybreak and sunset.

The next productive point (MRW16) is a long jump down the river, on the north side. This point is actually a concrete wall, lined with riprap at the base. Be careful when casting here, as any lure that touches bottom is usually snagged and lost to the rocks. But it's worth the risk; this point often holds large numbers of stripers, as does the broken down pier on the upriver side of the concrete. You'll also catch white perch here, if you cast smaller lures.

The red #6 channel marker is an important marker to remember, as this is often one of the best spots in the river to take stripers, trout, and flounder. A shelf juts out into the channel here, and the bottom goes from 18' to 10' to 22' in a very short distance (MRW17). Both the top of the shelf and the sides will be productive at different times. When fishing this area you'll notice how the channel edge dips in towards shore slightly downriver of the marker; this is another spot that fish often congregate. Jigging, trolling crankbaits, and live-baiting are all productive along these drops.

At the mouth of the river, at the red #4 is another spot you'll want to check out. A bar at MRW18 runs from this mark to Thomas Point. Upriver of the bar where the depth is about 15' is a productive area for stripers and weakfish, and for some reason, trolling Rat-L-Traps at idle speed seems to produce exceptionally well in this area.

The Rocks on Thomas Point is the last South River hot spot we need to examine. A word to the wise: approach these rocks slowly and at high tide, until you feel very familiar with this area. There are several patches of rocks laying on the bottom, any of which will do a number on your prop. The first batch is just about 25 yards off the very end of Thomas Point, slightly over to the north side, and is marked by MRW19. These rocks take the most pressure because anglers can see the water breaking over and around them in most conditions. The other patches—one another 30 yards out and a third a half-mile from shore—are productive because they are not nearly as visible and do not get fished very often. On the downside, locating them can be tough. Often the first sign you've found the rocks is a bent prop or a snagged lure. Note also that there are scattered rocks lining the underwater ridge that runs from the visible riprap out to that last bunch of rocks, and running aground anywhere in this zone can be disastrous. Of course, approach and fish carefully and the rewards can be great.

To find these outer rock patches, idle on a 145-degree course away from the first bunch of rocks. Keep it slow, and post someone on the bow to look out for rocks. Every 50 yards or so stop and fan-cast a leadhead on light line off the starboard side of the boat. When it snags bottom, break it off and mark the spot. Then cast jigs to that same area, retrieving quickly enough to keep off the bottom. If you've found a rock pile, chances are you'll hook a fish. If nothing bites, continue searching with the same method.

The best way I've found to fish this series of rocks is to approach from the north side of the point, and idle up to within casting distance of the first batch. If there's another boat there I'll move on to the second batch, as this is a pretty limited area and in my book, whoever gets up the earliest in the morning wins the spot. In either case, if the first batch doesn't produce, move on to the others. You can hold your position around the rocks with either an electric motor or an anchor, but be forewarned that a standard Danforth will skip and drag here until it gets caught up in rocks. Then, you may have trouble getting it free. Instead, go with a grappling anchor. In calm seas with a small boat a cinderblock will work, too. Cast jigs, bucktails, and the like as close as possible to the rocks, and retrieve them at high speed. Go for a bottom-bouncing retrieve, and your lure won't survive the first cast—there are just too many snags here. And if you like the explosion of a striper hitting a topwater lure, this is a good place to try it.

If you do have good luck at the first batch of rocks, you're likely to fish-out or spook the spot after a dozen or so fish. When this happens, move out and start looking at the other rocks. They'll be holding fish at the same times. On a high tide, the riprap right against the northern shore of the point will be productive, too. Just remember to look for bank fishermen and stay clear if there are any in sight; you can move on, but they're stuck with that one spot. You can fish the northern side for about 50 yards before abruptly running out of water. The south side of the point is tough to approach on any tide. Even on a flood, there will only be a few feet of water and the small secondary point that you'll see jutting out into the south river has a very shallow, prop-eating shoal that sticks out from it.

Most of the fish taken at the Thomas Point rock piles are caught late in the fall. October and November are prime times to cast here, but daybreak and sunset during the summer and early fall can also be productive. I've seen people fish them in the spring and I've tried it a time or two myself, but never with much success. It should be noted, however, that a waterfront property owner I know who lives very close to Thomas Point catches a spring trophy or two each season, casting from his pier late in the evening or shortly after dark, baiting with big chunks of menhaden. Perch can often also be taken from around these rocks by casting Beetle Spins, two-inch grubs, and similar sized baits.

The Rhode and West Rivers are much like the South, in that they can run hot or cold year to year. Often the best zone these two small tributaries offer is the mouth where the two rivers come together at MRW20. During the summer this is a good area to try for weakfish (as usual during the heat of summer, it's best to try at night). Later in the year many anglers score on 16" to 26" stripers by trolling tandem rigs with small bucktails, Rat-L-Traps, and spoons. The basic tactic is to start at the mouth of the Rhode and troll to the northeast along the drop towards the green #1A marker. When you near the green, swing south and troll towards Curtis Point. As soon as it starts to shallow up turn west and head for the green marker #3. When you reach the green #3, turn north again, back towards the mouth of the Rhode. Continue trolling in this circle, and you should get into the fish.

Perch and smallish stripers can be taken inside either of these rivers by casting to piers, points, and riprap, but the West and the Rhode are not great rivers for anglers during most warm months of the year, because this is a very popular area with water skiers, swimmers and partiers. On weekends, in fact, it gets every bit as crowded in here as Annapolis Harbor. Swimmers will be everywhere, and fishing in the area just doesn't make much sense.

Just outside of these rivers, however, is another area that holds stripers; the stretch of land running from the easternmost point at the mouth of the Rhode River to the north, towards the South River, is covered with riprap, rock walls and also has a pound net. All of these structures will produce fish at different times. To fish the pound net, move in close and cast right up next to it with jigs and plugs. Many of the pound nets along the Western Shore in the middle Bay region are good fishing spots in some years, and are pretty dead in others. It's always a good idea to check out a pound net or two early in the fall, and keep coming back if you catch fish. If no takers appear on the second or third time you try the nets, move elsewhere and don't waste any more time on them, as they'll probably remain barren the rest of the season.

Rockhold Creek, which feeds Herring Bay, is certainly not a river and much of the time it runs muddy and is unfishable. However, it's worth noting for anglers who want to try for stripers fishing from a canoe, kayak, or other very small boat. There are two bridges on Rockhold, and one on nearby Tracy Creek. The bridge farther up on Rockhold is the most productive one of the three bridges, but all will produce a few fish if you cast jigs and bucktails dressed with twister tails or Rat-L-Traps, next to the pilings in late summer or fall. Note that some years the bridge pilings will be loaded with fish, others they will be more or less barren—this one's a coin-toss until you try it.

The Western Shore of the Chesapeake runs unbroken for many riverless miles, until you reach the Patuxent. The Patuxent River is significantly larger than most of the rivers covered thus far on the Western Shore, and so it has many more opportunities for different fisheries at different times. Everyone from bass anglers to crabbers can find what they like in the Patuxent.

Let's start upriver where perch, crappie, bass, and catfish are all available in good numbers, at different times. First a word of caution: after heavy rainfall, the upper and middle sections of the Patuxent will turn muddy and fishing will come to a halt. After a significant storm, it's best to wait at least four days before planning to fish the river. Boaters should also note that even when it runs clear the upper Patuxent is relatively cloudy, and there are plenty of submerged trees, branches and other boat-damaging items lurking just beneath the surface. It's best to cruise slowly and carefully.

From the Rt 219 bridge to the Rt 4 bridge in Wayson's Corner, most of the river is bass country. Crappie, sunfish, catfish (in huge numbers), perch, and pickerel are all present in this area, but most of the fishing action that takes place along this stretch is by dedicated bass anglers. Casting to visible structure such as fallen trees and root balls is the basic tactic, and it is effective.

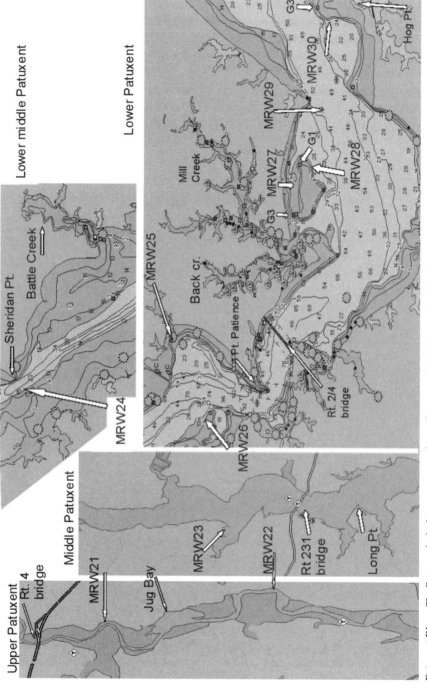

Upper Patuxent

Rt. 4
bridge

MRW21

Jug Bay

Middle Patuxent

MRW23

MRW22

Rt 231
bridge

Long Pt.

Lower middle Patuxent

Sheridan Pt.

Battle Creek

MRW24

MRW25

Back cr.

Pt. Patience

MRW26

Lower Patuxent

Mill
Creek

MRW27

G3

G1

MRW29

MRW28

MRW30

G3

Hog Pt.

Rt. 2/4
bridge

Patuxent River. The Patuxent is the longest western shore tributary entirely in the state of Maryland.

Near Upper Marlboro, where Rt 4 crosses over the river, sees an excellent yellow perch run in early March, followed by a white perch run a few weeks later. Just downriver from the Rt 4 bridge, the river takes a sharp bend to east (MRW21). Along the eastern bank, right in the sharpest part of the bend, there's a deep hole that both types of perch will hold in before staging the spawning run. This is also a good place to catch catfish. The fallen timber along the shores of this stretch of the river also hold largemouth bass, crappie, and sunfish. Most of the trees you see, however, will be barren. Look for those that either lay in eddies in the current, or create their own eddies, to hold the majority of the fish.

Then next hot spot moving downriver is Jug Bay, which is extremely shallow and is full of branches and fallen trees. Again, remember to take it slow and careful here. To leave the channel here and enter the Bay itself, you'll need either a canoe or similarly shallow-draft boat, as the water in many areas is barely a foot deep. There's also a lot of weed growth here in the summer, but if you can deal with it, you'll pull crappie, bass, pickerel, and sunfish out of this water. In the deeper areas, close to the western bank, there are catfish by the truckload. An interesting note: redfin pickerel, which aren't often caught on the Western Shore of the Chesapeake, are also present here in fair numbers.

Heading downriver another strong bend, this one pointing west at MRW22, has a deep hole carved into the riverbed. You'll find perch during the same spring run time frame here, though they'll arrive in this spot a few days to a week before they arrive near Wayson's Corner. Catfish can be caught here, too, year-round. The next stretch of river is an especially tough one to navigate, because the channel is less defined and there's a good deal more shallow water. Continue downriver, however, and the river deepens out again. Any of the fallen timber along this stretch can produce bass and crappie, but look for the areas of undercut banks, too. There are a few spots where the water has eaten away the soil between tree roots, providing fantastic cover. Drift baits through the holes under these root balls, and you'll find fish.

Where the river widens out and starts becoming much more noticeably brackish, there's a very important spot to note: Chalk Point. The power plant here—the largest generating plant in Maryland—has a warm-water discharge (MRW23) and in the wintertime provides a refuge for fish and anglers. Most of the fish taken here in the winter months will be small stripers, white perch, and catfish, but since the river here sees relatively strong tidal flow as well as a constant current, the warm water is disbursed fairly quickly and at times will be hard to pinpoint. Fortunately, the discharge canal is easily spotted. In years past it was possible to fish inside the discharge canal, and catch some pretty decent striped bass by bouncing jigs along the bottom. After 9/11, the regulations can change moment to moment. So while this does present an opportunity for winter anglers, you should only head for Chalk Point after reminding yourself that there is some possibility you'll be unable to cast your lures where you'd really like to.

From this point downriver, the Patuxent becomes much more like the Bay than like a river. Croaker will run as far up as the Rt 231 bridge some years, stripers become very common, and most of the fish in this zone are of the saltier nature.

Light tackle anglers can have a ball with stripers in the 14" to 28" class in this part of the Patuxent. Just below the Rt 231 bridge and all along the shores of Long Point there are docks and piers that hold fish. Even better is the area around Sheridan Point. Water over 40' comes right up to the point here, and there is a deep channel that continues above and below the point at MRW24. This is a great area to troll light tackle very close to the shore. Try to keep your boat in 15' to 20' of water, which is right in the middle of the drop. The mouth of Battle Creek is another good casting area for stripers, and up towards the headwaters of the creek you'll encounter largemouth bass and pickerel again.

The large stretch of water from Battle Creek down to Solomon's Island is striper, perch, and croaker water, with the occasional trout mixed in. Most of the stripers caught in this segment of the river will come from either trolling the channel edges or casting light tackle to the shorelines, piers, and creek mouths. White perch can be caught by drifting grass shrimp or bloodworm bits over the bumps and edges. But there are also some long stretches of very deep water that most of the time is fairly barren. Schools of weakfish may move in and out and you will find pockets of stripers along the drops, but don't spend too much time trying to search out the deep water in this zone.

Two shallow areas you will want to check out: the southwestern edge just outside of Hellen Creek (MRW25), and at the mouth of Cuckold Creek (MRW26). There's a fairly large stretch at MRW25 which is 15' deep, with a 7' plateau above it, and the deep channel below it. This 15' area and the edges above and below (to about 30') are flounder hot spots two out of three seasons, on average. Most of the flatties caught inside the river will be 14" to 17", and so you will catch many throw-backs. But weed through five or six undersized fish, and you should take a keeper or two. The same is true of the point of 10' water at MRW26; fish the plateau itself, the drop to its north and the drop to its south, and you should find some flatties.

Pt Patience and the Rt 2/4 bridge adjoin some incredibly deep water, and some of the holes here hit 120'. Occasionally schools of 16" to 26" stripers will hold along the mid-depth edges of these drops, but often fishing in this zone doesn't produce too much. Light tackle casters are better off casting jigs and plugs to the numerous piers and pilings behind Solomon's Island. While the river side shore of Solomon's does have piers as well, they aren't hot spots. Instead of spending your fishing time there, cruise around the island to Black and Mill Creeks. To catch flounder on jigs, look for the green #3 marker just northeast of the island. There's a secondary channel running close to shore here. Between green #3 and green #1 there's a sand bar, and drifting through the channel while bouncing a jig across the edge of the bar at MRW27 is a very good tactic. You can also work the eastern edge of this bar (MRW28) for flounder and because the drop goes down a little farther on this edge (to 25' deep) you'll often encounter stripers here, too. Late in the year, trout will also school along this edge. To catch croaker in the evening, anchor your boat just outside of the green #1 and cast baits into the secondary channel. As it gets darker send your casts closer and closer to the bar, into shallower water, and you can sometimes experience non-stop action here. There's also a man-made fish reef on the southern edge of this same bar. Try it if you like, but I wouldn't expect too much; in my experience, you'll loose a lot of tackle fishing around it, without catching many fish.

Small boat anglers in particular will be interested in a spot east of Solomon's and south of Drum Point, where there's deep water at MRW29 that is a good place to troll or chum along the drops from 30' to 50' on days when winds keep you from fishing the Bay proper. This spot will also see concentrations of seatrout most years, usually between late August and late October, and is a good backup jigging area during periods of rough weather.

Heading out of the river on the southern side of the mouth, there's a green marker #3 off of Hog Point. The bar inside of this marker is a must-stop spot for anyone who likes jigging for flounder and trout, or drifting bait on fluke killer rigs for these species. Croaker and spot will also be caught in decent numbers here. As you approach the marker you'll see a mass of crab pots between the marker and shore. Drive right to the edge of these pots, and keep an eye on the depth finder. You'll notice that the pots are set in shallow water, and end right at the drop-off. Using the crab pot floats as a point of reference, fish this drop from where the floats end into 22' or 25' of water on the western edge of this point, marked MRW30. Sometimes you'll end up catching more fish right on this edge than you will in any of the spots in the main-stem Bay—don't pass it by without giving it a shot at the beginning of the day, and stop here again as you head back into the river.

The next and last river of the middle Bay's Western Shore effectively divides the middle and lower Chesapeake, creates the Maryland/Virginia border, and is one of the most important tributaries to the Chesapeake. The Potomac River runs through Washington, D.C., winds all the way up into West Virginia, supports a vast selection of fishing opportunities for both freshwater and saltwater anglers, and also has a warm water discharge at the Dickerson power plant. In short, it's a microcosm of the Bay. However you most like to fish, whatever is your favorite quarry, you can find it angling on the Potomac. You should bear in mind, however, that the Potomac River Commission has its own set of regulations you must abide by. While they are similar to Maryland and Virginia regs, they don't mirror either, so do a little checking into the rules before fishing the Potomac.

Although you can't navigate there from the Bay, the first spot we'll cover on the Potomac is Dickerson. Why look at this area if it's not really a part of the Bay? For the same reason we took a look at Deer Creek off of the Susquehanna—it offers unique fishing opportunities that many Bay anglers will be interested in. In this case, Dickerson offers warm-water winter fishing, as well as a real shot at catching walleye, a purely freshwater fish that Chesapeake anglers won't be able to pursue elsewhere on the Bay or its tributaries.

Note that to approach the power plant's warm water discharge, you'll need a shallow draft, river-capable boat. If you're apt to be upset by nicking your prop on a rock or two, don't even attempt fishing here. In any case, keep your speed down and your eyes open. When you approach the discharge, it looks almost like a ramrod-straight tributary to the river, rather than a canal. You can poke up into the canal a little ways—once again assuming that they don't change the regulations for security reasons, the day before you get there—and it's not necessary to go up very far. Most of the eastern (Maryland) shoreline of the river here will post temperatures eight to ten degrees higher than the rest of the river. Casting baits into this warmer water, you can catch small and largemouth bass, catfish, sunfish, and tons of rock bass, as well as carp. Walleye won't orient to the warmth of the water as much as they will to water depth; to pursue these fish, stick to deep holes and sharp, rocky drop-offs.

In Washington, D.C., itself, there is more great freshwater fishing. Although this area is tidal, the bulk of the fish found by anglers here are largemouth bass and crappie. One exception: in the spring months when stripers are spawning, the Potomac does see its own spawning run. During March and April stripers in the 30" plus category will be caught in good numbers, particularly in the area from the Anacostia's mouth to Piscataway Park. Catch these fish by casting cut menhaden or herring into relatively shallow water, about 8' to 12' deep, particularly at sunset and shortly after dark. Set up over a flat with these depths near the river channel, and let your bait sit on the bottom on a standard chum rig. Remember, though, this is strictly catch-and-release, as the tributaries are off-limits to harvest during the spawning season.

Bass and crappie anglers in this stretch of the Potomac usually focus their efforts on one of two forms of structure: piers and bridges. Both are present in good numbers in the D.C. area. The Woodrow Wilson Bridge is particularly known to anglers as a hot spot; cast baits and lures on the upcurrent side of the pilings, or drift minnow suspended under bobbers on the slack downcurrent side (a great crappie technique). So far as fishing the piers goes, it's the usual game: fish your way up one shoreline and down another, tossing spinnerbaits, crankbaits, or minnow/jig combinations as close as possible or under the piers lining the banks. Catfish anglers will also have a lot of success in this area of the river, although eating bottom feeders out of this water is questionable, at best.

Anglers after tidal bass, crappie, perch, and catfish will be interested in the series of creeks that feed the next leg of the Potomac: Mattawoman, Quantico, Aquia, Potomac, and Nanjemoy creeks are all prime waters. These creeks are a bit on the brackish side for catching bass near their mouths, and most anglers will run up into the creeks for freshwater species. Crappie are usually found even farther up into the creeks. As a rule of thumb, don't plan on finding many freshwater oriented fish until you leave the wide main creek and enter the tight creek channel that probes into marshland. In Mattawoman Creek, you'll find plenty of catfish and perch in the main creek itself, fishing the channel bends. From January through mid-February, look for yellow perch between Sweeden Point and Marsh Island near MRW31. The creekbed makes a sharp bend here and the bottom is scoured out, particularly on the side of the channel closer to the island. The next big bend (MRW32) is also scoured out, and you'll find pre-spawn perch holding here during the same time frame. Some time in February these perch will move up a ways to a couple of holes in bends farther up the creek, at MRW33 and MRW34. They'll be catchable here usually until April.

MRW31 is also the start of the really good bass fishing water. Casting spinnerbaits and plugs to the points, old piles, channel edges and fallen brush is the way to score in this area. When casting spinnerbaits, note that gold is a particularly effective color for these waters, which are more often than not discolored.

While all of these creeks offer decent fishing, the next really spectacular one is Nanjemoy. In fact, this creek supports the best yellow perch fishery I have ever experienced on any Chesapeake tributary. During the run—which starts here earlier than most and ends later than most—it is possible to limit out on yellows of a pound or better with some consistency. In fact, when perch jerking here you should consider limiting yourself to fish of 12" or better only.

Most of the really good fishing here starts in the vicinity of Friendship Landing. Outside of this point, perch, bass, and crappie are tough to locate. In the open areas of this creek you will, however, be able to catch all the channel cats in the 5–10 lb range you can stand, by putting cut herring on the muddy bottom and allowing it to soak for a while. At Friendship, there is a ramp and public pier. Motor 65' or 70' directly off this pier, then make a 90-degree left turn and motor another 50' or so, and keep a close eye on the depth finder. There's a hole out here—MRW35—that drops to 14', and this hole is the first stopping-off point for yellow perch staging prior to the spawning run. I've located and caught good numbers of perch in this hole as early as the last week of December, and as late as the third week of February.

Once January arrives, however, the bulk of the perch will move into the first hole in the upper section of the creek at MRW36. This hole is without

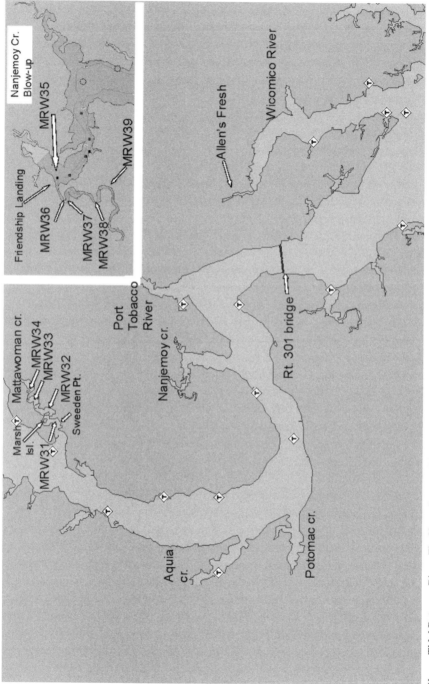

Upper Tidal Potomac River. The Upper Potomac River's tidal waters are rich with bass, perch, catfish, and stripers.

question the most reliable spot anywhere along the Western Shore of the Chesapeake to catch large yellow perch in the late winter months. Most of the creek channel is about 12' up to this point, and where the bend begins it abruptly drops to 20', then farther in the hole, to 25'. Cast all through the hole's deep water during a low or dropping tide, and up onto the adjacent tidal flat (MRW37) during a flood tide. There are numerous fallen trees lining the western side of the creek here, too. You'll catch some perch and an occasional largemouth bass in these trees, but the hole usually has the lion's share of the fish. Channel cats will also swarm into this hole for a two week period, some time during late January or early February. Oddly, when they're present in this hole they suspend at mid-depth and don't take a bait in the mouth. I have no idea what they're doing, but you will feel a twanging sensation on your line, set the hook, and reel up catfish snagged around the pectoral fin, time and time again.

The second major bend in the upper creek (MRW38) is similar to the first one, but is significantly smaller. You'll locate perch here through the same time period and up to a week after they depart the first hole. Although they'll be caught as far out as Friendship, the third big bend (MRW39) marks the start of the really good bass and crappie fishing. You'll see a couple of piers in this stretch, but more cover is provided by trees laying along the banks. Largemouth fishing here is no different than in other tidal creeks, though it should be noted again that like Mattawoman, Nanjemoy usually has discolored water and gold is the best blade color for spinnerbaits and spoons. Catching crappie up this creek is difficult, as there will be many spots that look inviting but hold no fish. When you do locate a good spot, however, the fish are usually large and present in good numbers. For this reason, you're best off doing a lot of moving and trying one tree or pier after another until you catch a fish. Then re-cast close to the same spot, and work it over hard before moving on. When you find a crappie in a specific spot, you should be able to pull between 6 and 10 fish from the same location.

It should be mentioned that you can score on perch, catfish, crappie, and bass in all of the other feeder creeks in this area, too. Port Tobacco and Potomac Creek, to name a couple, do have decent numbers of fish in them. I certainly wouldn't want to discourage anyone from trying them. However, past experience has proved that the above-detailed creeks have better fisheries on a more reliable basis. Allen's Fresh, at the headwaters of the Wicomico, is another area that sees a good perch run. It also supports a great largemouth fishery, as well as crappie, huge carp, catfish, and sunfish. Allen's Fresh, however, has a pretty strong river current and should be approached more like river fishing than Bay fishing. You'll need to take two cars, drop a canoe or kayak in up-river, and leave a second car near a down-river access point. There aren't really any particular hot spots to discuss, as most of Allen's

Fresh has undercut banks without visible structure. It's best to simply cast where you can while drifting downstream, instead of focusing on particular spots and trying to hold on them.

The next stretch of the Potomac anglers will want to examine is from Carters' Lumps to St George's Island. This stretch of the river is much more Bay-like, and you won't find bass, crappie, and other freshwater species from here on down. Stripers are the main year-round quarry here, with croaker present in decent numbers from mid- to late April on.

The unpredictable bottom of Carters' Lumps and Kettle Bottom Shoals marks the first area that's worthwhile for chummers and light tackle trollers searching for striped bass. No specific spot is identified as a hot spot here, because any of the bumps or edges could be the spot of the day. Instead of focusing on one place here, move around the area until you get some bites. In the summer and fall months, you'll also find a lot of snapper blues in attendance. Late and early in the year, bottom rigs baited with grass shrimp will produce white perch on the humps, too. When on the hunt for stripers here, remember that specific bump you choose isn't imperative, as long as you make sure you're fishing a drop of more than five feet or so. Trollers will do well towing Rat-L-Traps and lipped diving plugs. Light tackle anglers should also look for the pound nets in this area; there are several along the northern (Maryland) shore in this stretch. Cast as close as possible to the nets, retrieve quickly, and you should hook into a few stripers at each one during the seasons that they orient to them. Flounder will also make an appearance on these shoals some years, but this is a little more dependent on the season, and the quality of flounder fishing here can't be predicted very well.

The Virginia side of the river from Kettle Bottom Shoals to Nomini Cliffs has several areas of hard bottom that support oyster bars. While there is no one standout spot in this stretch, it's worth mentioning because croaker will often move up to this point in the river and feed along these bars from late spring through the fall. To catch croaker here plan on drifting cut bait and moving often until you locate a school of fish. Action here is hit or miss, but once you locate a school of croaker it'll often be red-hot until you drift off the school, or it moves on.

On the northern shore of the river, just upriver from where St. Clements Island marks the mouth of St. Clement's Bay, a nice drop-off runs from the red nun #14A down to the red/green nun HI buoy, at MRW40. All along this edge, you'll find good jigging for schools of medium-size stripers from June through November. Trout move in here too, usually by August, and blues will be scattered through this area from June on. On the opposite shore, Currioman Bay at MRW41 is essentially an 8' to 10' deep hole surrounded by shallow mud flats. This is a great area to cast light bucktails and jigs for shallow water flounder during years of high salinity. This area also sees

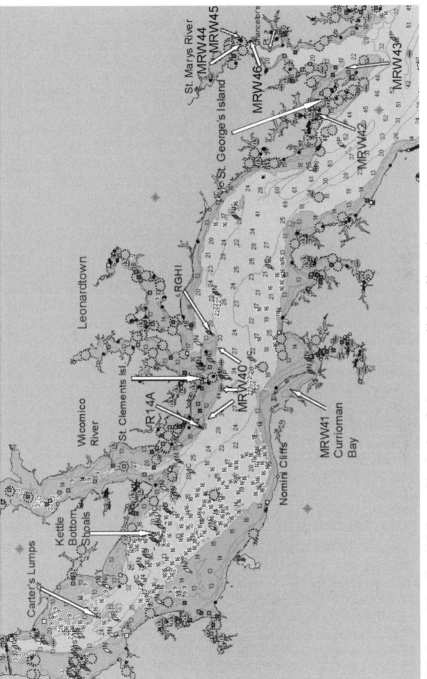

Middle Potomac River. The middle Potomac River has fewer freshwater opportunities, but saltier species are present.

mass invasions of croaker at times (forget about catching a flounder, when the huge school of croaker arrives!).

Both shorelines in this area of the river have decent drop-offs, and trolling along the edges where it drops from 10' to 20' or more is often a good bet in the summer and fall striper seasons. Near St. George's Island, however, you'll want to pull in the trolling lines and break out the light gear again. The channel between the island and the mainland has a great tidal flow, particularly near MRW42, and although the depths are not great, you'll find stripers, croaker, jumbo spot, flounder, and weakfish here. Cast jigs around the channel edges and near the rocks, any you will also find speckled trout some seasons. The channel between the northern edge of the island and Cherryfield Pt (MRW43) also has good water flow, and a bit more depth. This is a great spot to jig for weakfish from September on. Or better yet, night fish in this area from July on, and you'll see more than your fair share of trout.

There are also a couple of hot spots in the St. Mary's River that are worthy of note. The first is Church Point on Horseshoe Bend. From August on snapper blues, croaker, and flounder collect on the southern side of this point at or near MRW44. Some years, you'll also catch puppy drum here. There's a small salt pond on the point itself, with a tidal cut connected to the river that is small enough to jump across. However, fish will gather here to feed when the water flows out on a dropping tide. They won't be there in great numbers, but usually a predator or two will lie waiting by the outflow. There's also a strip of riprap between Church Point and the St. Mary's College's pier at MRW45, which usually has some flounder, stripers, and the occasional red drum hunting around the rocks. If you're interested in night fishing, note that the college pier is well lighted and if you set up 30' to 40' away from it with your own lights, you can create a huge fish-attracting area. Weakfish, stripers, croaker, and blues will all be caught here in the dark, and although the majority will be smallish, I know of one 9 lb gator trout caught right next to this pier.

There's more riprap and a pier for the Dove, a reproduction of the historic sailing ship, on the southern side of Church Point at MRW46. As with the riprap on the northern side, stripers, flounder, and occasionally red drum hunt around these rocks; the pier never seems to hold many fish.

The second spot in the river we need to cover is Chancellor's Point, which isn't as significant as Church Point, but for some reason seems to attract decent numbers of flounder, blues, and trout. The drop-off close to shore is very steep, and there's an oyster bottom around much of the point. Casting jigs up close to shore and bouncing them back along the bottom, or light tackle trolling along the drop-off, will produce plenty of strikes from August on through November. Exactly where they will gather on the point is unpredictable, so plan to do some hunting here.

Continuing along the northern shore of the Potomac, the next hot spot is Cornfield Harbor at Point Lookout. This area attracts a lot of fish, but note that on summer weekends, it'll be crowded with boats, too. There are three particular spots to pay attention to, here. First, Point Lookout itself. The southern side and much of the northern side are covered in riprap, which will be patrolled by stripers, flounder, and some years, red drum. Because there are a lot of shoreline anglers here, however, it's usually best to plan on casting to the riprap only on weekdays, or during inclement weather. The second spot is the drop-off at Cornfield Point. For some reason chumming doesn't seem to work well here, but bouncing jigs along the drop at MRW47 will produce stripers, trout and on the shallower areas of the edge, flounder. A chunk of soft or peeler crab on a fluke killer rig is also an effective choice here. The southern tip of the drop off Point Lookout (near MRW48) is the third spot to consider. There's a fantastic 20' to 50' drop here, at which trout and sometimes stripers will congregate. Again, chumming doesn't seem to do the trick here for some reason. But if you start at the top edge (which is easy to spot, as it's usually loaded with crab pot floats,) and drift down the edge with baits or jigs, you'll usually score. One note of caution: the wind and current tend to collide here sometimes, and the seas can get very big, very quickly. This isn't a small boat spot, except for the nicest of days.

The last spot on the Potomac that all anglers must be aware of is the long, unnamed slope on the Virginia side of the river. This edge sees a strong run of big stripers early in the season, and while many trollers will putt from here to the middle grounds to Point Lookout, spring chummers can score big-time here. The notch that reaches out to deep water at MRW49 provides a spectacular drop-off from 10' or 16' to 35' or 40'. Anchor along this edge and chum, and you should hook up with stripers in excess of 30". In the summer and fall schoolies will also congregate in this area. You may come here to chum and see a batch of boats a little farther towards the Bay, too. There's a green #3 can a few miles down from this spot, and often boats will bunch up and chum here. By all means try this spot if MRW49 doesn't produce, but I've tried it before and am convinced that boats gather there simply because there is a visible marker, and not because the spot is any better. (In fact, the drop there is not as well defined.)

This entire edge, from the Coan River to Smith Point, also is good flounder territory. Drift from 10' or 12' down to 22' or 25', and you should hook into numerous flatties from May on. Most will be throw-backs, but if you work for them, you should score a few keepers along this edge, too. Between it and Point Lookout there are also several deep holes that drop down below 60' near MRW50. In the fall you'll often find birds working over breaking stripers and blues, with Spanish mackerel mixed in during September. If you're fishing under these birds also make sure you try dropping a tandem rig down to the

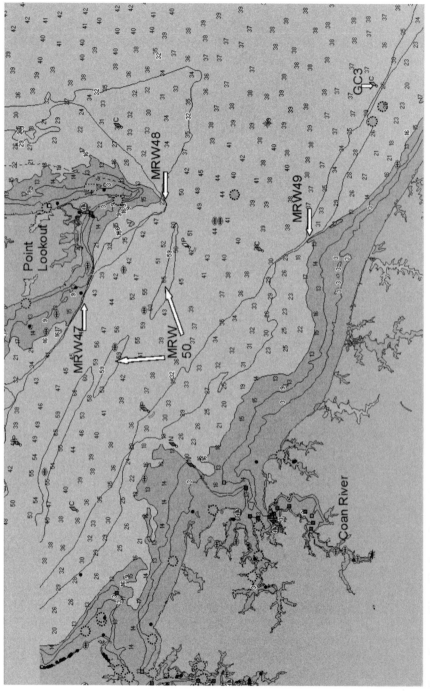

Lower Potomac River. The Lower Potomac has several excellent deepwater areas.

bottom, and probe around for trout. They'll often be lurking down there, waiting for injured or killed baitfish, which are missed by the surface feeders. Some years trout will school in these holes as early as August, too, but often they won't feed and will be holding too deep to effectively night fish for them. Usually, by mid-September they'll go on the feed again, and many years you can catch them here in large numbers.

The Eastern Shore Rivers

Eastern Bay is one of the most productive patches of water in the middle Chesapeake for catching a wide variety of gamefish. It has exaggerated currents thanks to the geography of Kent Island, plenty of water deeper than you'll find in other nearby rivers, and several sharp points and cliff-like drop-offs. Extra bonus: because it's protected by land on three sides, you can often fish here when the wind is blowing too hard to fish the open Bay.

To be technically correct, we should point out that Eastern Bay isn't really a river but is a small bay unto itself. The Miles and Wye Rivers feed into it, as does water from the Chester River, through Kent Narrows. Kent Narrows is a great place for small boat anglers to get in on the action, since it is completely protected from the wind. But be advised: on summer weekends during prime hours, there is usually too much pleasure boat traffic to fish here effectively. That said, stripers and white perch can be caught here virtually year-round. From June through November you'll also hook into blues, trout, flounder, croaker, and spot in the narrows. But by far, stripers are the main fishery here.

The main mode of attack is to cast jigs or plugs near the bridge pilings, pier pilings, and riprap jetty running out from the south side of the bridge. Fish all of these structures as you would the Bay Bridge pilings: cast upcurrent and retrieve at a fairly quick pace. In low light I've had success casting into the shallows in the Narrows, which includes the area along that long jetty. Note that if your boat has a draft of more than two feet, you'll have trouble getting in here.

When fishing the pier pilings in Kent Narrows, you'll have the best luck by placing your lure within a foot or two of the piles. Try to cast parallel to the piers, on one side then the other, as close as possible without hooking wood. Also try skipping your lure under the pier, which leads to many hook-ups—and lots of snags. You play, you pay.

Often another effective method for fishing the narrows is to live-line white perch in the four- to six-inch range. Rig them on a standard live-lining rig (see part II: Tactics and Tackle) and drift through the main channel. In my experience, this is much more productive on the south side of the bridge than on the north side.

Heading south about three and a half miles from the narrows, you'll find the entrance to Greenwood Creek. The northern side of the creek mouth has a

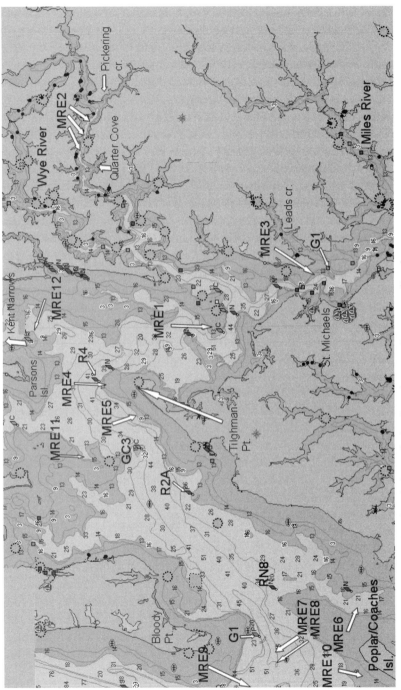

Eastern Bay. Eastern Bay is a good option whether you're hunting stripers, croaker, trout, or flounder.

rock jetty lining, which is worth checking out during the summer and fall months. (Charts say it's too shallow to get in here, but on the middle of the tide there's at least two feet of water.) Don't expect many keepers as most of the fish caught from these rocks tend to be in the 12" to 16" range, but the occasional 20" fish shows up here, too.

Continuing south along the southeast shore line, you'll soon enter the Miles River. There's an underwater point here marked by MRE1 that is a good spot to jig for flounder starting in late May, and stripers, usually starting in June. Many years you can also find trout in the deep water off the end of this point, from August on. Head east into the Wye River, and you'll note very deep water that goes right up to most of the shoreline. Light tackle trolling for stripers is effective here, and during the summer and fall you'll also pick up a lot of snapper blues. The Wye also used to be known for its strong perch runs, but in the past couple of decades, this run just hasn't materialized as it historically did. There is, however, a great late fall and early winter fishery in the Wye for stripers. Most run 12" to 16" but a few fish up to 26" show up, too. Catch these fish by bottom-bouncing very slowly with small feather jigs. From the mouth of Quarter Creek to Pickering Cove (MRE2) is a good stretch for this type of fishing, although it shouldn't be attempted on Saturdays while duck hunting season is in. Duck hunting is very popular in this area, and you'll hear shots fired close enough to scare you if you fish this stretch of the river.

Farther up inside the Miles River, there is plenty of opportunity for light tackle casting to piers and pilings for stripers. As with the Wye, most of the stripers you catch in the river will be on the smaller side, with a few keepers and larger fish mixed in. There's one Miles hot spot for trout, too—at the green #1 near the mouth of Leads Creek, the current has carved out a small bowl on the northern side of this point at MRE3. With depths over 40', trout gather here starting in August and can be caught up until they move out into Eastern Bay and orient under schools of breaking fish, in October or November. The best way to catch these fish during the dog days of summer is, of course, to set up with night lights in the shallower water closer to the point and fish in the dark.

Marking the northwestern side of the Miles' river mouth is Tilghman's point, MRE4, one of the most reliable areas in the middle Bay for flounder. Currents rip across this point that drops from 10' to 36" on the east side and 10' to 45 on the west side. One side or the other will be hot depending on what the tide is doing at any given moment, but it's rare that both sides are hot at once. Flounder will make their first showing at Tilghman's Point between mid-May and early June and will stay there until the end of October or the beginning of November. Position your boat on top of the point, using the red #4 channel marker to orient yourself, and allow the wind or current to push you into deeper water. No bites? Then try drifting the opposite side. Always keep track of the depth you take fish, as flounder usually hang in the same depth zone, and try to keep your bait in that specific zone for as long as possible. If you bounce jigs or bucktails for flounder, or use another active fishing method that keeps your lure moving rather than dragging along bottom, you'll also hook into stripers of all sizes here.

If you fish from a small boat, you should know that this is a tough place to fish on weekends. Many large pleasure boats and motor yachts cruise to St. Michaels, and they all pass by Tilghman's Point. At times, fishing here is like being in a washing machine due to all the boat wakes.

When it gets rough on the Bay, many local anglers use the 10' to 50' shelf that runs southwest from Tilghman's Point at MRE5 as a backup chumming spot. Both stripers and blues will be in the area. You might find them anywhere along this edge, between the red #4 marker and the red #2A marker. There's also a small channel running into shore from the red #2A marker, and this is another good place to try and catch flounder. Late in the year, I've also located weakfish on this edge. If you happen to hook into something extremely large here, don't assume it's a ray and break the line—black drum in the 40- to 60-lb class sometimes pop up along this edge in the summer months. In fact, this is about the northernmost point that Bay anglers will find big black drum with any regularity.

The entire edge from this red #2A to the red nun #8 is a fairly slow drop and is not a place I concentrate my efforts on. However, it should be noted that some very good anglers—including at least one professional guide—do work this water regularly for flatfish, and I've heard a lot of talk about scoring good numbers of flounder along this edge. Heading south, it runs into the channel between Poplar Island and the mainland. This isn't an incredibly deep channel, but if you search around it on the north/eastern side of the island at and around MRE6 you'll find plenty of holes and troughs that dip down to 22' or 23'. They will hold weakfish from August on, and many times you'll find small pockets of birds working over breaking stripers in this area. Unfortunately, in my experience they are usually smaller fish. This isn't true, however, of the trout you'll find in the Hill Hole, the deep fingers of water that run from the main channel of Eastern Bay to the east side of the Hill at MRE7. This hole hits 70' in some spots, and if you find working birds in this zone you're likely to have sizable stripers on top, with weakfish deep below the churning water. There is a 50' to 66' drop at MRE8. Work this area thoroughly, especially in October and November, to fill a cooler with weakfish. Between mid-November and early December, huge white perch also move into this deep water. They're usually large enough that they will hit the three and four ounce weakfish jigging spoons, which certainly look too large for white perch, upon first glance.

This area, as well as the main stem of Eastern Bay, is also a great place to locate schools of large menhaden in the fall. Always carry a bunker snagger—a treble hook with a lead ring around the shank—when you're in the area, and try to snag a couple of live baits out of the school when you find one. Slip a hook through an 8" live menhaden's back, flip it right back into the school, and hang on; some of the largest stripers taken from Eastern Bay fall to this tactic. Usually, it seems that there's only one or two really big fish hanging around each school. So if you catch one using this method and can't repeat the success quickly, move on without investing a lot of time and look for another school of bunker. If you want fish in the 30" to 40" range when everyone else is catching 16" to 22" fish, this is the tactic you want to try.

If you follow these fingers to the north towards Bloody Point Light you'll soon drop down to depths nearing 100' at MRE9. For some reason large white perch congregate in this deep water late in the fall, too. If you see working birds here check them out for stripers or blues up top and trout deep below the school. One year out of every four or so, they'll be found hanging around in this area.

From these deep fingers, Poplar Island is just a few miles to your south. Poplar and Coaches Islands were diked several years ago and are currently used for dredge disposal. As you might expect, the riprap dike is a good place to cast light tackle for stripers. There's enough of it that you could spend the better part of a day here, just casting to the rocks. There's another, lesser known fishery here, however. About 100' out from the north side dike the water drops to 14', then to 16' (in some places, 18') than comes back to 14' before beginning a long, gradual slope into deeper waters. Charts don't show this dip (at MRE10), running the length of the island, which accounts for its relative obscurity. It may have been created by the currents here, which were changed when they built the dike. In any case, early in the spring this dip sometimes fills up with croaker and a flounder or two. This area was also traditionally a reliable black drum spot during their late spring run. However, since the construction here changed the currents and prevailing water conditions, I have not experienced or heard of a consistent drum fishery off the north side of Poplar Island.

Bordering the northeastern mouth of Eastern Bay is Bloody Point. There is an extremely sharp drop from 10' to 70' or 80' that runs all the way from Bloody Point Light to the green channel marker #1. This edge is another place many anglers hunt for flounder, trout, and stripers and is another area where you'll often find breaking fish. However, don't spend a lot of time here if you don't have quick success, and don't plan on locating large schools of fish here. For whatever reason, most of the time fish on this edge seem to be scattered and do not often concentrate in one spot. If you do see working birds over breaking fish and they are among the crab pot floats, which are placed at the top of the drop in 12' or less, ignore them completely because the fish will invariably be between 6" and 12" long. Find birds working over the deeper water, however, and you'll usually be looking at larger fish with the potential for weakfish down deep.

At that green #1 mark, the channel takes a turn to the north. From this dogleg in the channel all the way down to the green can #3, there is a nice drop from 35' to about 60', which reliably holds trout and often stripers from August on until winter sets in. They can be found on either the western or eastern side edges, though the western edge is generally better in this zone. This stretch of channel is probably the most reliable place in the middle Chesapeake to find weakfish in any given year, from August through November. North of the green can #3 there is a piece of deep water called the Duck Head, because it's shaped exactly like the head of a duck. This area also holds trout on a regular basis and jigging for weakfish there at and around MRE11 is particularly productive early and late in the day.

There's also a man-made fish reef, in about 20' of water a half-mile or so from this edge, about two miles northeast of the green marker. This reef looks huge on the fishfinder, almost always has boats fishing around it, and people often tell me they've caught fish here. I've given it a dozen-odd shots, never had a verified bite, and lost several lures on snags. Try it if you like, but I wouldn't have huge expectations.

The same cannot be said for the drop from 15' to 30' on the eastern side of Parson's Island at MRE12. This edge produces flounder, stripers, and croaker early in the season, and trout can be added to the list from mid-summer on. Along the island's shore there are several areas where you'll see fallen trees reaching the water, and when the tide is high it's possible to sneak in and catch stripers and perch from around them. As with the jetty at Kent Narrows, don't try this in a deep draft boat.

With the exception of the channel going into Crab Alley Bay (light tackle troll anywhere through here with Rat-L-Traps and bucktails dressed with twister tails to take stripers in the 12" to 22" range), the water behind Parsons is too shallow to be of much interest while angling, but I just can't help mentioning its value as a crabbing area. If you ever feel the desire to take a fishing break (shame on you) this is a great place for running a trot line or even chicken-necking. From Parsons in to Kent Narrows there is a deep-water channel and you'll see charters bottom fishing here for croaker, spot, and perch. However, larger game fish don't seem to provide much action in this strip of water.

The next river heading south along the Eastern Shore is the Choptank. This is an astonishingly productive river, offering everything from bass fishing on its upper reaches to big black drum at the river mouth. Starting upriver, the first zone of interest is from the Rt 331 bridge to Denton. This stretch of the river offers tidal bass fishing, which improves steadily as you head upriver. It's at its finest in the feeder creeks and headwaters. One such area is Watts Creek, which has great bass and crappie fishing, plenty of catfish, and a tremendous late winter perch run. The second major bend in Watts, MRE13, has a 22' deep hole that will become packed tight with yellow perch as early as the first week of January. They will remain there until March most years, when they're joined by white perch. There's a large pavilion that is built out over a portion of this hole (see Shorebound Angling Hot Spots of the Middle Chesapeake). On the down-creek side of the pavilion, cast between the pilings and the rocks and you'll often find good sized crappie schooled up, with a bass or two mixed in. The third (MRE14) and fifth (MRE15) major bends also are decent perch holes—you can still catch perch in them a week after they've moved up out of the second bend, on their way to spawn—and there is plenty of downed timber along the shoreline to cast at for bass. Better bass fishing, however, is upcreek at MRE16 and 17. Some days, you'll catch a half-dozen bass out of the one hole at MRE17. Look upcreek from this spot and you'll see a large tree sticking out into the water; this tree has been in place for at least three years (I hope it's still there next time!) and also holds a lot of fish with regularity.

The stretch of river from Watts to Tuckahoe is standard tidal bass water. Casting to the brush, undercut banks, and pier pilings you'll catch plenty of largemouth, as well as some crappie. Put cut baits on the bottom, and catfish will prove plentiful, too.

The Tuckahoe itself is much the same, although it is a peculiar river in the same way Watts is: large stretches that look good will prove to be barren, then you'll suddenly locate a pile of fish in one specific spot. If pickerel is your target, three of these super-charged hot spots are the flats at MRE18, 19, and 20. Look for stumps and grassbeds in these areas, and cast Roadrunners tipped with minnow, or minnow on a shad dart or marabou jig suspended under a bobber. In the deeper water near these flats you'll find some bass, perch prior to the March run, and lots and lots of catfish.

One of the most productive spots during the perch run for both yellow and white perch, however, is in Hillsboro itself. This particular spot also holds good crappie fishing most of the year. Unfortunately, it's so far upriver as to be considered non-navigable, and doesn't show on the charts. Luckily it is easy to locate from the public boat ramp in Hillsboro, just a few yards after the Main St bridge over the river. This ramp is small and won't be usable for boats over 16'. But if you launch a small jon boat or canoe here and follow the bend downriver (away from the bridge) for about 100 yards, you will see a huge beaver dam on shore that is built out over a fallen tree that has been in this spot for several years. The tree has several huge branches that reach a good 20' or so out into the river. Tie off to one of these branches and jig right next to the tree, or cast up near the beaver dam, and you'll enjoy the very best fishing the Tuckahoe has to offer. On your way out, try the bridge pilings too: crappie often suspend around them.

Heading downriver from this point, the Choptank is a river in transition. During some years you'll catch bass beyond this point, some years you won't. Regardless of the particular year small stripers, white perch, and catfish are

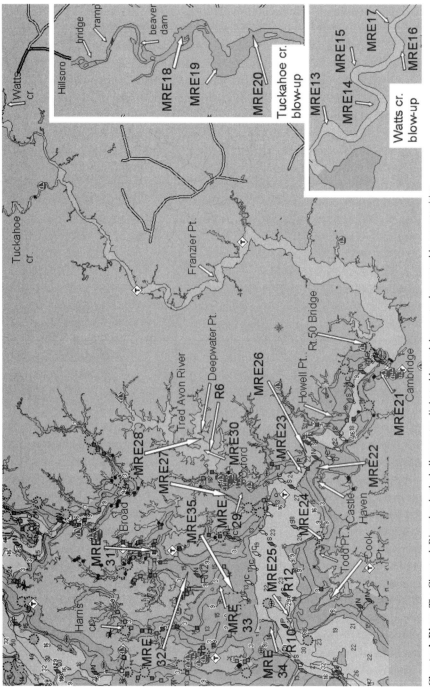

Choptank River. The Choptank River has both shallow water, light tackle, and deepwater heavy tackle opportunities.

available along this stretch, and most years, croaker are present in good numbers from May on from Franzier Point all the way down to the Rt 50 bridge.

The Rt 50 bridge in Cambridge is where the Choptank starts getting really interesting. At this point, you're far enough downriver to catch most Bay species unless freshwater flows are well above the norm. Even then, stripers, croaker, perch, and snapper blues are all possibilities.

Because of the numerous piers and pilings, Cambridge is an excellent place to cast light tackle for striped bass. Fish in the 12" to 26" range are available in the river year-round, although it must be noted that you can't fish the river for striped bass during the spring trophy season. The Municipal Yacht Basin (MRE21) is a good area to cast jigs, Rat-L-Traps, and similar plugs. Light tackle trollers will want to set up a pattern running from the bridge all the way down to Howell Point, zigzagging back and forth along the channel edges. This will be effective through the fall but this section of the river has a nasty habit of becoming swarmed with 6" to 10" snapper blues some years, and fishing for stripers in this way becomes practically impossible. Usually, this period runs from July or August through mid-September, then the blues start thinning out.

A couple miles downriver from Howell Point is Castle Haven, which is well known as a Choptank hot spot. In fact, it's the first of three points on the southern shore of the river that form an incredibly hot fishing zone I call the Choptank Triad. Weedbeds in the shallows on Castle Haven at MRE22 provide cover and feeding areas with great deepwater access for stripers, and anglers in shallow draft boats who cast light gear will enjoy success here most years from mid-June through the fall. Hop over the edge of the drop-off at MRE23 and you're in an extremely deep, sheer trough that provides prime trout water. This deepwater edge is popular with bait fishermen using Fluke Killers, particularly from August or September through November. Jigging spoons and tandem rigs are also effective on this edge.

The next point downriver, Todd Point, offers more great shallow water/light tackle action, with a unique twist: there are huge stone ruins here piled up in about four feet of water at MRE24, positioned such that there's usually a ripping current moving across them. There's one strip about 30' long running parallel to shore, a 20' wide swath of more or less open water, then a second line of rubble. Putt in close with a grappling anchor and position your boat so you can cast back to both sections of rocks and the open water between them, and you'll enjoy fast striper action. This spot is also important to anglers in the Choptank because it's one of the northernmost places to catch speckled seatrout. Specs move in here during years of low freshwater flow, usually in April and May. They get harder to find through the summer but often make a second showing in September or October. They are thick here perhaps one year out of five, but during times of drought historically they have appeared year after year.

Cook Point, the next downriver from Todds, also has a significant rip moving across it whenever the tide is moving. As you'd expect, this attracts stripers most of the season. Specs will be caught here, too, usually when they are also found at Todds, if there isn't too much freshwater flowing down the river. This is another spot where "double-dipping" is a good bet, because there's good trout and flounder water just outside of it. When the tide is really moving poke in close to the point and cast to the rips that are visible as long as there's a knot or more of current. After casting for stripers and specs, note the location of the two red markers, #10 and #12, about a mile to the north of the point. Move out and position your boat so you drift in or out across the drop running from the deep water where these markers are, to the 10' to 12' drop half-way to the point. This ledge (MRE25) is an excellent spot to locate trout and flounder, either by dragging baits or jigging. For some reason, there always seem to be some larger fish around here, too, and it's not uncommon to catch 20" flounder and 25" seatrout on the same drift. In fact, this ledge is one of the most productive spots in the entire river, if not the entire middle Bay. It also seems to hold the fish a bit longer than the surrounding areas. Trout move in as early as May, flounder during the same time frame, and two out of three seasons both fish will be caught here until July. One out of three seasons, you'll have good catches in this spot right through the summer months (particularly on flounder), before the trout kick into high gear again in September. It's impossible to overstress just how good the fishing along these three points is. Sure, some years none will hold fish. But each and every spring when you set out to discover where the fish have gathered for their early run, this is one of the best places to start your search—often, you'll look no farther.

The north side of the river may not be as hot as the Triad on a regular basis, but some days will surrender a heavier cooler full of fish. The first reason why is Chlora Point, directly across the river from Castle Haven, where fast-moving currents have scoured out deep water practically up to the banks of the point. The drop on the eastern side of the point (MRE26) is a good flounder spot from May on and will also hold seatrout and stripers once the fish school. Try casting heavy jigs right up to the shoreline and bouncing them back into deeper water for the stripers here; move off and vertically jig for the trout.

The Tred Avon River empties into the Choptank's northern shores, just downriver from Chlora Point. Although the Tred Avon is best known for it's awesome crabbing and for the cruising destination Oxford, it also offers some good angling opportunities. The fishing is usually not quite as good as in the Choptank proper, but it's protected from the wind and provides small boat anglers with a good shot at fish when the weather gets tough. Attack it as you would the Wye. Relatively deep water coming close to the shores makes it a good place to try light tackle trolling, and slow-trolling feather jigs. The shelf along the rivers' northeastern shore from the mouth up to Bellevue, at MRE27, is a good ledge to slow-troll feathers along for stripers from early summer through the end of the season. Most will be below the 26" mark, but plenty will be keepers. Same goes for the stretch between the red #6 and Deepwater Point (MRE28), at the mouth of Trippe Creek. Casting jigs to the docks along the shore in this area will also produce stripers.

If you want to target trout in the Tred Avon, move to one of the deeper holes in the river and drift baits or drop jigs. There are several such holes, starting with the 40' deep water at MRE29. Hope to locate trout here during the summer months when night fishing (move over to the edges, where the water shallows up quickly) and in daylight from September through the end of the season. This is a good hole but one word of caution: there will be a fair amount of boat traffic running past you on a sunny summer Saturday here. If that presents a problem, move up to the channel just outside of the red #6 to MRE30. The bottom in this section of the channel bounces between 36' and 40' and creates good fish-holding structure. There is more deep water in the center of the Tred Avon as you move upriver, and much of it holds weakfish. However, the farther away from the Choptank you go, the smaller the trout seem to get. In most areas farther upriver you'll have to weed through a dozen or more throw-backs to eke out a keeper or two.

Broad Creek and Harris Creek, the next two feeders moving downriver, don't have the same deep water as the Tred Avon and tend to hold fewer fish. One exception is the spot in Broad Creek at MRE31, where all of the creek arms converge, and the currents have scoured out a 35' deep hole. This is another good bet for jigging or drifting baits for trout. If you want to catch stripers in either of these two creeks, your best bet is to prowl the shoreline and toss lures at the docks. One other spot of note is the shallow shelf protruding into Broad Creek (MRE32) near the red #2 nun buoy. On an outgoing tide drift from the 20' water on its northern side and you can usually locate some flounder. On an incoming tide, move to the southern side of the drop. Most of the flounder caught here will not be doormats, but when you're trapped in the creeks and rivers by rough water, this is a good spot to get in a shot at flatfish.

A better bet for sizable flounder in the Choptank proper is to run to the large 10' flat that sticks well into the river at MRE33. The drops here are not dramatic, but particularly on an incoming or on a high tide, flatties will move up onto this bar to feed. The same is true of the shelf inside of Blackwalnut Point at MRE34. This spot does have a strong drop-off to the south, which also provides good action on low tide and outgoing water. Both of these spots will see flounder as early as May and will be productive through the fall most years.

In the center of the river, at MRE35, lies an airplane wreck. It's hard to anchor over the wreck itself, but if you can get right over it you've got a very good shot at weakfish, and stripers. Panfish such as spot, croaker and the occasional small sea bass will also congregate in the area of the airplane wreck. Off to the sides of the wreck you'll also score the occasional flounder, and usually the flatfish you find in this area are sizable fish.

The middle of the river to the south and east of the airplane wreck, sometimes known as "The Lumps" or "Choptank Lumps" is another well-known bottom fishing area for trout, croaker, and spot, with stripers and flounder often mixed into the catch. Croaker can be caught here in very, very large numbers from mid-April through the summer, and trout will join them en masse most seasons starting in late May or early June. Though this spot is called the lumps, it's the holes that are more dramatic, surrounded by areas of hard bottom. Often, trout will form small schools in these slightly deeper pockets of water and can be caught jigging or dropping peeler or soft crab baits. Note that at some times, particularly early in the year, there will be so many croaker in this zone that it's tough to catch anything else—as soon as a bait touches bottom, they're on it. Though you will catch some stripers here from the time that they start schooling in the spring through the season's end, this area doesn't really stand out as either a chumming or trolling spot.

Just to the south of the Choptank lies—no surprise—the Little Choptank. This river is a creek in comparison to the Choptank, but it does hold some good opportunities, particularly for small boat anglers kept off the Bay by rough weather. The first area of interest is the abrupt shelf at the mouth of the river, marked by the green #1 marker. This spot is pretty exposed, and particularly on a north or west wind, will be just as rough as the main Bay. The drop here goes from 5' to 30' in a heartbeat, and flounder will show up in this spot some years as early as the beginning of May. You'll also find some trout in the deeper water adjacent to the point.

MRE36, the relatively featureless, shallow area between Susquehanna Point and Ragged Island, doesn't appear to house any fish-holding structure. But for some reason, this area becomes rich in croaker starting in late May or early June, and usually remains full of them through the season. There are several more deep holes moving upriver from MRE36 and one would have to think that in some years they hold trout. But for whatever reason, croaker seem to rule this river most of the time, most years. One exception: there are a couple of strips of riprap along the western side of McKeil Point. Though the water is shallow along this shoreline, light tackle anglers will find stripers feeding on the rocks, particularly at high tide. Flounder can also be pulled from the riprap here, though the vast majority will be throw-backs.

The Honga River is the next major waterway heading south, and this river is one that every Chesapeake angler should check out. It holds excellent shallow water fisheries for stripers and speckled seatrout, croaker are everywhere, and it has several good weakfish spots and flounder spots, too. Plus, the

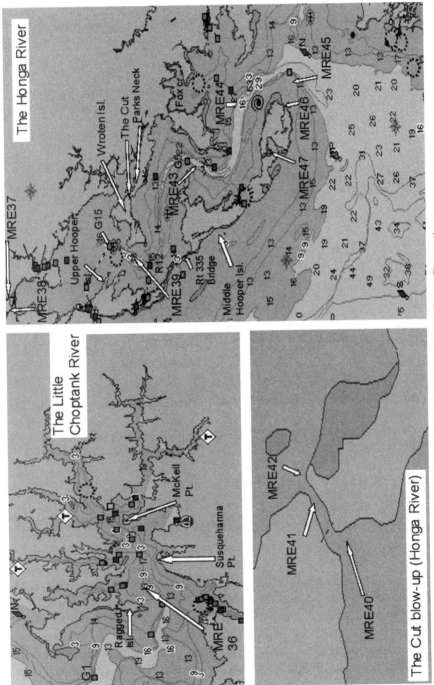

The Honga River

MRE37

MRE38

Upper Hooper

Wroten Isl.

The Cut

Parks Neck

Fox Cr.

MRE44

MRE43

G5 R2

G15

R15

R12

MRE39

Rt 335 Bridge

Middle Hooper Isl.

MRE45

MRE46

MRE47

The Little Choptank River

McKell Pt.

Susquehanna Pt.

Ragged Isl.

MRE 36

G1

The Cut blow-up (Honga River)

MRE42

MRE41

MRE40

Honga and Little Choptank Rivers. The Little Choptank and the Honga are excellent Eastern Shore options.

Honga is more protected than many rivers on the Eastern Shore, because Hooper Island gives it shelter from a westerly breeze.

The first two spots of interest on the Honga will be most important to anglers who enjoy fishing from kayaks, canoes, and car-toppers. Rt 335 has two bridges, the first passing over an unnamed cut at MRE37 and the second over Great Creek at MRE38. Both of these cuts are accessible at or next to the bridges, and both will hold croaker starting in mid- to late May. In the fall, stripers (mostly small ones) can be caught along the bridge pilings. More importantly, this is one of the few areas in Maryland waters where an angler can catch speckled seatrout from a canoe or kayak. In June and sometimes through the summer, you will find speckled trout along the edges of these cuts and will hook into them by casting curly tail jigs and bucktails up to the banks as you drift through. Note, however, that very strong currents (particularly in Great Creek) will make this type of fishing a real workout for paddlers when the tide is active.

The next Rt 335 bridge connects Upper Hooper Island to the mainland. The cut under this bridge has a tremendous current running through it at times. It looks like it should also be a great spec area, but for whatever reason few are caught here. But the opposite is true for stripers, smallish weakfish, and loads of croaker that can be caught in the channel running under the bridge. On the eastern side of the bridge the channel disappears rapidly and it's tough to find depths over eight feet, but on the western side of the bridge there's a nice channel and some undercut areas along the bank that drop down to 15' or so. No particular spot along this bank seems to out-produce another, so cast jigs all along it while drifting by the shoreline. You'll often catch lots of sub-legal stripers in here, with an occasional keeper fish. For whatever reason, large croaker will also stage in this channel. Toss just about any form of bait into the deeper water, leave it on bottom, and you'll usually hook up quickly. Flounder also come into this area during the summer and into the fall, and you'll find them on the less intense drop-off on the northern edge of this channel. The relatively deep water continues for a ways along the bank before meandering into the center of the cut, then back across to the bank again, forming a rip that can be spotted by eye when the water is moving. This spot will also produce stripers and the occasional flounder. Note that this area is another that is subject to strong currents when the tide is pumping and although the water is protected it is also connected to the main Bay, so this area isn't prime for paddlers unless you're very experienced and in good shape.

The next hot spot in the river's main channel, between the green marker #15 and the red #12, at MRE39. This is a great spot to tuck away in your brain for windy days, as the fishing here can be as good as many areas on the main Bay for weakfish. One difference: most of the fish will be on the small side. While its reliability is high—four years out of five you'll find trout schooled here—the majority of the fish are between 10" and 16". Plan on catching five or six fish to get to one keeper.

Although the charts don't show it clearly, the main channel at MRE39 is mostly 20' to 24' deep water. There are numerous humps, however, which rise to 14' or 16' scattered throughout this channel. Jigging and dragging baits over these humps will produce the trout and an occasional flounder. During periods of high tide, also check out the shelf on the eastern edge of this area, up towards the bank of Wroten Island. Sometimes you'll find the trout in 12' to 8' of water, outside of the channel, along this edge. This edge is also an excellent night fishing spot for seatrout.

The cut running between Wroten Island and Park's Neck may look small but it is the single best speckled trout spot in Maryland waters, period. Limit catches of speckled trout are possible here, and often the fish are much larger than you'd expect. In fact, 3 and 4 lb trout are caught here regularly, and trout all the way up to 10 lb are caught in the cut on occasion. File it under strange but true—virtually all the trout in this cut will be specs. Catching a weakfish here is extremely rare. Stripers often are mixed in with the specs and sometimes outnumber them, and a flounder or two can often be pulled off the bottom from the deep water at either end of the cut (though not usually from inside the cut itself). While the stripers in the cut are usually not jumbos, the opposite is true of the flounder. It's rare to catch more than two or three in a day here, but it's also rare to catch a throw-back. In fact, most of the flatfish prowling at the ends of the cut range between 2 and 4 lb.

Fishing at the cut varies radically with the tide. You can spend two or three hours there without a single bite, watch the tide change, and then get strikes on each and every cast for the next two or three hours. Both the specs and the stripers will change their hunting techniques depending on the current flow in the cut, too. Usually they will be feeding at or near the surface through the slack water, then close to the bottom during moving water. However, at times they will display the exact opposite behavior. So when you first arrive at the cut, vary your retrieval techniques until you discover which gets the fish biting. Commonly, the best way to fish here is to go to the upcurrent end of the cut, then cast towards either shore as you drift down it. The shorelines on both sides of the cut have great drop-offs, and you will locate fish all along them. However, you may need to anchor your boat and fish in a single section of the cut either because there are too many boats in it to drift (this area does become crowded, especially on weekends) or because the fish are stacked up in a single spot. This can happen just about anywhere in the cut, but there are a couple of spots that you should be especially aware of.

The first spot to pay special attention to is the rip on the south side, about 25 yards outside of the cut's mouth on the western end, at MRE40. There's a nice drop here from 4' to 15'. Jigging on the ledge is the way to find a flounder or two, and casting and retrieving at the rip will produce stripers much of the time. Four-fifths of the way to the eastern end of the cut, look along the northern side for a bar, with a visible rip on a strong flowing tide. Both stripers and speckled trout like to congregate in the area near the rip at MRE41. The point on the northeastern edge of the cut also forms a rip during an outgoing tide and will produce both stripers and trout. The point on the southeastern edge is even better, however (MRE42). It comes out 20' or 25' off of the shoreline. Anchoring in the deep water just outside the cut's mouth and casting back into this shallow water often produces trout and occasionally produces stripers, too. The drop off of this point is probably the best flounder edge to jig over in the cut. Although the water shallows up quickly outside of the cut, blind-casting away from it into open water will also produce fish at times.

Across the river from the cut, there's one last Rt 335 bridge, this one connecting Upper and Middle Hooper Islands. There is a fairly long stretch of deep water on either side of the bridge (the charts show 10', but you'll find 14' and in some spots, 16' of water here). Croaker can be caught in this deep water from May on through the season, and a few weakfish can also be found meandering through the channel. Casting up to the bridge pilings, you'll catch stripers of all sizes. Flounder will also be found here, when the wind is calm and the water is clear. Unfortunately, since this area is exposed to a westerly breeze, clean calm water is the exception rather than the rule in this spot. One other problem: there is good-looking riprap and steel bulkhead on either side of the bridge, but there are almost always shoreline anglers here. Yes, you will find fish near the structure, but only at the expense of the anglers stuck in one spot. Best to move elsewhere and give them a break.

Another good location that is protected from west winds is the squeeze in the channel just downriver from the green #5 marker, at MRE43. This is a good area to jig or drift baits for weakfish, which, like those at MRE39, will usually be on the small side but plentiful. Because this spot has deeper water, you'll also be able to find trout here most years right through the summer—though it can be a challenge to get them to bite during the dog days.

Chummers can find productive water at MRE44, on the edge at the mouth of Fox Creek. Particularly on an incoming tide, fish will often congregate in the 15' to 22' zone. Flounder can also be caught on this shelf some years, and croaker practically any time during the season. But if you're more interested in light tackle casting for stripers, continue downriver to MRE45. There are a couple of pound nets here that provide an opportunity for tossing jigs and plugs for stripers. Directly inshore from MRE45 there's also a tiny cut running back into the marsh, at MRE46. Depth in the cut ranges between 3' and 8', even though it's barely 15' across, and you will find stripers and specs feeding in it at times. MRE47 is a much larger cut, has a much stronger tidal flow, and provides a better opportunity for catching large numbers of fish. However, it's also more heavily pressured and on weekends may be crowded. If you're after numbers of fish go here first, but if you're interested in fewer, larger fish, start at MRE46.

The Nanticoke River is less interesting than the Honga as a saltwater fishery, but is much more interesting as a brackish one because it has a far more significant freshwater flow. In fact, it runs all the way up to Seaford, Delaware, where you can catch bass, crappie, and pickerel. Many Eastern Shore bassers consider the Nanticoke prime water.

In its saltier areas, the best known spot in the Nanticoke is without a doubt Roaring Point, and with good reason. Croaker usually make an early showing here, take up residence starting some time in April, and remain through the season. Trout arrive shortly after the croaker and will be present in ever-increasing numbers until they peak, usually in October. The good fishing area isn't just right at the point, but stretches from the river's mouth upriver, past Roaring Point itself. This point is noted for a second reason: it's a good drop to catch flounder on, from mid- or late May through the season. The Roaring Point zone also has a late season and winter fishery: white perch will often collect in large schools and stage here through the cold months, before making their spring run up the tributaries.

Along the western shore of the Nanticoke, there are several creeks that are of interest. MRE48, 49 and 50 each mark creek mouths with significant water flow. A good tactic is to hit these just after a high tide has peaked and turned, when water rushes out of the marsh. Speckled trout, striped bass, and occasionally even red drum show up at these mouths, grabbing bait that's flushed out of the creeks. The mouth of Wetipquin Creek, on the river's eastern shoreline, may also produce stripers at times. There's also a bridge a short ways up the river that will hold both perch and stripers (usually small ones) particularly during low water flow. However, for some reason this creek always seems to run dirty and more often than not—particularly after heavy rains— visibility in it is very low. Perch, of course, will often bite on bait no matter how ugly the water may be, and just before the perch make their run in the spring, you can intercept them in the deep water on the downcreek side of this bridge.

Moving upriver from Wetipquin to Long Point you will find plenty of croaker and some trout here and there, but most years the action isn't reliable enough to focus on and anglers in this area will travel downriver to enjoy more consistent fishing. Quantico Creek is another feeder that can be targeted for the perch run in early spring. Most of the fish will stage in one of the three major holes at bends in the creek, at MRE51, 52, and 53. Catfish will also be found in these holes.

At this point along the Nanticoke, the riverbanks close in and the water becomes significantly deeper, as the river makes a series of sharp bends.

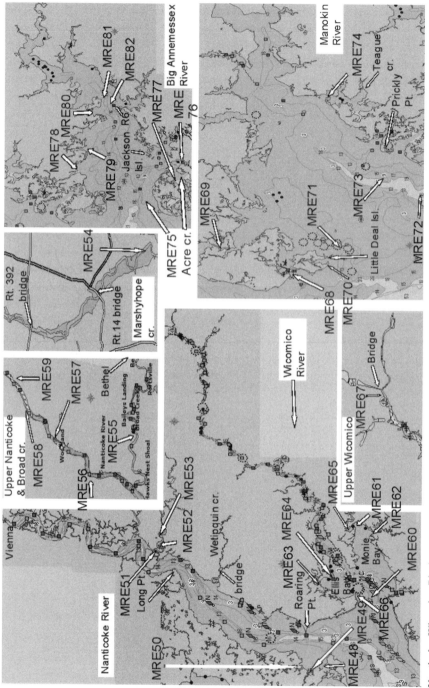

Nanticoke, Wicomico, Big Annemessex, and Manokin Rivers. The rivers off the Tangier Sound have a huge variety of angling opportunities.

During the summer croaker and perch can be found in many of these deep-water sections, but trout don't usually go upriver this far. Stripers can be found on the points through this section of the river, usually by casting jigs up into the shallow areas and retrieving back down the drops. The next noteworthy hot spot is at the river's junction with Marshyhope Creek. The Marshyhope is well known as bassing water. It also sees a white perch run in the spring, usually a week or two later than the main run. There's also a spring striper bite from Vienna upriver, as the Nanticoke supports a fairly significant striper spawning run. It's catch and release only, and as with other striper spawning areas, these fish must be handled with great care. Be sure to check the current regulations, too, since these change from year to year.

Bass anglers will want to start off in the Marshyhope by cruising upcreek to the fallen trees along the shoreline on the southwestern shoreline, at MRE54. Early in the year most of the bass will come from the timber, but there are also a few lily pads and weedbeds in this area that attract fish as well. Fish these after the sun has been up for a while; the pads and surrounding water will warm up more quickly than the surrounding open water, triggering more aggressive feeding. The water in this area is often off-color, especially during periods following rainfalls. If you notice that the water is brown or rusty in color, stick with brown, red, and orange lures. In clear water, bladebaits and white or chartreuse is the way to go.

If you like catching pickerel, you'll also like this area. The Nanticoke watershed is excellent pickerel territory, and you can pick them up by casting minnow, small spoons, and Roadrunners dressed with minnow to the edges of the weedbeds and lily pads. Some will also come from the fallen trees, but in general, pickerel prefer green matter over wood as cover.

The Rt 14 bridge over the Marshyhope is another good place to shoot for bass. Casting tube jigs, bladebaits, and at times crankbaits to the bridge pilings can all be effective. Most anglers will simply work their way upcreek from this point, casting to the fallen trees and branches in or overhanging the water. There's a second bridge over the creek at Rt 392, and the creek ends not far above this bridge. Again, pick your lure color according to the water color.

The second creek on the Nanticoke that all bass anglers need to know about is Broad Creek. It's significantly shallower and slower-moving than the Marshyhope. In most years, it produces bass in the 2–3 lb range more consistently, too. The slower, shallower water warms more quickly, providing a better environment for lily pads and weeds. Starting at MRE55 there's great pickerel fishing in the shallower areas of the creek, wherever green is visible. Fallen timber from this point on provides most of the bass cover. The entire creek provides plenty of targets to cast at from here all the way up to the bridge at Bethel, Delaware. The bridge pilings hold fish, and there's some good timber just past the bridge that also holds bass much of the time.

Farther up the Nanticoke at Woodland, there's more good bassing territory at MRE56. Most of the cover here is provided by the docks and piles downriver from the Woodland ferry. Although they're too small to show up on the charts, from this point upriver you'll note several small creeks feeding into the river at MRE57, 58, and 59. All of these are also good bassing spots; cast lures up into the creek mouths and retrieve back by the points on either side. This far up the river you'll also find some crappie in residence, mostly hiding under the piers or fallen trees, and next to pilings.

The Wicomico, like the Nanticoke, is less significant as a saltwater fishery than it is as a brackish one. Terminating in Salisbury, Maryland, it offers prime crappie, pickerel, and bass fishing. But in its mouth, the Wicomico is best known as a croaker area. The deep hole at MRE60 loads up with croaker in May, and also with smallish weakfish many summers, usually starting in late May or early June. This spot will produce some flounder and stripers, too, but wouldn't exactly be called a "hot spot" for these species.

The Wicomico quickly runs out of depth beyond this point, but the two shallow bays—Ellis and Monie—both provide a shot at speckled trout. Usually some will be caught in the spring from mid- to late April through late May, particularly around the cuts at MRE61 and 62 in Monie Bay and 63 and 64 in Ellis. You'll need a shallow draft boat and light gear to effectively fish each of these spots. MRE61, at the mouth of Monie Creek, however, is a little easier to access—and is one of the best of the spots to find specs in this area. Strong water flow makes the mouth of the creek and the bend at MRE65 an excellent places to find these fish, particularly when an incoming tide shifts and first starts running out.

There's another good spec spot at the mouth of the river at MRE66. You'll have to be careful here—the water is shallow and there are old pilings, and in a few places rocks that love to eat props. But approach this zone by either poling or using an electric motor, and most shallow draft fishboats can access it effectively. Don't bother making the run to fish here on a west or strong southwest wind, however, because the water will become churned up fairly easily here, discouraging the spec bite.

The middle and upper sections of the Wicomico are much like the Nanticoke: in the summer you can find croaker in most of the deeper downriver areas, calm grassy areas house pickerel, farther up the river bass can be taken from fallen timber, and catfish can be found in most of the holes. But there isn't much stand-out fishing that will make it a destination. The leg of the Wicomico where it hits Salisbury, however, is quite interesting to freshwater guys. There are pilings, wharfs, and wreckage littering the edges of the river (literally—this is not the most picturesque zone of the river), which provide cover for bass and crappie. At MRE67, there is a series of pilings along the northern shore of the river that are equally spaced along the channel edge.

These piles hold crappie—good numbers of them, and good-sized fish. Catching them, however, is tough if you don't use a minnow/bobber combination. For some reason, the crappie here like to hold extremely close to the piles, and they don't move very far off of them, even to chase down dinner. Casting lures or baits and retrieving them past the piles is rarely effective. Instead, you need to cast a bobber to within one foot of a pile, and don't disturb it either until it drifts away from the pile or disappears via crappie power. Keep your baits up close to the wood with this method, and you can catch them by the dozens here.

Toss spinnerbaits and tube jigs to these pilings and the wharf just down-river, and you'll also locate some bass. The fixed bridge in Salisbury is the end of the road, but don't leave this area without casting to the pilings, whether you're after bass or crappie. You'll also take an occasional yellow perch at the bridge, wharf, and pilings.

South of the Wicomico lies the Manokin River. This river has a more interesting bottom and (speaking for the saltier species) holds a few more fish than those to the immediate north, more seasons than not. The first point of interest is Deal Island, on the northern side of the mouth of the river. The cut separating the western side of the island from the mainland has a strong current ripping through it, and although you can't see it on the charts, 12' of water running right up to an undercut bank in several areas. The section of the cut marked by MRE68 is often chock-full of croaker, and at the northern and southern end, you can catch stripers, flounder, and an occasional speckled seatrout by casting to the points on either side where the cut widens out. The mouths at either end of the cut at MRE69 also has specs most seasons, but requires a shallow draft boat or local knowledge to get through without running aground. The same is true of the cuts and points on Little Deal Island; fish can be found here with regularity, but only if you don't run aground first. MRE70, on the west side of the island, is one exception. There's enough water here than most shallow draft boats will be able to get in and out easily, and a fairly nice rip forms along this point attracting stripers and specs.

Just to the south of the island, a channel runs into the river and forms a great stretch of water at MRE71. Most years weakfish will move in here late in the spring (following the croaker, of course) and steadily increase in numbers through the summer, and good numbers of flounder can be taken dragging baits or jigging on bottom along the edges of the drop.

The trout will be most active here on low and falling tides, but on a flood tide move over to the edge of the hole. The large shallow flat to the south of MRE72 has a hard sand bottom, and this is often a good area to fish shallows for flounder. Particularly early in the year, when most of the surrounding water is still in the lower 60s, on calm sunny days the flat will warm up quickly and draw in the flatties. Cast up into 4' or 5' of water and retrieve bucktails dressed with minnow, or bounce a four-inch paddle tail jig along the bottom, and you stand a good chance of entering flounder heaven. Some years this area will also be full of croaker, however, making it tough to focus on the flatfish.

In most cases you'll only want to fish MRE71 to get protection when the wind's out of the north, because this same high/low water, trout/flounder game plan can be applied on the south side of the flat, too—and in the 40' and 50' deep water at MRE73, you also have a shot at finding some larger tiderunner weakfish. Trout can be located in any of the deeper sections here, and during flood tides you'll usually have better luck moving upriver from MRE73 into the 20' to 30' deep water. When the water level is falling, focus on the deeper sections.

Shallow water anglers will be interested in several of the cuts and points along the southern side of the Manokin. The cut at MRE74, running into Teague Creek, is one such spot. You can locate specs here in the spring and fall, although most years you'll catch more stripers casting to these points. Prickly Point, slightly farther south, is another point you'll want to check out. This is another fairly shallow spot, but it can be approached during most tides directly from the west. Most of the action here occurs during the end rush of an incoming tide.

Below the Manokin is the Big Annemessex that offers superb light tackle angling with deeper jigging territory side by side. In fact, it's one of the most underrated, under used rivers on the Eastern Shore. When the wind is out of the north or south, this area provides excellent cover for small boats, and seas here rarely become too tough to handle—but the fishing remains exceptional. The lower section of the river's open water doesn't have any stand-out features, but the shallow flats at MRE75 swarm with croaker early in the spring some years. Fish bait here on a high tide in late April, and often you'll experience faster action that you will in the sound itself. A little later in the year, usually mid-May, specs can also be found by easing into Acre Creek, and casting to the cut mouths at MRE76 and 77. Just a short hop upriver, casting to the edges of Jackson Island will also produce specs in mid- to late May. But the best spec spots on the big Annemessex are on its northern bank. MRE78 (fish this one on a falling tide) MRE79 and MRE80 all mark productive creek mouths. Even though it doesn't look incredible on the charts, the creek mouth at MRE80 is one of the best spots on the river. Approaching is tough, as there's barely a foot of water in the end of this cove at low tide, but the creek itself is 4 or 5' deep just inside the mouth. If your boat is narrow enough, it's possible to poke into the creek and cast into a hole at the first bend to the left, where another feeder creek joins it. Big specs come into this hole and will feed here through the high tide. When leaving the creek always take a few moments to cast jigs to the eastern edge of this cove, as stripers often feed along the edge of the marsh here. They are usually small, but numerous.

The point at MRE81 is another exceptional spec spot. It's usually feast or famine here—some seasons you won't get a hit here, others you'll pull in a dozen speckled trout in an hour, every trip. And unlike most of the spec spots near by, the fish don't seem to move in here until late in the spring, yet often remain in the area through the summer months. Then, when most other spots pick up again in the fall, this one usually fails to produce late in the year. It's best fished by anchoring to the southwest of the point about 50' from shore, casting back up to the marsh grass, and bouncing jigs across the bottom.

When the tide drops and the shallows become less active, move to MRE82 near the red #6 marker. Although the charts don't reflect it, the channel here drops down to 24' in a couple of places, and most summers mid-sized weakfish move into this trough. Bouncing jigs on the drop-off right next to the red #6 will also produce flounder during the summer and fall months.

The Little Annemessex—the last river along the Eastern Shore of the Tangier—serves as the waterway running into and out of Crisfield, Maryland, so it sees a good bit of boat traffic from watermen during the week and from pleasure boaters on weekends and isn't usually thought of as a fishing destination. There are still opportunities here, however. Pitching lures at the numerous piers and bulkheads of Crisfield will produce small stripers, and some years, even a speckled trout or two. Most anglers will save this approach as a backup for extremely windy days, when the larger nearby rivers and the sound can't be accessed.

Middle Bay, Main Stem, Western Zone

From the Bay Bridge to Point Lookout, the main-stem Chesapeake covers a huge area. To make it easier to digest, the mid-Bay section is divided between eastern and western zones. This section of the Bay is almost 70 miles long, and the width of the Bay varies between 4 miles and 15 miles across. But pinpoint the hot spots in this massive body of water, and you'll catch fish. Lots of them.

South of the Bay Bridges, Hacketts Bar (MMBW1) is the first hot spot on the western side of the main-stem Bay that you need to know about. Quality of fishing tends to vary greatly from year to year in this spot, and some years it seems to attract nothing but snapper blues. Other seasons, big stripers are taken here in big numbers. This is also a good spot to locate white perch and sometimes, croaker.

Just after the turn of the century, Hacketts produced some very interesting catches, and for some reason the past few years it seems like this spot is on the upswing. Puppy drum in the 15" to 20" range showed up in good numbers here in 2002, an event no one could remember happening before. In '03 they returned, though in lesser numbers. And stripers in the 30" to 38" range appeared in chum slicks in October, an unusual time frame for catching big fish in the middle Bay. Interestingly, the best fishing here is usually not right on the edge of the bar, where it drops off into the 30s, but up on top of the bar itself in 18' to 25' of water. This holds true for both chumming stripers and catching perch, although you'll do best on perch by drifting along the shell bottoms in 12' to 18' well inshore of the edge.

Just outside of the mouth of the Severn River there are several nice shelves and humps. But this is also an anchorage area for the Naval Academy, and since 9/11 you'll need to give the ships anchored here lots of elbow room. This area also becomes clogged with traffic from sailboats, especially on weekends. Sunny afternoons, it will be all but impossible to fish here. Considering these factors, the mouth of the Severn is not a great place to plan on fishing extensively.

The next point south is Tolly Point (MMBW2) that has a dramatic bar running all the way out to the green #1AH marker. Drifting from 25' up to 14' and back to 25' over the point just inside of this marker is a great way to fish for white perch, croaker, and small stripers. Trolling the edge that forms a concave shape from Tolly to Thomas Point produces decent catches of keeper stripers at times, usually in June and again during the fall. Move your trolling pattern out slightly to 30'-plus deep water in the spring time, and you're in a prime trophy zone. In some years trout also show up along this contour or hold right along the 15' to 35' drop at Thomas Point, but the last time they made decent showings here was in the late '90s. Working birds will also be spotted at and between Tolly and Thomas Points. Nine times out of ten, these will be in relatively shallow water, over small stripers in the 10" to 14" range. Unless you see birds working near deep water—at least 30'—it's usually best to ignore these patches of fish.

Directly east from Tolly point is MMBW3, an anchorage area for commercial ships waiting to pull into the port of Baltimore. They may be anchored from two miles north of Tolly to a half mile south, anywhere the water is deeper than 35'. The water ranges from 35' or 40' on the western side to 50' near the main shipping channel, and there are no major drops or structure I know of in this zone, which may partially explain why the ships anchor here. In any case, the big ore carriers, tankers, and containerships are good for more than looking at—they hold fish, and at times, lots of them.

Remember the classic spring trolling pattern for trophy stripers in this area: back and forth across the Bay from the bridges to Bloody Point to Thomas Point. As you can see from looking at the charts, this anchorage is smack-dab in the middle of this pattern. When you pass through it, troll right up to any ships you see and parallel them. Pass as close as is possible and safe, while remembering that they will have a rig-snagging anchor line down. By June smaller school stripers and blues will collect around the ships, and sometime after August, trout gather here too. These ships are required by law to maintain deck

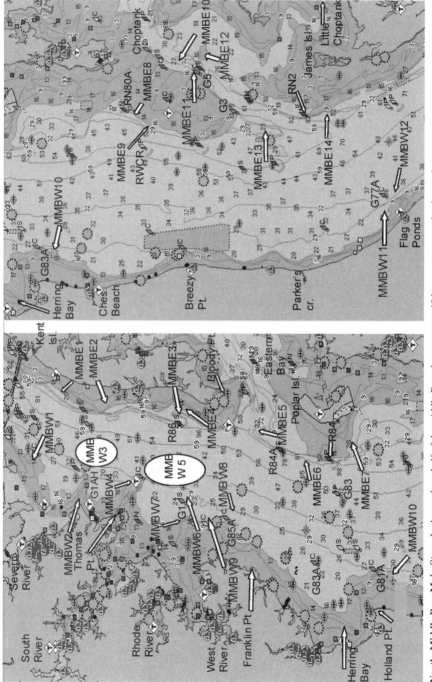

illumination and all night long they splash the water with their bright deck lights, attracting schools of Bay anchovies and menhaden. As the sun comes up the fish don't usually scatter, but stay near the ship for cover. The longer the same ship stays in the same place, the more fish it will gather. Sometimes there will be four or five ships anchored at the same time, and all of the fish will seem to have collected around one of them—usually, it's the one that has been anchored here the longest. So if there's more than one ship at anchor and the first doesn't produce for you, don't hesitate to move off and try the next one. Some ships stay for just a day, some for a few days, and in rare cases you'll see the same ship anchored up here for a couple of weeks in a row.

Drifting is the best way to take the trout, stripers, and blues that gather here from mid-summer on. When approaching the ships, stop and first identify the speed and direction of your drift so you know where to safely position your boat. Then circle the ship, with one eye pasted on your fishfinder screen. You'll want to get in close, preferably within 10' or 15' of the ship's hull. For some reason one or two specific areas of a ship usually seem to hold all the fish, and most of the time, this is either along the upcurrent side amidships, or right at the bow. At times, you'll also locate fish 20' to 50' behind the ship's stern.

If you want to target stripers and blues stay a little farther away and cast up to the ship's hullsides. Immediately begin a fast, erratic retrieve. If no strikes come, on the next cast give it a five-count before you start retrieving, on the next cast, a ten-count, and so on. To target trout, get as close as possible and drop a tandem rig, spoon, or hammered metal lure (like a Stingsilver) down to the bottom and jig it. For some reason, the trout hanging around ships seem to respond well to dead-sticking at times, too.

I've seen boats try to anchor right next to a ship, and even tie off on them, but for obvious safety reasons I don't recommend this tactic. Plus, the specific spot where the fish are holding will change with the tide. If you anchor next to a tanker amidships you may have good action for a few minutes, then nothing. Keep on the drift, however, and you'll be able to follow the fish as they move from amidships to the bow, or the stern. I do recommend looking carefully along the sides and particularly at the stern of the ship before setting up for a drift, because often the crew onboard will have fishing lines over the side. They are usually friendly if you wave and smile, but few speak any English.

South of the anchorage, the next hot spot along the western side of the main-stem Bay is the drop on the north side of Thomas Point. About 100 yards dead north of the lighthouse, the drop from 16' to 36' (MMBW4) often holds stripers but more often than not they're sub-legal. As mentioned earlier, in the past this area has supported trout, perhaps one season in four. In the mid-90s we used to catch flounder here, and on a flood tide found them all over the 12' to 18' area surrounding Thomas Point Light. Sadly, flatfish haven't made a serious showing here for six or seven years. Of course, that could change at any time.

Drifting this edge while jigging or trolling along are usually the best methods. Chummers can also score here if they can anchor the boat in the deep water very close to the edge, on an outgoing tide that sweeps the chum slick up onto the bar. Chumming seems to increase the proportion of keepers to throw-backs in this spot, too. Up on the bar can also be a productive spot for croaker, particularly at night, late in the spring and early in the summer.

What about casting to the rocks at the foot of the lighthouse? It sure looks like an awesome chunk of structure to throw lures at, and it does often attract stripers. However, they're usually on the small side. As a general rule of thumb, if you're fishing in a mobile fashion you should swing by and take a few casts, but it's not worth a huge time investment.

The outer edge of Thomas Point, the center of which is marked by green can SR, can also hold fish. However, it gets more pressure than the northern edge (markers seem to attract anglers, as a general rule) and in my opinion, holds fewer fish. Move about ½ mile to the east, however, and you're over a muddy bottom at and around MMBW5 that is prime for chumming or trolling for stripers early in the season. Many years, trophy fish move through in May, then seem to disappear. Then in mid-June or even as late as July they reappear here and stick around for a month or two. This is true of the mud bottom from this spot all the way down to the green can #1 outside of the mouth of the West River. It can be potluck, since there is no particular structure or drop-off to focus on, but once you locate fish in this zone, they usually stick around the same general vicinity for a week or two at the least. This muddy bottom zone is one of the best two mid-Bay areas to look for big cow trophy stripers during the spring season (the other being the Love Point mud flats).

Why do those big, fat fish hang out in an area with no structure and no other obvious fish-attracting feature? I can't say I know for sure. However, I have noticed that many of the fish caught in this area have crushed up manoes (sometimes called steamer or soft clams) in their belly, and I've pulled in clam shells stuck to my anchor. So, it stands to reason that they are feeding on clams here, which leads one to believe that clams should make a good bait. So I've tried them—many times. I have yet to catch a fish on one while chumming the mud. This could be because the stripers smell the chum and want to eat menhaden, or it could be that they come to this area shortly after feeding on manoes elsewhere. Or maybe there's another reason that's beyond me—I don't have the answer, but I can tell you one thing for sure: fresh menhaden will out-fish clam baits in this situation every time.

Spring trollers in this area will usually follow a triangular trolling pattern from Thomas Point to Bloody Point to the Bay Bridge. Anglers slightly to the south use a triangle running from Thomas to Bloody to the green #1 marker, or Horseshoe Point. The exact pattern you follow when trolling for spring trophies isn't really that important as long as you make sure you're covering the different depths until you run into some fish. This makes it important to have more east-west in your pattern than north-south. If you know fish have been located in a more specific area, by all means of course you should focus your pattern on that area.

Two miles south of the Thomas Point lighthouse, there's a green channel marker #1 that is usually referred to by locals as "old green number one." This marks a drop from 24' to 32', which sometimes holds stripers and blues. Many years—maybe one out of two—this spot is also productive for chumming up spring trophy stripers, and many trollers hook trophies in this area, too. However, it's more important because it marks the northwestern most hump (MMBW6) in a series that runs for a little more than a mile and a half to the south and a quarter mile to the east. These are not huge humps; most go from 30' or 32' to 26' or 28' and they do not show up clearly on most charts. But they do attract fish, and local anglers take both spring trophy stripers and fall schoolies on them.

Year to year the quality of the summer and fall bite on these humps varies greatly. Some years they are dead, others fish are stacked up over them. No matter how many fish seem to be around them, though, either trolling or chumming is the way to go. For some reason drifting bait and jigging never seems to produce here.

Travel a half mile or more to the east, and you'll be over more of the mud bottom that produces spring trophies in the southern section of MMBW5. This section of the mud flat sees a late run of large fish one year out of three, usually in the 26" to 36" range, some time in mid- to late June and some years into July. Run from the green #1 in the opposite direction, and you'll find a dip (MMBW7) down to the mid-30s surrounded by 22' to 24' deep water. The western edge of this dip is an excellent spring croaker spot, especially in the evenings. When the tides are running strong, you may also get into legal schoolie stripers chumming or trolling Rat-L-Traps at very slow speeds in this area. It's not commonly the most productive place in the world to catch keeper stripers, but when a strong west wind blows, it provides an area of relatively sheltered water with decent depths and a good shot at fish.

The humps near the green #1 peter out just north of Franklin Point, where you'll find two more main-stem Bay points of note, the green #85A can and a clearly marked artificial fish reef. The can, like the green #1 marker to its north, continues marking the 4 to 6' shelf where the bottom changes to a gradual, muddy, featureless slope as you run eastward, until hitting the channel. The one unique feature here is the two-foot trough at MMBW8, which runs east-west from the mark for about a mile. It's not a very big trough, just a few feet across and a couple feet deep, and it does not show on the charts. In fact, its small size makes it tough to locate sometimes; start off just a few yards north of the green can, 50 to 60 yards east of it, and idle to the south. If you get more than 50 yards to the south, make a U-turn to the east and idle north. The trough is almost impossible to identify until you get ¼ mile or so to the east, but it's best to work a slow, steady pattern to find it. Otherwise, you're likely to start too far out and miss it entirely. This tiny, insignificant trough is an exceptionally good place to find summer stripers in the 30" to 36" range. When the dog days hit and big fish seem to disappear, try chumming here. Anchor upcurrent of the trough, with the stern of your boat as close to it as possible, and chum with large baits on the bottom—the results might surprise the heck out of you.

The same time and effort is not necessary to search out the artificial fish reef just to the northwest of the green can. Unfortunately, this reef is rarely productive, at least in my experience. Generally speaking, you'll find white perch and the occasional weakfish hanging around it, but not in great numbers. As with most of the artificial reefs in the area, this one reaches out and grabs your lures and baits—plan on snags and lost lures if you spend a lot of time here.

In the late '90s, when this region of the Western Shore saw strong runs of flounder from June through October, one could find some flatfish hanging next to the edges of this reef, and around the nearby drop-offs. The 15' drop to 20' marked by MMBW9 just off Horseshoe Point was a particularly productive area several years in a row. However, since the century turned flounder haven't made such showings in the area. Keep your fingers crossed; maybe next year they'll come back.

The waters off of Franklin Manor, the next zone of interest to Chesapeake anglers, enjoy a slow, steady drop all the way out to the middle of the Bay. Near shore along most of Herring Bay and just off Franklin Manor you can find schools of croaker from late April through the spring, but you won't catch many before sunset. It seems as if they roam the deeper waters of Herring Bay—where they can be caught on crab or bloodworm baits—when the sun's shining, and move in to just a few feet of water to feed late in the evening. Whenever fishing the shallows for these fish in the dark be sure to toss out a big hunk of menhaden, too. Stripers also move in shallow to feed when the sun goes down, and although most will be undersized during trophy season, every spring a few guys take home keepers while croaker fishing here.

The open water outside of Herring Bay is traditionally a good zone to troll for early spring trophies using standard spring trolling techniques, and often you'll see much of the Deale charter fleet meandering around in 30' to 50' of water anywhere east of Franklin Manor to Holland Point. Fish usually move through here and are caught in waves, much as they are at Thomas and Love Points, and Chesapeake Beach. One week it can be incredibly hot, the next week it might not be. In the past few years, however, they've been caught in this zone in large numbers through most of the trophy season. The "Old Gas Buoy," a green #83 channel marker, is a popular starting point and often you'll see charters trolling in circles around it.

Another standard trolling pattern many good anglers run in this area is similar to the Bloody/Thomas/bridge triangle, but this triangle runs from the green #81A can off Holland Point to the red #84 channel marker west of Poplar Island to green #85A can at MMBW9. Early in the day and in low light conditions, however, you'll notice that many of the charter boats will stick close to the Western Shore. In fact, they sometimes won't even go beyond the 35' contour running between 85A and 83A. When the light is dim and the stripers are willing to meander along in shallower water, this area tends to collect a lot of fish. Savvy anglers will make their first few passes of the day here, then stick around in the shallows only if the sun doesn't break through. Seeing several charters sticking in close and shallow in this area should tip you off, too.

At the southern point of Herring Bay, off of Holland Point, you'll see the green marker #81A. There's a nice drop running north/south here, at MMBW10, which is a good flounder edge most seasons. They often show here as early as mid-May and stay through June. Croaker and sometimes trout and/or stripers will also show up here at times. There's a marked fish reef just a couple hundred yards to the south that produces limited catches of fish some years, too.

Chesapeake Beach, another port that's home to a large charter fleet, lies a few miles to the south of Holland Point. The bottom of the Bay here is pretty featureless, with a long, sloping drop from 10' all the way into the middle of the Bay. As with the waters east of Herring Bay, this entire zone is often a productive spring trophy trolling zone. It's also an area you're likely to find breaking blues and stripers once the fish are schooled, and during the late summer, they'll often have Spanish macks mixed in. Trolling and running to working birds and breaking fish is the name of the game in this zone; bottom fishing in this area is tough, because there aren't any ridges, humps or features to focus on. Fish in this zone for a few years, and you'll notice that when the Chesapeake Beach charters go bottom fishing, they usually head across to the Eastern Shore. The one exception is croaker, which can be caught from or near the shoreline in evenings.

From Chesapeake Beach south to Flag Ponds (MMBW11), a stretch about 10 miles long, the Western Shore of the Chesapeake remains pretty blasé. The drop is slow, the bottom is muddy, and there just isn't a whole lot of structure around. The entire zone will produce spring trophies, which are passing through the area on their way up or down the Bay. Trolling is the favored method. (Although there's no obvious reason why chumming the mud wouldn't work here, I've never tried it and no one I've ever spoken with has, so I can't vouch for its effectiveness in this spot.)

At Flag Ponds, the drop becomes a bit more dramatic south of the green can #77A, at MMBW12. Just west of the can there's a series of bumps that usually attracts spring croaker, some trout (more later in the fall) and small stripers. As with the Western Shore areas to the north, flounder used to make a good showing here but in the past few years, their numbers have been lackluster except for the period from mid-May to late June.

The Gas Docks (MMBW13) are located a few miles farther south, and in past years this was one of the hottest places in the middle Bay to chum up schoolie stripers. Fish in the 18" to 28" class gather here as early as mid-May, and they're usually in the area right on through the fall season. This isn't really a "dock" but is a natural gas unloading facility, with huge pipes and rigging towering above the water. A boat could anchor next to a support leg—a series of massive steel spider pilings—or inside the 90-degree angle on the northwest corner of the facility. Often the docks would be so crowded it was tough to get a good spot, but just as often the action was so fast that all you had to do was idle around for a few minutes until someone limited out and left, vacating a position. But shortly after the turn of the century they reopened the gas docks, and anchoring right up next to the facility is no longer legal. However, you can still manage to draw fish away from the structure by anchoring upcurrent and chumming hard. The stated minimum distance has changed several times since they reopened it and could change again at any time, but at the time of this writing is 500'. At this distance, it is possible to chum in the fish.

If you take your boat to the west side of the Gas Docks and go a little less than halfway to shore, you will pass over the pipeline. Watch your depth finder as you pass between the structure and shore, and you'll note a ridge running 12' feet deep with deeper water on either side of it. The closer you are to the docks, the deeper the water, all the way down to 40'. Like most of the artificial reefs in Chesapeake Bay, this ridge usually holds more snags than fish. But if you jig a couple of feet over the ridge, you can usually save your rigs and catch stripers. Croaker, spot, and other bottom feeders are also found along this ridge sometimes.

About a half-mile to the south Cove Point lighthouse sits on shore. The point it marks (MMBW14) is, during many years, the best flounder spot in this section of the Bay. The top of the point is 8' to 12', and the edges around it drop quickly off into the 30s. It's easy to locate the edges, even without a fishfinder, since crab pot floats litter the bar above the drop-off. And since it sticks out into the Bay in an easterly direction, no matter which direction the tide is flowing you can usually position your boat so it drifts from deep water, up onto the point, then back down the other side. One side or the other usually holds the lion's share of the flatties. If flounder are your species of choice, checking out Cove Point is a must; I've seen catches of 40-plus flounder on one cycle of the tide here. Another great tactic is to try drifting the point once or twice, to determine if the flatties are biting during the tide cycle you're in. If not, move off towards the Gas Docks and try chumming up stripers for a while. Then a couple hours later, try drifting the point again, and so on. By alternating you can usually catch each species during its period of strongest feeding, which, in the case of stripers and flounder, do not overlap. (Stripers usually react to chum best during the last hour and first hour on either side of a tidal change, while flounder bites tend to pick up with a strong, steady current.) Using this tactic, you have a real possibility of filling the cooler with both species.

From Cove Point to the mouth of the Patuxent there aren't many radical features. You might, however, find birds working anywhere through this area. In shallower areas (20' or less) almost without fail these will be foot-long or smaller fish, but if you spot them in deeper zones it's worth checking them out. Many years, you'll find marginal keeper stripers feeding over 30' or 40' of water and in the late summer and fall Spanish mackerel (as well as blues) will often be mixed in with them. In the spring and again late in the year trout can also be found, along the edge that drops from 15' to 33', just south of Cove Point at MMBW15. Stripers may also show up here, at just about any time of the year. This sharp edge is very productive some years and is always worth slowing to check out or jig over for a few minutes if you're leaving the Patuxent and heading north for either Cove Point or the Gas Docks.

The area outside the mouth of the Patuxent is known as the Chinese Mud (MMBW16), and fish can usually be found in this vicinity most of the season. In early spring stripers are often intercepted by trollers who drive in a huge circle, following the mouth of the river on the western side, going three quarters of the way across the Bay, and back around again. In fact, much of the Solomons Island charter fleet follows this routine and quite often makes limit catches. One note about catching spring stripers here: either there is a distinct group of fish that holds in this area—separate from the bulk of the migrating fish going up the Bay—or fish passing through here during trophy season headed north to spawn are behind schedule. Perhaps there is some other scientific reason I can't fathom, but whatever the cause, most of the spring trophies you catch here during the trophy season and even into early June will be full of roe. This is not usually true of the fish caught farther north in the main-stem Bay. In fact, the reason the trophy season is main-stem Bay only is to ensure the fish get a chance to spawn before getting caught. But while just 10% of the trophies I've caught in the rest of the middle Bay had roe, over 80% of the trophies I've taken outside of the Patuxent had roe. Note also that for some reason, trophies taken on chum over the mud are most often males, and I have seen just four roe-laden female while chumming over mud. Maybe they don't stop to feed on the mud bottoms until post-spawn, maybe males like the mud more. Who knows—but I can say for sure that chumming trophies, while it results in fewer fish than trolling, doesn't prevent the big cow females from spawning.

Trout can show up in the same Chinese Mud zone any time from spring through fall, and croaker are almost always available somewhere in this area from April through July, or later. Note, though, that as with other croaker hot spots, most of the real action takes place at dusk or in the dark.

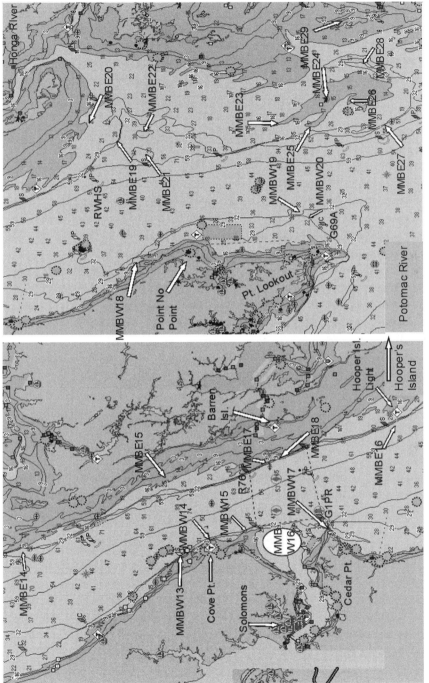

South, Middle Bay, Main Stem. The southern portion of the middle Bay is Maryland's southernmost portion of the Chesapeake.

For some reason, the trout here seem to respond better to baited rigs drifted across the bottom than they do jigs. Who knows why, but past experience has proven that drifting soft crab on trout scouts is the best way to go on the Chinese Mud.

The southern point marking the entrance to the Patuxent is Cedar Point, and this is another great flounder area. Search the drops between the old lighthouse ruins at MMBW17 and the green #1PR buoy, and work on the drops from 12' to 25'. Light tackle casting to the ruins can be fun and productive late in the year when stripers move up into the shallows, and sometimes during the spring and summer at daybreak and sunset. The ruins are strewn about underwater, however, and the visible parts are not the only obstruction out there—approach slowly, with caution, and only in a shallow draft boat.

From Cedar Point running south to Point No Point is another long, mostly featureless area. As with those to the north, this zone is a good area to troll for spring stripers as they move through the Bay, but there isn't much structure to target after the spring trophy season has past. Off Point No Point, however, the bottom starts getting a little more interesting. Just north of the point, there's a section of bottom ranging from 8' to 30' at MMBW18 that attracts flounder many seasons. Stripers can also be jigged up and/or chummed for here once they've started schooling through the fall, and trout can be found along the deeper edges of the drops. These fish usually show up here in late May and June, then again in September or October. But this area is most reliable for croaker. From mid-April on, they are almost always present in this vicinity in good numbers.

The strip from Point No Point to Point Lookout doesn't look incredible on the charts, but is a great area to fish. From the Point No Point lighthouse to the green #69A can, there are several holes and edges that are consistently good for croaker, fall stripers, and spring and fall trout. Pay special attention to the deep water at MMBW19. Jigging here in May and June is a good bet for early trout, and although they usually disappear from July through early September, they'll be caught here again in the fall. Closer to shore the 15' to 25' drop holds flounder most years. And through the fall breaking stripers and blues often show up in this zone. During July and August Spanish mackerel will often be mixed in with them.

Another hot spot in this zone is the 25' to 35' drop at MMBW20. This is a great summer and fall chumming and/or jigging edge for stripers in the 16" to 28" range most seasons. As with MMBW18, trout will make an early and late showing here, commonly with a fishless gap in between late June and mid-September.

Middle Bay, Main Stem, Eastern Zone

To the east of the anchorage just south of the Bay Bridges, the water stays in the 50' zone until it drops down into the ancient Susquehanna river bed channel. The eastern edge of the channel, which we'll call the Kent Island edge is extremely sharp, and is a wonderful edge to troll along or jig next to. Since the drop is so sheer, anchoring on this edge is nearly impossible. That makes chumming a no-go along most of it. From just below the Bay Bridges down to Gum Thickets (recognizable by the red channel marker #86) this edge is pretty consistent, going from 15' or 20' all the way down to 70' to 100'. Zigzagging along this drop is prime spring trophy trolling water, and during the summer you'll pick up blues and smaller stripers in this area, too. Spanish mackerel will make a showing in this zone some years, maybe one in five or six, but this is about as far north as you're likely to see them in any given year. Unless there's a drought they usually won't be found much north of the Choptank.

Once the seatrout begin schooling in the fall, you can locate pockets of them by weaving along this edge slowly enough to spot fish on your fishfinder, then dropping jigs. Don't worry about marking the spot, because one of the advantages of fishing along this drop is the presence of crab pot floats at the top of the edge in 15' to 20' of water. Just 50' to the west of these floats you'll be over deep water, but it's close enough to eyeball the floats and use them to keep track of exactly where you—and the fish—are. When chasing those pockets of trout here don't expect them to sit still in one place. But as long as the prevailing current remains the same, you can usually follow a school as it works its way northward or southward along the edge. If you lose track of the fish, check the tidal conditions and often you'll note that the tide quit or changed. Then, start looking for the fish in the opposite direction.

Most years—though not all of them—the lion's share of the trout action along this edge will take place to the south of Matapeake. Matapeake is easily recognizable because it has the first visible water tower on the shoreline south of the bridge. The 15' to 20' drop just south of the Matapeake entrance (MMBE1, shown earlier on the northern chart) is worthy of note because this is the northernmost area of the eastern shore of Chesapeake Bay to regularly catch flounder in decent numbers. Some years there won't be any around, some years there will be more flatfish caught in this zone than any other spot north of the Choptank, but every year it's worth checking out.

Anywhere along the Kent Island drop, you'll often see groups of birds working in the shallow water just to the east of the deep water ledge. These are usually stripers and blues in the 10" to 14" range. However, keeper-sized stripers can sometimes be caught in the shallow zone by casting up to and around the pound nets in this area. There are several but their exact locations seem to change every five years or so. One exception is a net that has been maintained in the same spot for as long as I can remember, at MMBE2. Try casting Rat-L-Traps and jigs as close as possible to the net, and rip them back with a fast, erratic retrieve.

Working south along the eastern side, the next important spot to learn about is Gum Thickets. As mentioned earlier, Gum Thickets breaks the straight Kent Island drop, just before it ends altogether at Bloody Point, the southernmost part of Kent Island. At different times and with yearly variation, Gum Thickets has it all. You can chum, troll, jig, and drift baits here with amazing success for everything from seatrout (the biggest I've ever taken on the Chesapeake, a 10 lb 6 oz fish, came from Gum Thickets) to rockfish to croaker. If you look closely at the chart, you'll notice that MMBE3 is on a little arm of deep water that cuts into the edge of the Kent Island drop, clearly marked by the red #86 channel marker. This pocket is a good place to jig for trout in the fall, and for schoolie stripers through the season.

The bottom and current are not correct to chum for early spring trophy stripers here; to catch those fish in this zone, you're better off trolling. But once the schoolie season starts in June, you can chum up both stripers and blues at Gum Thickets. Interestingly, the best chumming here seems to take place not in the finger at MMBE3 but along the inner edge of the feature at MMBE4, which is neither the sharpest drop nor the closest to exceptionally deep water. For whatever reason, however, this is where they often congregate. When approaching this spot, zigzag from 30' to 18' and look for fish on the meter, then drop the hook where you see the most marks.

Flounder, croaker, spot, and other bottom feeders are more commonly found on top of the hump just north of the red #86 marker. Drifting over this hump with bait or jigging a leadhead/twister tail will both produce fish. Note, however, than in June this entire area is inundated with rays some years, to the point of being practically unfishable with bait. You'll also find them up in the shallow water on the eastern side of that finger of intrusive deep water. This spot is particularly good for catching croaker around sunset, or after dark.

With seatrout at Gum Thickets, all bets are off. I've found them in the shallows where I expected croaker to be in the evening, in the deep water of the channel to the west of Gum Thickets, on top of the hump, in the finger of deep water, and on the edges to either side of the finger. If you want to target trout here, just maintain your mobility and search around until you see fish. Don't stop too long or too often to work hard on ghost images and small returns, but move, move, move. When you do find a good, solid school of trout it should be relatively easy to keep track of your position, since there are several visible marks (the red channel buoy, Kent Island, and Bloody Point Light) as well as significant underwater features. Also remember that Gum Thickets does not commonly have a strong showing of trout in the spring; it's usually a fall fishery here.

About two miles south of Gum Thickets, the Kent Island Drop ends at Bloody Point. Many spring trophies are taken from the deep water in this area by trollers. Despite the fact that the drop is sheer and looks like a good edge, however, it's rare to find large numbers of keeper fish holding and feeding right on this edge during the summer and fall. The potential exception is late in the year, when you may see flocks of birds over breaking stripers and blues, with trout below. It seems to happen about one year in five or six.

At MMBE5, you can see a large underwater hill that is surrounded by extremely deep water on the western, northern, and eastern sides. This isn't just any old hill, this is The Hill. It is without question one of the most popular, productive places to chum for stripers and blues from late spring or early summer through late fall. On a beautiful, sunny day in August or September when the fishing is good, you may see as many as two hundred boats planted on The Hill. On a windy weekday when the only captains out are those earning a paycheck, you can still usually find a dozen or two charter boats from Kent Narrows, Tilghman's Island, Deal, and/or Chesapeake Beach, working their magic on The Hill.

If there's any one secret to being successful at this spot, it's to get there early. Preferably, at first light. This will allow you to roam over the transitions from 35' to 25' deep water and search a bit for the large schools of stripers here. Since the stripers seem to congregate on and around different specific parts of The Hill from season to season (sometimes from week to week) you'll want some flexibility in where you set up. Arrive later, particularly on a weekend, and you usually have to choose a spot depending on where there's room instead of where there are fish.

Stripers and blues will be found all across The Hill, but usually the very best area—and often the hardest one to find a parking spot on—is the northernmost edge, in 28' to 32' of water. For this reason, it's best to approach from the north when beginning your search pattern. If you search the northern edge without success, the next most likely area to find fish will be the eastern edge, where The Hill's shallowest area (22') is located. At times, the stripers will move up onto this slightly bumpy region and hold here through a particular tidal cycle. Which particular tidal cycle? That seems to change from year to year, and some years it seems to have no effect at all. The same is true of each specific region of The Hill. Once you have the pattern, however, it will usually remain the same for a matter of weeks, or more.

The western edge of The Hill is another zone that will at times be the most productive, though with less regularity than the others mentioned. One important exception: move south a half mile along this edge, which we'll call the Poplar Island Drop, directly in line with the red channel marker #84A, and in late spring (usually early to mid-June) you can intercept trophies running slightly behind the generally accepted migration schedule with chunks of menhaden set on the bottom. This is also a good spot to check out when The Hill becomes overcrowded. The deep water immediately west of this spot is worth noting for fall trout, which will school and hold along this edge one year in four or five. Check it out every fall, though, because history shows that when the trout do show up here, they usually stay in the area until migrating south for the winter.

With the exception of spring trophy season, standard chumming techniques rule throughout this area, and trolling takes a definite backseat since it's usually too crowded with chummers to troll through without raising a few hackles. Trolling doesn't seem particularly effective here, in any case, perhaps because there's fresh ground menhaden available so often. And although undersized fish often swarm around The Hill, particularly in the fall when you may have to weed through a dozen throw-backs just to find a single keeper, chumming here provides some nice surprises. Spanish mackerel, black and red drum, and even cobia are caught on occasion at The Hill. All of these fish are rare visitors, sure, but every year The Hill manages to startle a few mid-Bay anglers. During the same time frame that black drum arrive at the Stone Rock— the last two weeks of May through the first two weeks of June—The Hill is often also a flounder hot spot. In fact, the flounder that briefly hold along the edges of The Hill, sometimes as deep as 35' or even 40', are the real lunker flatfish of the mid-Bay. They are sometimes caught by chummers, and by June it's usually impossible to target them by drift fishing because of all the boats at anchor. However, if chumming is slow and you're parked on one of the edges during this time frame, it's worth fan-casting a jig or bucktail dressed with a fat bull minnow. Just let it sink, then slowly bounce it along the bottom.

Before moving along from The Hill, I should stress again that this is one of the most productive chumming spots in the middle Chesapeake, and it's often worth putting up with the crowds to get in on a lot of fast action. We must also note that in a strong wind, particularly a south wind combined with an incoming tide, it can be very tough to get a Danforth-style anchor to set on the hard bottom. With a north, east, or westerly wind you can always drop anchor in deeper water and it will usually hook as it drags up the edge, but a southerly breeze means your anchor will always be traveling down-hill.

Combine that with an incoming tide, and a Danforth will just bounce along the hard shell bottom. Now picture this situation: 100 boats are anchored on The Hill in a five knot northerly breeze with an incoming tide. Then the wind switches and blows 15 knots out of the south. In a moment, half of the boats are going to start dragging anchor, and the result is a real mess. The solution to this problem is to carry a grappling anchor. On any oyster shell or hard rock bottom, these have superior holding power to other traditional style anchors. On The Hill, a grappling anchor will usually grip and hold the bottom on the first pass—and keep that grip.

One more caution about The Hill: some years, setting up a chum line here means getting bluefished to death. At times your boat will be swarmed by 8" to 12" snappers, chewing up baits and shredding leaders. When this happens it may be best to just suspend your chum line and wait a few minutes for the snappers to move over to someone else's slick. You will also notice that the blues usually come on strongest when the striper bite peters out, and vise versa, so you usually don't miss out on too many quality fish by holding back when the little snappers are in a frenzy.

Although the drop between The Hill and the red 84A marker is productive, it is not as sheer as the same ledge another mile south. About half way between 84A and 84 at MMBE6 the drop is a little more abrupt, and it's easy to keep track of because crab pot floats are usually set right at the top of it in 18' or so of water. This stretch of water is one of the best spring flounder spots in the middle Bay. It's not an easy ledge to fish, because that drop is so fast that at times the bow of your boat will be in 20' and the stern will be in 30'. That makes a drift sock an invaluable tool here, and it can slow you down just enough to be make-or-break. Try bouncing jigs from 12' to 35', or drag Fluke Killers tipped with minnow/squid combinations to hook into the flatfish here. The biggest flounder will show up some time during May and stick around for two to three weeks. After the doormats move through, you'll find more common sized flounder along this edge for another two or three weeks, usually well into June.

Schools of stripers in the 16" to 24" range also seem to love this edge. Sometimes you'll find them holding at mid-depth in 40' to 45' of water just off the edge, other times they'll be schooled up in 16' and you'll have to dodge crab pots to catch them. A quick search usually discloses their location, since you can cover these depths and all in-between with a few short turns of the boat. Stripers found in this spot are usually active feeders and jigging tandem rigs, twister-tail jigs and spoons often produces limit catches in short order. During June a great game plan is to jig this spot for schoolie stripers, fill the cooler, then move up right against the edge and pound on flounder to put some icing on your cake. That's not to say big stripers are out of the question here—I've seen several trophies up to 38" jigged up along this edge while targeting smaller rock and flounder.

Deeper along this same edge, you may also find schools of weakfish. Some years they are marked by flocks of birds over breaking stripers and blues, other years they are not. This is not a reliable place to find them, but like Bloody Point, it seems that one year in every five or so, a school will show up here and stick around through the fall.

One would think that with all the fish that can be jigged up here, it would be an awesome place to chum. I've dropped anchor here several times and experienced some success, but not enough to choose chumming over jigging in this spot again. That's just my experience—give it a shot for yourself, but don't be surprised if you find yourself catching fewer fish than you did on the drift.

South of the red #84 the edge takes a turn to the east, then runs south parallel to Tilghman's Island. This area is generally known as The Hook.

MMBE7 is a spot on The Hook worth checking out once or twice a season, but if you don't find fish here relatively quickly move on. While they do school up here some years, more often than not you'll find better numbers of them either to the north along the Poplar Island edge or to the south near Stone Rock or Sharp's Island.

Three miles to the south from here, find the red nun #80A and you'll be looking at the Stone Rock. It gets its name because there is some hard, rocky bottom here that is very recognizable with a quality depth finder. Legend has it that the rocks were ballast dropped by sailing ships centuries ago. To find the rocks just watch on your fish finder for the bottom line to become very skinny, very quickly. (Remember that counter to common sense, on most depth finders a thick bottom line indicates a soft bottom, and a thinner line indicates a harder bottom.) This hot spot is famous for attracting big black drum from mid-May through June. Drum fishing can be intense—when the fish are located everyone piles up, and you might find yourself holding a fishing rod with one hand and pushing off of a boat with the other. It can be very rewarding, too, as many of the early season drum that show up at the Stone Rock run well over 50 lb.

The Stone Rock edge drops from 15' to 35' but the abruptness of this drop varies greatly. The part of it that seems to be the most reliable is marked by MMBE8. The drum could show anywhere in this area, however. Flounder can be found here also, by locating one of the sharper edges and drifting from 15' to 25'. Generally speaking there isn't usually a lot of action at the Stone Rock after the drum depart in late June, and through the summer. However, in some years, maybe one in five or six, stripers school here after the heat of summer passes, providing chumming bite from September on. It's also worth noting that there are a couple of pound nets located just to the north of the Stone Rock, which are sometimes worth casting to for stripers in the 14" to 24" range. You may also find birds working in the area, but unless they're located on the deep side of the Stone Rock, you're probably looking at fish in the 10" to 16" range—and nine times out of ten, the birds will be over the shallow stuff.

South of the Stone Rock you'll note deep water runs into the Choptank, then it shallows up again as you reach Sharp's Island Flats. This hot spot is terrifically exciting, because it attracts a great variety of fish, and usually holds one variety or another from early spring right through winter. You might locate fish anywhere along the entire edge of the flat and up on the flat itself, so no particular part of it is identified as a hot spot—think of the whole area as one.

The first excitement of the year comes from trophy stripers that can be trolled up in the deep water anywhere along the western side of the flats in 40' to 100' deep water. From mid-May through June black drum can be located along the same edges, though they'll be shallower. As with the Stone Rock, most of the drum you'll catch here will be in 15' to 35' of water. They don't usually hold on a specific spot, but wander this edge; the best way to find them is to slowly putt along until you see good marks on the fish finder and don't concentrate on any specific spot until you see those fish.

During the same time frame flounder can be found along the drops, and the edges off of Sharp's Island also provide a historical early season chopper bluefish bite. While it's true that this fishery has been less productive in the past decade than it was before the striper resurgence, it could return to its former level at any time. These fish are scattered, and like the drum, could be intercepted anywhere in the general area by trollers.

Croaker, spot, and trout will also be found along the edges of Sharps' Island Flats and when stripers school up, this is another good chumming zone. But up on the flat itself is the favorite area for horse croaker, usually caught with peeler crab or bloodworms on bottom rigs at night. Jumbo spot also roam the flat some years, although they haven't run in serious size or numbers in years of late. Some years stripers in the 14" to 26" class gather around the lighthouse itself and are caught by anglers casting jigs up to it.

Now find the red and white CR buoy on the chart and draw a line directly to Sharp's Island Light. Along that line a finger of slightly shallower water that sticks out into deeper water, at MMBE9. This is a prime place to chum for stripers during late summer and fall. Late in the year, it's also a good bet you'll find trout holding here out closer to the CR buoy in deep water. Anywhere in this entire area you could also encounter breaking stripers and/or blues—with the potential for Spanish mackerel mixed in during August and September, and trout schooled beneath them from September on.

To the southeast of Sharp's Island Light is an area known as the Diamonds (MMBE10). Like The Hill, this is a traditional chummer's haunt that has produced countless fish through the years. Virtually every season you'll see charters working the Diamonds for schoolie stripers and blues. There's a small but great pair of lumps here at MMBE11, almost within casting distance of the green #5 channel marker. They come up to 18' and are surrounded by 35' to 40' on three sides with the 8' flats (usually marked here by a field of crab pots) to the northwest. Both are great chumming spots whenever stripers are schooled in this zone of the Bay, but neither can support more than a couple of boats. You'll also catch plenty of stripers and/or seatrout jigging these lumps at times. On the south side of the channel, there's a large lump that comes up to 16' and is surrounded by 23' to 25' of water (MMBE12). This bump holds plenty of fish and can support many more boats. It's almost always better to locate on the smaller lumps, however, simply because they are harder to find and thus get less pressure from other anglers.

Running southwest from the Diamonds there's a green marker #3. The drop-off on the south side of this marker is tremendous, going from 10' to 75' in a matter of feet. It certainly holds fish—flounder and stripers in the spring and summer, and trout in the fall—but it's so steep that you'll need calm winds and a slack tide to fish it effectively. The underwater point that follows this edge to the south is known as The Summer Gooses (MMBE13), another very reliable chumming spot once stripers have schooled up in the summer and on through the fall. The depth here runs 25' and drops to the mid-40s to the west and all the way down to the 80s to the east. Start looking for fish in this spot on the southernmost edge and run an east/west pattern, working your way northward, until you locate some fish. You can also catch flounder in the shallower areas of the Gooses, but once the stripers start hitting, you may encounter too many anchored boats to set up an effective drift—this is another one of the most consistently chummed spots in the middle Bay.

Another mile south of the Gooses, look for the red nun buoy #2. The edge running south from here, the St. James edge, can be extremely productive. Searching for spring trout along this edge and particularly near MMBE14 from some time in May through mid- to late June is a good tactic—many mid-Bay anglers score their first weakfish of the year here—and some years they stay in the area through summer and fall months, too. Jigging for stripers once the size limit drops to 18" is a good bet, but chumming in this area can get tough because the stripers usually seem to move around in clusters. Anchoring in one place here can be the kiss of death, as the stripers move around and swarms of little bluefish move in to chew up your baits. This edge is very rugged, with craggy drops and sudden depth changes—and this zone of bumpy bottom is often a place you can intercept the black drum a week or so before they show up at Stone Rock. Some years they pass right through and you might only find them here for a few days, other years they'll stick around for a few weeks. In either case, drifting soft crab on the bottom usually produces stripers and trout, when the drum don't cooperate. And as the season progresses, if you drop crab baits on Fluke Killers it's a good bet to catch stripers, trout, croaker, and flounder. Once the dog days of summer hit, the deep water west of the edge is also a good area to look for Spanish mackerel (trout usually seem to move out of this spot by the end of June, and don't usually return until the fall).

This edge remains well-defined for a good five miles or so, until you reach Punch Island Bar and MMBE15 (shown on the south, middle Bay, main stem chart). All along this stretch, you can locate scattered pods of stripers and trout in the spring and fall, and flounder from mid-May on. In the summer, try trolling along it with a zigzag pattern to intercept Spanish mackerel and blues. The edge drops a bit more gradually at Punch Island Bar, which gives you the ability to anchor and chum with ease, and many anglers have success here. This is also a good area for evenings spent croaker hunting. In the fall, anywhere from The Gooses down to Punch Island Bar you have a good shot at locating working birds with stripers, blues, and/or trout below them.

The next stretch of this edge, from the red channel marker #76 to Hooper Island Light, provides similar opportunities. There's some tremendously deep water to the west at MMBE16, dropping all the way down to 120'. Early in the spring and again late in the fall, don't be afraid to spend some time searching over this deep water. You'll sometimes find pods of trout holding tight to the bottom, even in the deepest zones. Often, this means deploying a drift sock while jigging with thin diameter superline and a four or five ounce lure to stay deep enough. Do so, and you can often make banner catches of trout. Higher up on the ledge you'll start to encounter more stripers and blues than trout, and drifting peeler or soft crab anywhere along this edge usually produces croaker from early spring through mid-summer. Flounder may also be found in the 10' to 30' zone and some years they seem to carpet the area along the top of this ledge, particularly just west of Barren Island between the MMBE17 and MMBE18 marks. One year out of three you'll find good sized fish here with regularity; unfortunately, the rest of the time the flounder seem to be on the small side.

Troll the deep water anywhere west of this edge in the spring, and the fish you catch will be anything but small. Trophies roam this zone from the opening of the season through June, and standard spring trolling techniques will produce well here.

The western edge of this deep water zone also holds fish at times, though they're usually less concentrated and move around more. It's a stretch to even call it an "edge," as the rise from water in the 80s to water in the 40s is long and slow. For this reason when using any method other than trolling, the best bet is usually to start hunting fish along the eastern edge, where it's easier to pinpoint the particular depth the fish are holding at.

As you move south from Hooper Island Light, this edge deteriorates. However, a couple miles to the south, just inside of the red and white HS buoy, there's an abrupt change in the contour at MMBE19. This spot attracts weakfish during both the spring and fall runs. For some reason, particularly in late May or early June, the trout holding here are often super-deep. Don't be afraid to jig or drop a bait in 90' or 100' of water, if you see good returns on your fishfinder. Move in shallower to MMBE20 and you'll find schoolie stripers in the summer and fall, and croaker through most of the season.

About five miles to the south of the lighthouse there are twin humps marked by MMBE21 and 22 that rise to 30' from 50' to 60' of water. These are big humps, and the larger western one is almost a half mile wide. On the southeastern edge it drops all the way to 65' and on an incoming tide, this is a great place to chum once the stripers have schooled up. You'll find spring croaker and spring and fall trout here as well, but flounder don't seem as attracted to the spot. During the summer, plan on hitting lots of bluefish in this zone.

These humps, like many areas that come up into the lower 30s from deeper water, are an especially good place to find large numbers of fish in late August and early September during years that large anoxic zones form in the main-stem Bay. These zones of "dead" water, which contain low oxygen content, can form any time during summer and remain for a matter of weeks or months depending on weather conditions. Generally speaking, the warmer the weather the more anoxic water that forms. But years of heavy rainfall—which feeds unusually high levels of phosphates and nitrates into the Bay—can also have a dramatic impact. Most years, the anoxic zone doesn't start until the water is 35' or so deep and runs to the bottom. With the warm weather the fish are seeking cooler conditions, so they try to go deep. But they can't survive in the anoxic zone, so they move down to 30' to 35' and hold at these depths. Find humps like these, which meet the barrier zone between cool temps and anoxic water, and you'll often locate good numbers of fish.

Hop another five miles south and you'll enter a zone known as the middle grounds (MMBE23). This area, the farthest south fishing spot still considered to be in the middle Bay, stretches north/south for another five miles, and is at least a mile wide for most of its length. Smack in the middle of it lies the Target Ship (MMBE24), which the navy uses for bombing practice. The middle grounds are covered with humps, peaks, ridges and drops varying from 50' all the way to 10'. They all may hold stripers and blues once the fish school, croaker can be found here from mid- to late April on, and trout will show up here shortly after the croaker do. The stronger edges will also hold flounder for most of the fishing season. On occasion, a cobia can even be found here, as well as surprise visits from sea bass, red drum, black drum, speckled seatrout (usually in the shallower areas) and other oceanic species that spend time in the lower Bay.

Locating schools of stripers, blues, and trout here is often rather easy, as two relatively large charter fleets (out of Point Lookout and Crisfield) fish here quite often. Most days, numerous charter boats will clue you in as to where the bite has been hot. However, you certainly do not have to follow the crowd to be successful here. If they're on one ridge in the middle grounds, they'll be on others, for sure. Some of the best specific spots to try chumming include the 18' to 30' drop at MMBE25; the numerous small humps at MMBE26; and the western drop from 30' to 50' at MMBE27. When jigging for seatrout or drifting chunks of peeler or soft crab, the edge at MMBE25 is a good bet.

A short run to the west of the middle grounds lies the Mud Leads (MMBE28). This is really a trench of deeper water that runs between the middle grounds and Smith Island. Chumming on the outer edges can be productive for stripers and blues, but what this area really stands out for is good seatrout fishing. It's wide enough that you can make long drifts across it, but narrow enough that you won't spend too much time drifting over featureless areas of flat bottom. Try hitting this spot when there's an east or west wind, so your drift takes you down one side of the trench, across it, than back up the other side again. Another tactic you'll find effective here is to start in 20' to 21' of water, bouncing a jig on the bottom for flounder with the rod in your hand. Lower a second rod rigged with a trout scout/peeler crab rig and set this rod in a holder. Once the jig bounces off the edge and the water drops over 30' switch rods and concentrate on the baited rig while moving through deep water. When the bottom rises back up on the other side, it's time to pull the switch again and go back to bouncing the jig. Using this technique, you can often catch a flattie or two on either side, and a trout or two in the middle.

The last spot we want to examine in the middle Bay, main stem— MMBE29—is two miles to the east of the Mud Leads. This area, just outside of Kedges Straits, sees some strong currents and has a hard bottom and many bumps and ridges. None are particularly sharp and most are in relatively shallow water, running from 10' to 20'. This spot is worth noting, however, because every few seasons you can literally load the boat with croaker here during the spring run. This area also holds good numbers of flounder, and during years of drought, you'll sometimes catch sea bass here as well, though most are small. Puppy drum are another possibility around these bumps, particularly for anglers using Fluke Killers baited with peeler or soft crab. Kedges Straits itself holds some different possibilities, but since it's part of the Tangier Sound we'll save that for the next section.

Tangier Sound

Tangier Sound has to be one of the greatest places on Earth to go fishing. It's got it all: light tackle shallow water fishing, deep water jigging, trolling zones, chumming spots, and gobs and gobs of fish. The water here is salty enough that most years you'll find oceanic visitors, and the variety of species you catch on any given day is at its widest range in the Bay. In Tangier Sound, it's not unusual to catch ten different types of fish in a single trip.

Starting at the northern end of the sound along its western boarder of marsh islands, Hooper Strait is the first area to note: it's all potential trout water. Practically every year the fish will move in and hold somewhere between the red #4 and red #8 markers. T1 is often the best starting point when you go to look for them here, but each season and sometimes week to week their exact spots of choice will change. Scattered pods of stripers in the 16" to 26" class can also be found roaming around in this area. Flounder are more likely to be found on the drop-off from 10' to 20' on the northern side of Bloodsworth Island. But the real stand-out fishing at Bloodsworth is more light tackle casting, for stripers and speckled seatrout. Virtually every point and cut mouth at Bloodsworth can produce fish. Speckled trout will move in starting in mid- to late April, depending on the weather. As the season progresses the fish will move in and out of the shallows according to changes in the weather. The shallow water warms and cools more quickly than the Bay and sound, and the specs only take up residence in the shallows when the temperature is to their liking—between 60 and 80°F. Once the temperature rises over 80°F, the fish will usually move out of the shallows and take a breather in deeper water. So once June hits, fishing for specs become harder and harder in the shallows barring a few unusually cold evenings that pull down the water temperature. After the commonly slow months of July and August, the water starts cooling off again in September and the specs will return to skinny water.

The best spots to try are those with visible rips, which will usually occur during the peak hour or so of each tidal cycle. Cove Point at T2 is a good place to start. You'll often have a visible tidal rip here, and fishing is best when the water is roaring by the point strongly. If you have a boat with a shallow draft, you may be able to poke into Northeast Cove and, after hitting T2 at the moth, fish T3 and the other cuts that run into the marsh here. Any and all of them with water flow can be holding specs, and you'll find some stripers hiding in there, too. Unless you have a real flats boat, it's best to only enter these areas on a rising tide. Do it on a falling tide, and you may find yourself stuck in the mud. T4, on the northern end of the island, is a little easier to approach and also has a rip during the right stages of the tide, which both speckled trout and stripers will feed in.

Holland Straits is another spot that's reliable for weakfish just about every season, though most caught here are usually on the small side. The deeper water at T5 and T6 is often where you'll find the fish. As with Bloodsworth, the points and cuts of South Marsh Island provide an excellent opportunity to light tackle cast for specs and stripers. You'll also find both species as they hunt for small crabs and other critters in the weedbeds on the flats between South Marsh Island and Spring Island. The trick to fishing this area is to pick a sunny day with little wind, so you can spot the edges of the weedbeds. Casting into the weeds is hopeless, as your lure will become fouled seconds after you cast, each and every time. But retrieving a lure parallel to the edge of a weedbed will keep your hooks clean until a predator attacks. "Potholes" in the weedbeds (open areas with exposed bottom) can also be productive, if you can toss a jig into one and retrieve across it.

Kedges Straits is larger and less protected than Holland Straits, and it also commonly holds more fish of significant size. Weakfish, stripers, flounder, and croaker are all common catches here, and weakfish in the 4 to 6 lb class are not unusual. During the early '80s, when weakfishing in the Sound was notably better, limit catches of fish in this class was the norm. Puppy drum in the 2 to 10 lb class also are fairly common in Kedges; they make a serious showing perhaps once every four seasons and are present to some degree virtually every season. Bait fishing—either large bloodworms, cut peeler crab, or soft crab put on a Fluke Killer rig—is the method most commonly used in this area, but jigging and bouncing plastics along the bottom is still a viable option. You'll also start to see a few oceanic oddities here: sea robins, sea bass, and if you pull a clump of seaweed into the boat, there's a good chance it'll have pipefish or a sea horse hiding in the sprigs.

Any of the relatively deep water along the north side of Smith Island will hold fish, but the hottest hole around is usually the eastern end of the finger of deep water at T7. Fish both sides of this trench, and if the results aren't to your liking, move slightly to the west and try another drift across it. Slowly work your way from east to west until you identify the hottest area, then stick with it. There's also a bar at T8 that flattie anglers should take note of. This is a good spot to try casting and retrieving soft plastics or bucktails dressed with peeler crab, particularly on a rising tide. Drop baits here after nightfall, and you'll catch plenty of croaker, too.

The countless points, cuts, and rips of Smith Island provide another opportunity to cast light tackle for speckled seatrout and stripers, and this far south you're a little more likely to run into red drum, as well (particularly during the spring run). The island shouldn't be approached on a point-by-point basis, for one simple reason: there are zillions of spots fish will feed along the islands shores, and you simply can't fish all of them in one day. Sure, some points may be better than others, but anglers familiar with this area know that the fish can appear at one spot one day, and another the next, and in these shallows, they do tend to move around a lot. You should plan on dedicating whole days at a time to fishing the shallows here, and slowly check out each point, cut mouth and channel as you come upon it. As with the shallows around South Marsh Island, you'll run into a lot of weedbeds that also provide good opportunities if you cast around their edges. That said, here's a run-down on the spots that are most likely to be productive on any given day.

At T9, several cuts come together into one mouth exiting the marsh. You'll have to be sneaky to get in here, but once you do there's a good bit of water in the mouth and in the cuts themselves. Cast to the mouth on the approach, then (if you have a small, shallow draft boat) poke up into the western arm of the cut with an angler posted on the bow. He or she can cast up the cut as you slowly move through it, alternating casts to the right and left shorelines. Remember to try this tactic only on an incoming or high tide; you don't want to be up inside the marsh when the tide's dropping, or you could get stuck there.

At T10, again, there are several cut mouths that merge. Cast to these as well as the points immediately to the north and south of T10. Although it doesn't get as much tidal flow, the entire shoreline of Twitch Cove (T11) and the southernmost cut mouth in it is all worth casting to. There's more flow at the next cuts south (T12 and T13, the Thoroughfare), but the Thoroughfare does have a channel, so there will be some boat traffic here. It's worth putting up with, however, as this cut is one of the deepest around and you'll find the specs sometimes hit here on an off-tide, when the shallow points and rips are

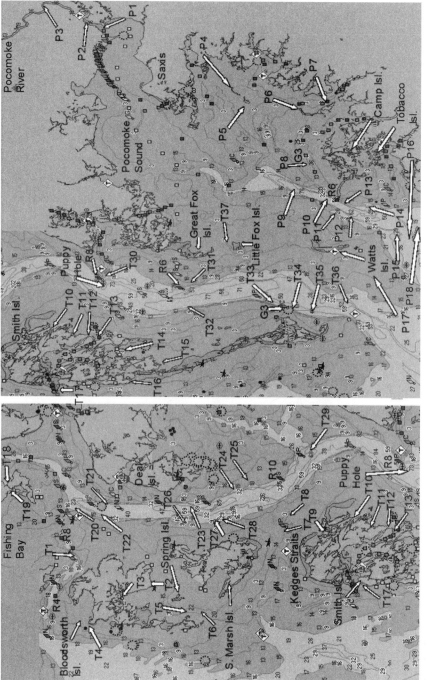

Tangier Sound and Pocomoke Sound. The Tangier Sound is one of the fishiest places on Earth.

nonproductive. The same is true of T14. Note that you could spend a day merely fishing the inside of the island here, poking in and out of cuts. Again, it is smart to approach Smith Island as a day-trip, and plan on spending many hours gunkholing as you fish, instead of rushing from hot spot to hot spot—there are just too many potential hot spots here to rush things.

T15 is a spot you'll want to hit on either an incoming or outgoing tide, so long as the water's moving. Same goes for the small point at T16, on the western side of the island. Remember that on a west wind, it will be hard if not impossible to fish the western side of the island. The breeze will have a long fetch across the entire Bay, and if the waves don't make it impossible to fish the shallow water, you'll find it next to impossible to get in more than a cast or two before being blown aground. There's a breakwater at T17, which is a good bet if you're hoping to hook stripers. Speckled trout, though, won't congregate here as the rockfish will. Slide in-between the islands here and there's more deep water. As with the Throughfare, there will be some boat traffic here, mostly crabbers, but this is a good place to be during a slack or changing tide as fish will feed in these deep inland holes when they won't be as active in the shallows and around the rips.

Throughout this entire area, you will find a lot of grass beds and at times, it will be hard to keep the grass off your hooks. Just remember to downsize your jig heads so they don't sink as quickly and cast around the edges of weedbeds, not right into and over them.

In the open-water section of the Tangier, there are many opportunities for deep water jigging, flounder fishing, and still more places to find weeds with predators prowling the edges of the beds. With a few exceptions, croaker won't be mentioned specifically in this section of the book because simply stated, every one of these spots is usually a good place to find croaker. Many years the Sound will be inundated with them, and your biggest challenge when hunting weakfish, flounder, stripers, and reds will be keeping the croaker off your hooks.

The northern end of the sound runs into the mouth of Fishing Bay, which provides more light tackle action. Fishing Bay itself is mostly shallow and in years past had lots of grasses, making most of it more or less unfishable, though very productive nursery water. Unfortunately, in the recent past the Bay-wide die-off of grasses has affected this area as well, and the grass beds are not what they used to be. The spots with the most consistent potential here are T18 and T19. This cut has a nice flow that attracts speckled trout and at times, puppy drum as well. Cast into the mouth and probe your way up into the cut, to get in on these fish.

Sharkfin Shoal (T20) is one of the better known hot spots in the northern end of the sound, with good reason. Trout move in here during May. (Again, remember that, as with most portions of the Sound, their numbers will start low and steadily increase as the season goes on. Peak trout fishing will usually occur in September or October.) The tip of the fin is usually the most productive spot, and fishing is best when you can drift east/west across it.

The ledge at T21 is an excellent spot to fish deep water for weakfish, and you'll find big tiderunners in this area more seasons than not. The favored method here is to locate a school of fish, drop anchor, and lower crab baits to them. But the best anglers I know will not anchor unless strong winds force them to do so, in order to hold position over the fish. When calmer conditions allow, stick with drifting instead of anchoring. It will allow you to cover more water and move with the schools, as they rarely remain in one exact spot for an extended period of time.

The ledge directly across the channel, T22, is another productive zone for seatrout. The fish can be found anywhere along this drop, on any given day. You won't usually find big schools of trout in the open water between the ledges, however, you will run into schools of breaking blues and stripers during the fall. And if you're changing spots during the summer months, it's a good idea to put out some small spoons and troll rapidly across the deep water, instead of just running through it—Spanish mackerel can sometimes be found wandering through the open water, searching for baitfish.

An area known as The Chain Hole, at T23, is another hot weakfish spot that produces large fish many seasons. As with T21 and T22, drift over the drop to deep water for the best success. To the south along this ledge T24 and T25 are spots that produce some decent chumming catches of stripers in the fall, too. Although these two edges will also produce some flounder, a better bet for flatties is to hop across the sound and fish the bumps at T26, 27, and 28. Each of these hot spots is a hump that comes up to between 10' and 15' and is surrounded by much deeper water. Starting in May or June, these bumps are an excellent place to bounce jigs or drag Fluke Killers with a minnow/squid combination to catch flounder.

The deepwater edges on either side of the trench running from the Chain Hole down to the red #10 marker are always worth scouting for trout from mid-season on. There's a more contained finger of deep water at T29. This slot often contains trout, mostly from July on although some seasons they will appear here early, too. The entire stretch running from here to the red #10, on both sides of the deep water, are also productive trout ledges. As with the edges to the north, schools of trout may choose to take up short-term residence anywhere along these drops, and whenever you fish this area they should be scouted with the fishfinder.

The Puppy Hole, just outside of the lighthouse, is an extremely popular place to fish. Yes, the fishing here is good, but the main attraction is that it's the closest hot spot to the boat ramps at Crisfield. As a result, you should expect this area to be more crowded than other spots on the sound. Just below the

Puppy Hole, however, is one of the best flounder edges in the Tangier, at T30. Many seasons, particularly on an incoming tide, the 10' to 20' drop here is often carpeted with actively feeding flounder. The majority of the fish will be throwbacks, and you may need to weed through a dozen fish before you catch a keeper. Don't let this deter you, however, as there will also be some larger flounder mixed in. Because the action here can be so fast and because you'll need to rack up high numbers to get a cooler of keepers, this spot is best fished by bouncing jigs or a bucktail. If you use bait, you'll often spend too much time getting out deep hooks and re-baiting, resulting in a lower overall catch rate.

Another exceptional flounder edge is located at T31, just south of the red #6 buoy Again, the 10' to 20' zone is your best bet. The flounder don't seem to stack up in as great numbers here as they do at T30, but the throwback-to-keeper ratio is usually a bit better.

The eastern edge of the drop to deep water from T31 to the Pocomoke Sound is not as well-defined as it is in other areas of the Tangier. This doesn't mean that you won't find trout in large numbers here, it just means that they'll stage in less specific spots and will be harder to locate and relocate throughout the season. If you're in the area, by all means, look for fish. But the drop in this zone is not a good planned destination, in and of itself.

This is not true of the drop along the western edge, which is sharper and much more dramatic. As with the edges farther north, schools of weakfish can be found holding along these drops pretty much anywhere. There are, however, a couple of particularly productive points along this stretch. The first is at T32, which is the first spot that the edge really forms into a cliff-like drop. You'll find trout here, as well as schools of stripers and blues in the fall, but the drop is a little sharp to focus on flounder as you'll be out of the fish's preferred depth very quickly most of the time due to wind or current.

If the results at this spot aren't up to snuff, slide down to T33. At this spot the cliff-like drop-off hits a slope at 50' before dropping to deeper water more gradually. Where the steep drop intersects with the more gradual slope, you'll often find congregations of trout.

The next spot to check out heading south is just south of the green #3 can, at T34 east of Tangier Island. The edge here goes from 3' to 70' in a very short distance, and trout can be found holding here most seasons between 25' and the bottom of the drop. Because it's such a steep drop, flounder fishing along this edge is all but impossible. But you will find scattered pods of stripers in this area, as well. Slide a bit farther south to T35 and the drop off is more gradual. Along this edge down to T36, you'll find good numbers of flounder. Puppy drum, stripers, and speckled trout can also be caught up on the 8' to 10' flat between the deep water and the weedbeds closer to the shoreline. Cast jigs and bucktails trimmed with peeler crabs and bounce them along the bottom on this flat, and you've got an excellent shot at weighting down your cooler. At T36 the drop re-forms into another cliff. As you'd expect, this is another good trout spot, but again the drop here is so sheer that it's all but impossible to fish for flounder, and the stripers you find in this are usually in relatively small, scattered schools.

A bit farther to the east of this ledge lies Watts Island, which forms the eastern boarder of Tangier Sound. Like the other islands of the sound, Watts holds speckled trout and stripers from mid-spring until the summer and again in the fall. This area of the sound, however, tends to have a stronger run of puppy drum as well. Watts Island is small, and there aren't too many points to cast at, but just to its north lies Little Fox and Great Fox Islands. The shallows of all are a good bet for specs early in the year. The best way to fish these islands is to simply skirt the edges, casting towards the shore line. Fishing here becomes tough once the summer sets in, however, because there are usually too many weedbeds around the islands to cast to them.

Between Little and Great Fox Islands, look for the slight channel at T37. Although it's no deeper than 8', on warm, sunny days with calm winds in the late spring (usually the middle or the end of May) flounder and speckled trout will move in here to feed. This presents a great opportunity for light tackle casting for flatfish, with small bucktails and jigs.

Pocomoke Sound

The Pocomoke Sound is similar to the Tangier, except that it's smaller and shallower. Vast stretches of the sound are 4' or 5' deep flats, and while there are areas of good weedbeds in these shallows, there are also tracts of mud that don't support much angling.

The Pocomoke is notable for another unfortunate reason: it's where pfiesteria was first identified in the Chesapeake region. Runoff from poultry farms raised phosphorus levels in the river complex significantly, and most biologists feel that the nutrient load caused algae blooms and the much-feared pfiesteria to appear in the late '90s. Pfiesteria causes lesions on fish and can get people sick too, particularly if an open cut or wound comes in contact with a sore on an infected fish. At one point the disease was prevalent enough that a seven-mile stretch of the river and a small section of the sound were shut down to recreational and commercial fishing, swimming, and watersports. Several fish kills were recorded, the largest being 11,000 fish, mostly menhaden. In the last few years pfiesteria has not been as notable a problem in the Pocomoke. But any angler fishing in this area should surely be aware of its existence. If you catch a fish with sores let it go immediately, without touching it if at all possible.

The Pocomoke River, feeding into the sound's northeastern corner, supports a couple of fisheries. Like the rivers feeding the Tangier, it has a yearly spring perch run. For some reason it's usually a bit later than the runs on many nearby rivers, starting in earnest in late March. Most of the fish will be caught in one of three areas: the mouth of the river, the first big bend in it, and near Pocomoke City. Look for them early on at P1 in the river's mouth, in the 12' to 17' deep channel area. At P2, the channel deepens to over 20' and perch will stage in the deepwater areas before making their spawning run in earnest. You'll also find perch at the deep hole at P3. Between one and two weeks after the perch start biting in these areas, they'll start to show up near Pocomoke City, where the river's northern bend creates more current-cut holes for the fish to stage in. From this point upriver, bass, and catfish fishing becomes fairly good. While the Pocomoke is not known as big-bass water, fish in the 1–3 lb range are commonly caught by anglers casting to piers, fallen trees, and undercut banks. Interestingly, the Pocomoke also seems to support a better crappie fishery than many of the other eastern shore rivers.

The northern edge of the sound itself is bordered by Cedar and Great Fox Islands on the west side, and the town of Saxis to the east. Between these two areas, most of the sound is shallow flats. Year to year different areas support good grassbeds, however, and provide some territory for chasing speckled trout and in some years red drum. The specs arrive as early as mid-April, slack off in the dog days, and then feed heartily again in the fall. Red drum also arrive in mid- to late April, but these fish remain in the area and bite well through the heat of summer, usually peaking in mid-August. Unfortunately, it's virtually impossible to predict exactly where the weedbeds will be thick and where the fishing will be best in this area of the sound. You'll have to search around here, looking for grassy areas and casting to the edges. You may, however, want to head farther out into the sound—truth be told, the northern section of the Pocomoke is not known as a hot area.

In the sound's middle region, however, there is a more reliable speckled trout and croaker fishery, with drum showing up in good numbers about one year in three. The islands on the eastern side of the sound mark most of the hot spots. Upper and Lower Bernard Islands (P4 and P5) and Halfmoon Island (P6) support grass beds in the nearby shallows, and usually are productive areas to try. Most seasons, the shallows around Halfmoon are the more productive areas. Webb Island will also be an active location, on the eastern edge at P7; the western edge of the island is too shallow to access most of the time. Just south of these small islands lies the Camp and Tobacco Islands marsh and cut complex. Any of the edges and cut mouths through here can produce speckled trout. There are so many cuts, points, and small islands here that it should be approached as a day-long event to fish these shallows, rather than concentrate on any one or two specific locations. Simply cast to the shorelines, cut mouths, and weedbed edges.

Just north of Camp Island there is a deep hole at P8, near the green marker #3. Weakfish will usually move in here by mid-spring and remain through the fall, though as usual, they often won't bite well during July and August. One exception: night-fishing along the channel edge here during the summer. Put out a spread of lights, drop soft or peeler crab in 8' to 15' of water along the drop, and you have a good chance of seeing some hot action in the dark.

Between P8 and Watts Island, in the center of the lower Pocomoke, are several reliable hot spots. The northernmost is known as Robin Hood, at P9. This sheer drop-off into a trough running up the lower Pocomoke is probably the best area of the sound to fish for weakfish on a year-to-year basis. Crab in one form or another is the usual bait, and vertical jigging is also effective. Just south of Robin Hood are a couple of ledges on either side of the trough known locally as Beach Rock (P10) and Stone Rock (P11). Ironically, like it's northern twin the Stone Rock here is also a black drum spot. Though it's a long way from Stone Rock to Stone Rock, the drum usually appear here and at P12 at the same point in time: mid- to late May. There's also a chance of finding drum on the edge at P13, near the red #6 buoy, but the drop here is steep and this area is better known as a striper and seatrout destination. Beach Rock will also see a few drum, but the bulk of the sportfish caught on and around the 20' plateau here will be flounder. This is a good place to hunt for them in late April or early May, a week or two after the first early flatfish have been caught in nearby deep water and a couple weeks after they make a strong showing in the coastal ocean bays like Wachapreague and Quimby. Sometimes these early flatfish can be located simply by shuffling to the deeper section of the drop on the west edge of the 20' plateau, but better spots to search for them when they are holding in deep water are the drop-offs at P14, 15, and 16.

Watts Island, forming the western boarder of the sound, is another great area to try for speckled trout, croaker, and in good years, red drum. The name of the game for specs and reds here is casting to the edges of weedbeds in shallow water. Bait can be used in the early season, but most years by mid-May a lot of rays move into the area and it becomes necessary to cast lures only. When the water warms up, you'll also encounter large numbers of stripers in the shallows here in the 16" to 24" class. For croaker, fish the 10' plateau at P17, particularly in the mornings and evenings. You'll also pick up a few casting lures in the shallows, but many years, if you drop a chunk of crab or bloodworm in the area of P17, you'll catch all the croaker you can stand to catch in a couple of hours.

There's an artificial reef at P18 that, unlike most of the northern reefs, actually attracts a few fish. In the late spring and summer you can sometimes catch sea bass here, though most will be on the small side. Croaker, weakfish, and (unfortunately) sea robins also move on and off of this reef through the season. On occasion, you may even catch a tautog here. Fishing around the edges of the reef, flounder can be found in this area, too.

Shorebound Angling Hot Spots of the Middle Chesapeake

Even anglers without boats can get in on awesome action in the middle Chesapeake region. Piers, bridges, and parks in this zone will give you a shot at everything from trophy stripers to flounder. In some years, Shorebound anglers might even catch more fish than those running out into the Bay on boats—when it comes to fishing, you just never know.

WESTERN SHORE

• QUIET WATERS PARK: On the northern shore of the South River, Quiet Waters Park runs along one side of Harness Creek and along a small section of the river itself. Although you may find a few perch or small stripers in the creek (and plenty of crabs), the stretch on the river is the interesting part of the park to anglers. A large bluff overlooks the river's shoreline, which is a dog-walking park. By walking along the beach and casting jigs or topwater lures, you can catch stripers in the 12" to 22" class. You may luck into a fish or two here at daybreak or sunset in the summer, but this spot will produce best late in the fall, from October through December. In the spring there is another window of opportunity, when the grassbeds form near shore here. Cast to the edges with bloodworms for spot and croaker. Unfortunately, the grass beds in this area usually die out by summer.

• JUG BAY: At Patuxent River Park, just south of the Rt 301/Rt 4 intersection, there is a boat ramp and public pier just off of Jug Bay. The pier has enough room to support a dozen or so anglers. Most people who fish this spot will show up during the perch run, in March and/or early April. Yellow perch run first, followed by white perch. On a nice weekend day, this spot will usually get fairly crowded. The other fishing opportunity this section of Patuxent River Park provides to anglers is a shot at catfish, year-round. Chunks of cut herring set on the bottom usually do the trick. Occasional crappie, bass, and bluegill are also caught here, but not in high enough numbers to make them targeted species.

• SOLOMONS' LAUNCH RAMP PIER: In the shadow of the Rt 4 bridge over the lower Patuxent, there's a huge public pier adjoining the public launch ramp. This spot will pan out in croaker, spot, stripers, snapper blues, and a few flounder and weakfish, from mid- to late May through the fall. It can get crowded on weekends, but the pier takes several 90-degree turns and has a ton of surface area to fish from. During the week, you'll have enough space to bring a dozen friends without ever tangling. For those who want to fish for saltwater species, this is probably the best spot to try between Sandy Point and St. Mary's County. It's also a great place to try crabbing as you fish.

• **FRIENDSHIP LANDING:** When you need a cure for cabin fever in the deep of winter, Friendship Landing is just the place. This is the boat ramp most convenient to anglers launching in Nanjemoy Creek, and there is a pier here that can accommodate up to a dozen anglers. There are also several shoreline spots near the parking lot and boat ramp. Try casting minnow or grass shrimp on bottom rigs from the shore here, from mid-January through March for yellow perch, and mid-March through early April for white perch. Catfish anglers will also score from this pier, year-round, by casting out cut herring or menhaden.

• **ST. GEORGE'S ISLAND:** This little-known spot has room for several anglers, plenty of parking, and good fishing for spot, croaker, small stripers, snapper blues, and flounder. In the evenings, trout also become a good bet. Go down Piney Point Rd until you go over the bridge to St. George's Island. Turn into the parking lot at the base of the bridge, where there is a public boat ramp. Park and walk back under the bridge. A strong current pushes between the mainland and the island, creating a good feeding situation for the fish. Croaker and small stripers move in here as early as the first of May, and by June, most of the other species can usually be found here. Try casting out bloodworms for the pan fish, cut bait for the larger predators, and minnow or minnow/squid combinations for the flounder. One note of caution: there is a lot of broken glass in and around the parking lot, so this is not a great area to bring the kids.

• **CHURCH POINT:** Historic St. Mary's City, located at the St. Mary's College of Maryland campus on the St. Mary's River, includes a spit of land that juts out into the river. From July through November, snapper bluefish, smallish flounder, croaker, and the occasional striper or trout can be caught by casting from the beach here. Walk down the bluff next to the historic city, and (facing the water) head to the right until you walk out onto the point. Set up sand spikes anywhere along it, and cast cut bait straight out to catch the blues. For weakfish and stripers, cast live bait on a fishfinder rig. There is a drop from 6' or 7' to 13' or 14', within casting distance of shore. This drop often holds flounder, but you'll catch mostly 12" to 16" fish. Plan on a ten-to-one ratio of throw-backs to keepers.

Although large weakfish and stripers are not the norm here, I know of several in the 10-lb class caught from this location, and all came using the same technique: live-lining small spot after dark. Puppy drum can also be caught near the riprap closer to the historic city during the summer months, but it's hard to fish these rocks effectively without a boat.

• **POINT LOOKOUT STATE PARK:** This is a fantastic facility with a huge fishing pier, a long causeway and a riprapped point, all of which offer excellent fishing opportunities from late April through winter. The causeway is the stretch of road entering the park, at which you'll see huge boulders lining the road. Stop and park on the shoulder anywhere along the road here. Walk out onto the rocks—be careful, as one false step can lead to a nasty fall—and cast out as far as possible with bloodworms early in the spring; you'll catch croaker, the occasional striper, and once May arrives, the occasional (usually small) flounder. From mid-May through the season plenty of snapper blues, flounder, stripers, croaker, spot, and weakfish are caught here, mostly on cut menhaden. The bulk of the weakfish and keeper-sized stripers will come at night. Bluefish is the mainstay here, and on a decent day you can expect to land many 1–2 lb blues. Although the causeway is a great spot to fish from, you should know that on sunny weekends you will have a lot of competition. Sometimes, dozens of anglers are lined up 10' or so apart, all the way down the rocks.

The fishing pier at Point Lookout is one of the finest in Maryland. It has built-in rodholders on the rail, bait cutting stations, and benches. It runs hundreds of feet out into the Bay, but over a large plateau. Even at the end, the water is not much more than 6' or 7' deep at high tide. Still, a lot of fish are caught from this pier. Yes, it is often crowded, but less so than the causeway. The catch will be much the same as that of the causeway. For some reason, however, some seasons large numbers of very small flounder (6" to 10" fish) move in near the pier. Bluefish remain the mainstay, and a half-dozen keeper fish during one good tidal cycle is a common catch. Most of these fish will be caught by anglers casting out from the end or the last third of the pier. Anglers searching for spot and croaker should drop bloodworms right next to the pier pilings. One other feature of this pier is that it's lighted at night. Fishing after dark is the best time to catch weakfish here, which tend to move within casting range of the pier during late April or early May. Once warm water hits their numbers usually thin out until October. Cast fluke killers or bottom rigs baited with soft or peeler crab, to catch the weakfish.

One area of Point Lookout that is usually not too crowded is the rock point on the Potomac River side of the park, just before you reach the gates at the end of the park road. Walk out onto the beach (it will be to the right, if you are facing the fence) and you'll see a riprapped point that you can cast from. All of the same fish are available, although bluefish numbers do usually seem reduced here as compared to the Bayside. You can also bring sand spikes and cast from the beach, but during the warm summer months this can be tough as you'll have a lot of beachgoers around.

EASTERN SHORE

• **WYE MILLS:** Where Wye Lake begins the Wye River, a spillway below the dam provides good perch fishing at the tail end of the spring run. Usually beginning in mid- to late March and lasting for about two weeks, anglers casting shad darts, minnow, or grass shrimp into the river immediately below the spillway often connect with good numbers of perch. Walk downstream into the woods, and you can also locate a few holes that hold crappie and small bass.

• TUCKAHOE CREEK: There are two places on the Tuckahoe that are good bets for shoreline anglers. The first is at the Rt 404 bridge where it crosses the river. There is room for about a half dozen cars to park on the side of the road here. Walk down on either side of the bridge, and cast bottom rigs or suspend marabou jigs or shad darts dressed with small minnow under a bobber. Yellow perch are active here from March through mid-April most years, and a two-to-three week white perch run partially coincides and follows close behind. Cast near the bridge pilings and you may hook into crappie, bass, and catfish as well.

The second good spot is located in Hillsboro. On the side of the road along Main Street, there are parking spots and fishing spots for a couple hundred feet along the river. This area will get crowded during the peak of the perch run that coincides with the Rt 404 bridge run (these two spots are not very far apart) but there is usually enough room for everyone who wants to fish. Drive over the bridge, follow the road to the right, and you'll see the public boat ramp. There is another 100' or so of shoreline between the ramp and the bridge, which is also fishable by the public. Fish this area exactly as described above for the Rt 404 bridge area, but pay more attention to the bridge pilings. Quality crappie can often be found hiding around the pilings of this small bridge. They are usually all the way under the bridge, so you are best off using a bobber rig and allowing it to drift by the piles.

There is a spillway similar to the one at Wye Mills at the base of Tuckahoe Lake as well. However, you really have to time it right to catch fish here. The perch usually show up, then disappear in a matter of a week or two. Like the spillway at Wye, you can catch crappie and bass by walking back along the river. Pickerel are also present in good numbers in this area.

• WATTS CREEK: One of the best places to find winter yellow perch and crappie from the shore is at Watts Creek, off the Choptank River. Martinak State Park has a pavilion built out over the water, as well as several hundred feet of productive shoreline. The pavilion is located down the path to the left of the boat ramp, about 100 yards through the woods. It's large enough to hold about eight anglers comfortably and most days during the winter competition will be light. This changes in March when the weather warms up. However, since the pavilion has a roof and a sturdy rail, even kids will be able to fish here on snowy winter days. Straight out in front of the pavilion there's a hole that drops to 20', and yellow perch stage in here from mid-January through March. Cast minnow on bottom rigs, or grass shrimp, to entice the perch. The point directly across from the pavilion has a great drop-off and is an excellent place to cast to. The left side is all shallow and will be exposed mud during low tide, but the right side (between the pilings and the riprap) often holds good size crappie and the occasional bass, as well as perch. Any of these areas can produce catfish, on just about any bait.

The shoreline between the ramp and the pavilion, as well as the shore along the point to the right of the ramp, is mostly productive when the perch are running—not when they are staging over the winter. Early March through early April is the time frame when this occurs. Pretty much any time of the year, however, you can catch catfish in this entire area. Anglers casting to the riprap between the ramp and pavilion will also take the occasional bass. This entire park is well-maintained, trash-free, and is an excellent place to take children.

It should be noted that in the past few years the winter operating hours of this park have changed a few times. The gates used to open at 8:00 A.M., but this past season they were closed until 10:00 A.M. so you may want to call the DNR (800-628-9944) before planning an early morning here. The close time is sunset.

• **THE CHOPTANK RIVER BRIDGE:** One of the best things the state of Maryland ever did for shoreline anglers was to turn the old Rt 50 bridge at Cambridge into a fishing pier. This bridge may hold as many as 200 anglers during a summer weekend, yet the structure is so long that everyone has plenty of elbow room. There are benches, bait cutting stations, and even porta-potties spaced out along the bridge. There's also good fishing.

During years of heavy rain, much of the year catfish can be caught from the bridge on cut fish. From mid-May through September croaker is the main catch, and they can be caught by the cooler full here. White perch, weakfish, stripers, spot, and the occasional flounder are caught during this time frame and on through November. From mid-June through November, snapper blues are the second most numerous fish to be caught from the bridge. Many anglers also bring collapsible crab traps and catch crabs as they fish. It's a long drop from the bridge to the water, so you should bring a bridge net if at all possible, for landing the keepers.

Both sides of the bridge offer good fishing, but the water is fairly shallow (8' to 12') unless you walk halfway out along the bridge. For white perch and croaker, you'll find a good area by walking just 60 or 70 yards out on the north side of the bridge and casting up towards the new bridge. Near the center there is a deeper channel, which will be the best spot for weakfish during the daylight hours. After dark, they can be caught anywhere along the lighted bridge. Unfortunately, there is a fair amount of broken glass and old, abandoned hooks on the bridge so you should wear shoes at all times.

• **BLACKWATER:** The Blackwater River, which feeds into Fishing Bay, has a couple of spots that are productive for crappie year-round and perch during the March to April run. There is enough parking for a couple of cars along the roadside at the Goldon Hill and Maple Dam road bridges. The park seems to enjoy changing the parking regulations at each location regularly, so look for signs before you walk away from your vehicle. Some big crappie come from these areas every year, but they will only bite well when the water quality is good. Commonly, especially after rainfall, the river runs muddy and dark, and it can take up to a week to clear. Consequently, you're best off planning to fish here only after an extended dry spell.

• **COLBURN CREEK:** The launch ramp at Colburn Creek, off the big Annemessex River, has a small pier that can accommodate a half-dozen anglers. It rarely gets crowded, and most of the time, no one fishes from it. There is good croaker fishing here in the evenings, usually from early May through September. Small stripers, white perch, and very small snapper blues are also caught here sometimes.

• **CRISFIELD PIER:** In the heart of Crisfield, there is a large public pier that is mostly covered. Croaker, weakfish, small stripers, snapper blues, small flounder, and spot can all be caught here in varying numbers. The ferry boats to Tangier Island moor on the left side (when you are facing the end of the pier) so it's best to stay away from this section and fish directly off the end of the pier. There is a small area on the right side of the pier where you can cast to pilings and a bulkhead. Toss Rat-L-Traps out next to the bulkhead, and you have a shot at catching a striper or two in the 12" to 20" class.

• **SALISBURY:** In the heart of downtown Salisbury, you can fish along the banks of the Wicomico's feeder creeks. Where Rt 50 crosses the river, shortly after going past the 50 Bypass, you can see the park off to your right as you go over the bridge. The fish here are mostly freshwater, with crappie and bass ruling the roost. Crappie fishing, in particular, is excellent if you cast small grubs or minnow to tree branches and brush on the river's edge. In the spring you can also encounter perch runs here.

Salisbury's city boat ramp on the Wicomico, also off to the right but slightly down river when you cross the river on Rt 50, also has some space for bank anglers to try their luck. Unfortunately, you'll often find broken glass and other garbage spoils the surroundings here; the park is much cleaner and more family friendly.

• **RT 335 BRIDGE/HONGA RIVER:** The Rt 335 bridge crosses a cut between the open Chesapeake and the Honga River, between upper and middle Hooper Islands. Although you can't fish from the bridge itself, you can walk down to the riprap at the base on either side of the bridge, and cast out for stripers, seatrout, flounder, blues, croaker, and spot. There's good current and good depth within casting distance from either side, and there's plenty of room for several anglers to fish without crowding each other. The fishing can be really good here, too. In fact, this is one of the better Bay front shoreline spots to look for large flounder, especially when the current is flowing from the river to the Bay. On the down side, you'll have to bring lots of extra weights and rigs, since there are snags just about everywhere. Sitting on riprap is also uncomfortable, so make sure you bring a pillow or cushion if you plan to fish here all day.

• **WETIPQUIN CREEK:** Although the water is often dirty in Wetipquin, there is a bridge at the boat ramp that offers good structure, and there's plenty of room for shoreline anglers as well as a small pier. You'll find stripers occasionally by casting up to the bridge, but the better bet here is to try for early season white and yellow perch, or the rest of the year, catfish. Note that the bridge sustained hurricane damage in 2003 and has been unusable since. Although it was being worked on during 2004 progress seemed very slow, and as of this writing, you would be best served by approaching this spot via Rt 478 to be sure of easy access.

Lower Chesapeake Bay. Virginia's portion of the Bay begins at the Potomac and runs down to the Atlantic Ocean.

THE LOWER CHESAPEAKE BAY

While the upper and even the middle Chesapeake Bay are unique in their ability to offer anglers freshwater and brackish opportunities, the lower Bay is just as unusual in its ability to provide brackish and semi-oceanic fishing. Here you can still reap the benefits of the Chesapeake's one of a kind spring trophy striper run and the usual east coast warm weather quarry, but there are species found here that are rare or unheard of farther to the north. Cobia, tautog, spadefish, sheepshead, puffer fish, and even shark venture into this section of the Bay with regularity.

Two features every angler should be aware of in this region are the numerous grass beds that attract speckled trout and puppy drum, and the VMRC (Virginia Marine Resources Commission) oyster reefs. The oyster reefs attract just about every type of game fish found in the lower Bay that ventures into the rivers and bays, and on the Western Shore these are major target areas. In fact, they have received nationwide attention from the media, including *Sport Fishing Magazine,* for the excellent light tackle fishery they provide.

When plotting out a trip to Virginia's tidewater Western Shore, I suggest that you use the Internet as well as this book. Go to www.mrc.state.va.us, and you can find a map of the oyster reefs the VMRC has planted. On www.vims.edu/bio/sav, you can find a map of the grass beds in this area. The oyster reef map is naturally a little more reliable than the grass bed map, since grassbeds shift, appear and disappear every season. It's still a great help, however, to an angler scouting out this territory.

Before we get into the Western Shore rivers, there's an area on Virginia's Western Shore comprised of several small creeks, bays, and rivers we must look at in detail. Fleets Bay is neither a river nor is it part of the main-stem Chesapeake, but it is an incredibly productive area. Most of the channel edges and drop-offs in Fleets Bay will hold the usual bottom fishing suspects—croaker and spot, with some weakfish and flounder mixed in—but of greater interest and uniqueness is the speckled trout fishery here. First we should point out that any of the hot spots included here have the potential to hold red drum, as well as specs. But during the average season the majority of the catch will be trout.

The unique nature of this area has to do with its combination of small cuts and large grass beds. Note that the exact location and sizes of the grass beds will shift from year to year, and in any given season you could discover a "new" hot spot in Fleets. That said, the small cut mouth between the mainland and Bluff Pt, at F1, is a good place to try during a falling tide early and late in the year, and on a rising tide in the summer. The entire flat at F2 is also good spec territory, as much of this area will be covered in grass. A traditional method of catching specs here is to troll along the edges of the beds by rowing a small boat that gives your lure erratic speed and motion. Pink Mir-O-Lures are a favorite plug for this task.

The flat at F3 is another reliable grass bed, and most years it is relatively large. Long edges provide plenty of opportunity for trolling in a method similar to that described above. Casting lures along the edges of the bed near the drop-offs is also productive. During the sluff, when large numbers of crabs are shedding, this is the place to be. Puppy drum in notably larger numbers will also move in when the crabs shed. Fishing with soft crab is a viable option unless the rays have already moved into the area, in which case you'll be better off using artificials.

The creek mouth at F4 is another good bet, particularly on a falling tide. Approach this one from a distance and cast as you move in because specs will often take up residence outside of the cut itself along the surrounding grass bed edges. The point at F5 is also spec territory some seasons. Drift through this zone while casting jigs, and when you locate some fish, drop an anchor and concentrate on the area. Expect the exact location of the fish to shift with the tide, and as usual with specs, expect the trout to strike either fast moving lures high in the water column or slow moving lures low in the water column depending on the current.

The Western Shore Rivers

The Great Wicomico River—one of the three Wicomicos found on the Chesapeake—is not among the best producers of Virginia's Western Shore, but it certainly is worthy of note. If you're after croaker in particular and it's a blustery day, this is one body of water you'll want to consider.

Far upriver where the croaker don't roam, there is a limited bass and pickerel fishery. "Limited" is the key word, though, as the Great Wicomico does not have a huge freshwater flow. In fact, the freshwater fish found here will be in the headwaters, and the headwaters of the creeks. If you want to catch these types of fish, you're better served by heading for one of the more major rivers.

The first important spot to note in the Great Wicomico is Rt 200 bridge. You'll catch stripers casting to the pilings here, and often perch will also take up residence next to the pilings. Downriver at Rouge Point there is a nice drop

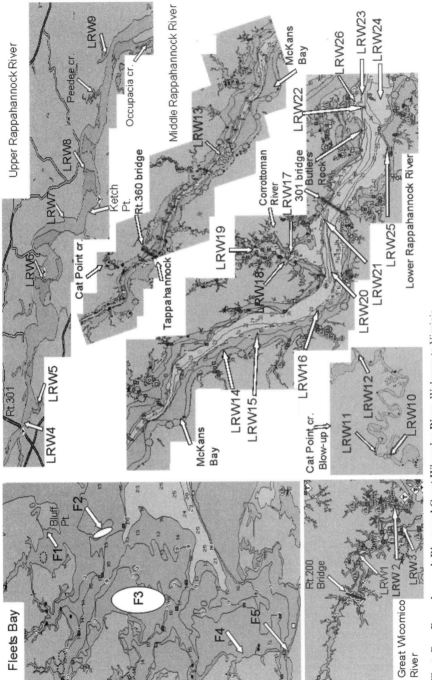

Fleets Bay, Rappahannock River, and Great Wicomico River. Welcome to Virginia.

from the end of the point straight off to 20' at LRW1. This is a good croaker hole, and late in the summer it will also hold spot. Some years weakfish also wander into the Great Wicomico and can be caught off this edge, but this is not exactly a sure thing. Like the trout fisheries in most Western Shore rivers in the middle Bay, the trout either move in or they don't on any given year. If they don't, you could fish here an entire season without catching a trout. If they do, you catch on weakfish every trip. There's no way to predict what each season will bring, but after trying the area once or twice, you can make an educated guess as to whether it's worth fishing there for the rest of the season. Even less often, flounder will move in here for the season.

LRW2 is another long shot, but worth checking out if you're limited to the river. This little creek mouth has a decent flow of water on a strong dropping tide, and you'll sometimes encounter a speckled trout or two here. A slightly better bet for trout—but the gray kind, not the speckled kind—that will also hold croaker in large numbers most years is the hole at LRW3. Since there usually isn't too much breeze here (unless there's a northerly going right down the river) this is a spot where it's possible to jig deep with light gear; a ½ oz jig head dressed with a chartreuse/pumpkinseed four-inch screw tail can be deadly.

The mouth of the Great Wicomico is well known as reliable croaker territory. Spring evenings and into the summer you'll find it productive to drift baits over the edges throughout the river mouth.

The next river south of the Potomac, and the northernmost river of significance entirely in the commonwealth of Virginia, is the Rappahannock. This is one of the larger rivers entering the Bay, and as a result, carries a good deal of freshwater. Naturally, this means that angling far upriver will produce fish such as bass, crappie, and perch. From Port Royal upriver is almost entirely freshwater, and it should be fished as other tributary headwaters. Plan to cast the banks with spinnerbaits, lipped plugs or plastics for bass, look for crappie in brush piles and fallen timber, and expect catfish just about everywhere. For some reason the Virginia rivers don't seem to produce pickerel as well as the rivers to their north and east, but you will encounter these toothy torpedoes as well.

LRW4 is located in Port Royal, on the south bank just downriver of the Rt 301 bridge. Many years ago there was a steamboat landing here, and some of the old pilings still exist. Look for them right on the channel edge, where it drops from a couple of feet into the main channel that goes better than 30' in this area. Cast and retrieve lures up to the pilings for largemouth bass, or toss small minnow suspended under bobbers to catch crappie.

The stretch from Port Royal to Ketch Point is fairly unremarkable, with one exception: this is some of the best water around for finding big, fat blue catfish. Bass will still be found in this area, as will pickerel and perch. In the spring, the Rappahannock also sees herring throughout this area. But there's no doubt that whiskers rule this zone. Cast cut herring or bunker and let it sit on bottom in deep water during the summer months, to hook into these fish.

In the spring, starting as early as April and certainly in March, a more effective method of catching these big cats is to fish marsh creek mouths on a falling tide, as the sun-warmed marsh water is funneled into the river. Blue cats will gather near these creek mouths to enjoy the rising temperatures. LRW5 and LRW6 are two such creek mouths that are good bets for early season blue cats. Slightly downriver at LRW7, 8, and 9 the same is true. Note that creeks having freshwater feeding them, such as Peedee and Occupacia, will also have strong flows. But the water here will be cooler since it isn't draining exclusively from the sun-warmed marsh, as it is at the spots listed earlier. This isn't to say they don't hold blue cats—they most certainly do—but they will have less action during the early spring and should be reserved for warmer months.

A little farther downriver, you'll find Cat Point Creek, an amazing offshoot of the Rappahannock that should be visited by every Bay-lover at least once. It is a winter roosting area for bald eagles, and dozens of eagles can be spotted in a single day here. The depth of the water in this creek is amazing; although the charts don't always show it, several bends in the creek go deeper than 30'. As you might expect, perch can be found in these holes in the pre-spawn months, and catfish most of the year. Where the creek first splits at LRW10 and the next bend at LRW11, you'll find deep holes and good fishing. LRW11, known to some Bay aficionados as the JPW hole (named for Chesapeake Bay naturalist John Page Williams), is always a great place to look for the blue cats, too. Later in the spring when the spawning run begins, move up the creek to LRW12 for white and yellow perch. Upcreek from this point, there is also a limited largemouth bass fishery.

The Rt 360 bridge just downriver from Cat Point Creek is worth casting to for stripers. At this point in the river stripers become more prevalent, and you'll find them holding along the pilings of this bridge. This bridge also marks the transition zone where saltier species become more common and freshwater species start to thin out. You'll still find those bruiser blue cats at this point, but expect their numbers to thin the farther you travel downriver.

The first good bottom fishing spot in this area is the channel and channel edge near Bowlers Rock. Try drifting bloodworms, peeler crabs, and grass shrimp for white perch, croaker, and later in the season for spot, along the edges at LRW13.

LRW 14, 15, and 16 all mark VMRC (Virginia Marine Resources Commission) oyster reefs that create excellent fish-attracting structure. Depending on the tide either the reef or a rip in the current above the reef may be visible. Cast to the edges of these reefs with screw-tail jigs, bucktails, or swimming plugs and you'll find rockfish. Some seasons, speckled trout and puppy drum will also make their way upriver to these reefs. Cast baited bottom rigs near them and you can often catch croaker by the boatload.

Near the mouth of the Corrottoman River you'll find another VMRC oyster reef, at LRW17, which is located adjacent to a nice drop to 27'. Jig or drop soft crab baits or live peanut bunker against the edge of this drop and you should locate weakfish most of the season. Casting and retrieving to the reef edges produces similar catches as the other reefs do. You'll also find trout with some stripers mixed in, as well as croaker, if you fish the nearby hole at LRW18. Up the Corrottoman at LRW19, the deep water holds croaker and in the saltier seasons, trout will move up this far as well. If you're after weakfish, however, and you want to stay inside the Rappahannock, you're better off jigging the edges of the deep water trough marked LRW20. On an incoming tide pay particular attention to the edge at LRW21 that catches the current and can cause fish to stack up. On an outgoing tide, expect the downriver end of the trough near the bridge at Rt 3 to be more productive. When the trout stop feeding—or if it's earlier or later in the season—move over to the bridge pilings that, as you might expect, will hold stripers. A little less expected is the presence of puppy drum near this bridge. For whatever reason, they seem to gather at times along the shorelines on either side of it.

The most famous hot spot in the Rappahannock is, without a doubt, Butler's Rock. Because it's so well known this spot does get a lot of pressure. The number of fish that gather here, however, makes it worthwhile in any case. Weakfish, especially, seem attracted to Butler's Rock. On an outgoing or low tide first look for them in the deep water immediately to the east, at LRW22. On an incoming and high tide, you're more likely to find them at the drop to 40' and just past it, at LRW23. Drop baited top and bottom rigs in these spots for spot and croaker, but note that early and late in the day you'll catch far more croaker by moving a bit shallower to LRW24. This edge is also a good place to chum for stripers and in the summer, blues as well, especially when there's a stiff northern wind you need to stay out of. Bounce jigs or drag minnow up and down this same drop-off, and you should encounter flounder as well.

Across the river from Butler's Rock, along the edge at LRW25, there's another VMRC oyster reef. This one will hold puppy drum, stripers, and speckled seatrout through much of the season. This is also a good reef to target croaker, because it's possible to fish bait on the flat on the northern side of the reef without snagging bottom all the time.

Just south of Windmill Point, at LRW26, there's another VMRC reef. As with the others it holds stripers, croaker, specs, and sometimes redfish. The important item to note about this particular reef is the arm of 14' water just below it, which is surrounded by 22' water on three sides. This is an excellent hump to fish for flounder; expect to find them on and at the bottom of the drop during low and outgoing tides, and up on top of the hump on high and incoming tides.

The Piankatank is another Western Shore river that is small but very productive, thanks again in no small part to the VMRC oyster reefs found here. Many of the reefs in this river are close to the channel edge and actually come out of the water at low tide, so they are marked with "Hazard to Navigation" markers. When you see one of these floats in the Piankatank, it's a dead give-away that there is an oyster reef. The first spot to note, however, has nothing to do with oysters. As with most bridges over Chesapeake tributaries, the Rt 3 bridge over the Piankatank attracts stripers. Cast to the pilings as you would at other bridges, with jigs or plugs. Slightly down river at LRW27 lies a VMRC reef on a great drop-off; the bar extends close to the edge of the drop to 21', and you'll find the usual suspects in attendance. Since this is such a sheer drop, most years you can also expect to find flounder along this edge from late spring on through the season. Another good flounder spot in this area is the hump surrounding the red #12 marker. Surrounded on all sides by water 20' or deeper, it rises to 10' on the top. Drift across this hump's lower edges on a low tide, or across the top on a high tide.

There are several other oyster reefs along the channel edges as you move down river, which are marked with "Hazard to Navigation" floats. All can be productive. But LRW28 is a fairly unique spot that sees an excellent current when the tide runs, and the channel becomes pinched here, creating a great spot to jig for seatrout from mid-season on or fish for croaker from early spring through the summer. On the edges of the drop you'll find flounder, and drifting the channel while casting into the shallow water between the #8 marker and Stove Point is a good bet for speckled trout.

The southern side of the Piankatank cuts a channel behind Gwynn Island, creating Milford Haven and Stutts Creek. The deeper water in the cut behind the island can produce just about any south Bay species during any given season, but on a regular basis, it's chock-full of croaker. The real interesting area in this neck of the woods, however, is the large area of shallow water just south of Gwynn Island. This area and the adjacent deeper water heading into the Bay proper, marked LRW29, is commonly known as the Hole In The Wall, and it provides some of the best speckled trout water along the Western Shore of the Chesapeake. While any of the common speckled trout tactics will work here, a favorite local tactic is to cut a soft crab in half, rig it on a three to four foot leader, and drift it weightlessly along a weedbed edge. Known as "letting it ride in the tide," large specs can't resist the offering.

Just to the south there's a tiny cut—LRW30—running behind a marsh island into Winter Harbor. This cut appears on the charts to be just a few feet deep, when in fact several sections drop down to 20'. As the current courses through here, rips form at several bends, creek mouth junctions and openings. Rig up a bucktail with a twister or pork rind as a teaser and cast to these rips, and you'll often enjoy furious action from 16" to 26" stripers.

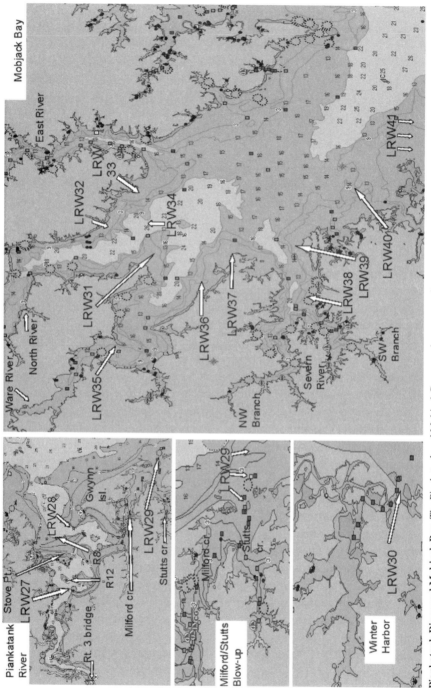

Piankatank River and Mobjack Bay. The Piankatank and Mobjack Bay are prime spec territory.

Mobjack Bay is the coming together of several rivers, the East, North, Ware, and Severn. Most of Mobjack runs between 10' and 20' and there isn't any particular deepwater channel that drops down significantly deeper either in the Bay or the rivers feeding it. Croaker can be found just about anywhere in Mobjack most seasons, but the real stand-out fishery here is for speckled trout. Again, the key is grass beds. The beds will shift from year to year, and you should expect their exact location from season to season to change. Instead of focusing purely on a specific bed or edge or two plan on moving around in Mobjack until you find the best beds each season. That said, there are a couple of areas that are more reliable than most. The water off Ware Neck Point, between the Ware and North Rivers at LRW31, is one such spot. The shore line across the North, between LRW32 and LRW33, is another edge that is usually weedy and productive for specs. Just outside of these areas at LRW34 you'll find some of the deepest water in the Bay and this is one of the best locations for croaker. Many seasons, perhaps one in three, good numbers of weakfish will also congregate at LRW34. Up inside of the Ware there are a few more of the ever important VMRC oyster reefs, including the edges off Jarvis Point at LRW35. These have particular importance because these are also weedbeds on the bar here most years, and the close proximity to both oyster bar and weed beds attracts good numbers of speckled trout.

Across the mouth of the Ware, the edge between LRW36 and LRW37 is another stretch that holds good grasses, and accordingly, speckled trout as well. You'll also find red drum along this edge many seasons. Same goes for the south side of the mouth of the Severn River, running from LRW38 to LRW39. This is another stretch that commonly sees healthy weedbeds, plenty of speckled seatrout, and some redfish each season. LRW40 is a much smaller area, but is an interesting area because it offers a shot at some different fish; during a falling tide, bounce jigs along the drop from the edge of the grasses down to 11', and you have a good chance of catching flounder. Move up into the cove itself during a flood, and you'll be casting at prime spec waters once again.

Another large stretch of water that has grass, specs, and reds is the flat at the mouth of Mobjack, marked by LRW41. This area is a little more exposed than most of Mobjack, especially on a southern breeze, and storms or heavy wind will rip up the grass beds here before those inside more protected areas. Often the grasses in this spot are patchy and not as well defined as in some other areas, but some seasons the grass beds will flourish here. Either way, local experts target trout in this area with the aforementioned traditional yet unusual tactic: they troll Mir-O-Lures in pink or chartreuse patterns from small boats while rowing them. Most people believe that trolling from a rowed boat gives the lures an erratic action that the speckled trout can't resist. Others mimic this action by trolling light gear with an electric motor, revving it up to wide-open throttle then dropping it back down to idle, then revving it up again.

The York River forms at the junction of the Mattaponi and Pamunkey Rivers, both of which have their own unequalled features. The Mattaponi offers anglers two unique experiences: first, an excellent April shad run that takes place far upriver along the stretch running from LRW42 to LRW43. Casting tiny lures and fly casting is very popular, and the run here is strong enough that it usually lasts for several weeks, attracting anglers from near and far. But for a truly strange fishing experience, move down river to LRW44 and fish bull minnow tight to the bottom. For some reason gar frequent this area, and there is no odder fish in the Bay region. In the spring white perch make a showing through this area as well, and they are present to some degree most of the year.

Interestingly, this section of the Mattaponi also has one of the greatest tidal ranges of any spot on the Chesapeake or its tributaries, rising and falling by as much as five feet on a full moon. Current, as you might expect, is stronger than on many other tributaries. This section of the river is also fresh enough to support some bass fishing, but it is less than stellar. There isn't much slow moving water with cover, nor are there many large creeks for bass to hide in. There are, however, a series of marsh creeks a little farther downriver that make for some interesting fishing in the early spring because the Mattaponi has a fairly large striper run. As these fish move in from the Bay and prepare to spawn, and again when they migrate down the river, they hesitate at the many small creek mouths during the falling tide. As the marshes drain through these creeks, each mouth becomes a potential ambush point for the stripers, many of which run in the 20" to 30" range. Later in the year, when the migratory fish have disappeared, residents in the 14" to 24" range can still be found at these creek mouths when the marsh drains, waiting for food to come washing their way. The creek mouths at LRW45 through LRW51 all provide good spots to cast jigs, plugs, and surface lures, when targeting these fish.

The Pamunkey sees less of a shad run but more of a perch and striper run in the spring. The holes at LRW52, 53, and 54 are all good spots to intercept white perch early in the season. Catfish anglers will want to try sinking cut herring in the deep water at LRW55. And stripers will hunt this area of the river with the same tactics as they do in the Mattaponi; try casting lures into the creek mouths at LRW56 through LRW62 early in the spring to intercept the larger fish, and later in the season to catch smaller resident stripers. Another spot catfish anglers should be familiar with is Cumberland Thoroughfare, at LRW63. The water running through here is fast and deep, in some areas well over 20', and late in the year and through Christmas catfish will sometimes stack up in the deeper holes along this stretch.

Where these rivers join to form the York the banks widen considerably, the currents aren't quite as potent, and common fishing tactics, therefore, change quite a bit. The straight channel edge starting at LRW64 and running all the way

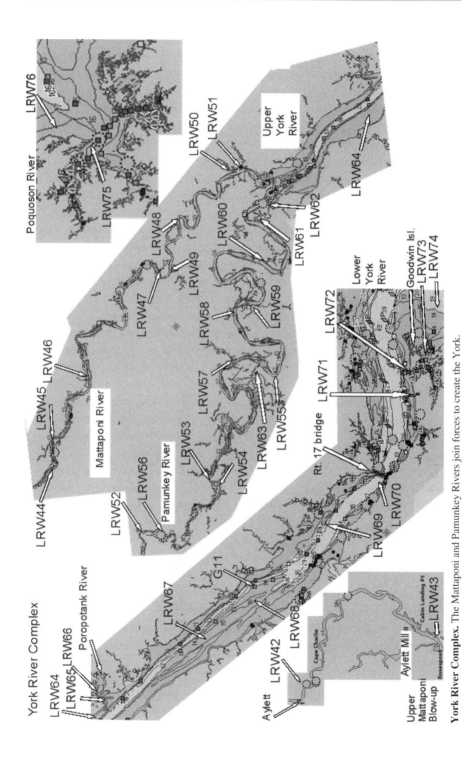

York River Complex. The Mattaponi and Pamunkey Rivers join forces to create the York.

down to the green #11 marker is productive striper territory. Most anglers troll along this edge, with Stretch 25s being the dominant lure of choice. Tandem rigs with bucktails and/or Sassy Shad bodies are another good choice.

The Poropotank River, which is really more of a large creek than a river, offers anglers a good shot at perch during the spring run. Fish the bends where the current has scoured out holes at LRW65 and the creek junction at LRW66 with minnow or grass shrimp on top and bottom rigs. After the spring perch run ends, fish these same holes with cut bait on the bottom and you'll hook into good numbers of blue cats.

Beyond this point the York begins showing a more brackish nature, with good numbers of croaker, spot and perch present most of the season. At LRW67, 68, and 69 croaker can be found in the shoals near the channel in the evenings. Where the Rt 17 bridge crosses the York the channel drops down— way down—to depths of greater than 70'. Weakfish can be found in the deep waters at LRW70 but they usually won't move into this area until mid-summer. Like the trout that move into other deepwater tributaries, they can be cranky and often bite poorly unless you fish for them after dark, with tempting peanut bunker or soft crab baits.

An unusual winter fishery for redfish and speckled trout exists a little farther downriver at LRW71, where a warm water outlet from an oil refinery keeps temperatures high enough for fish to collect and stay in the area, often right through the winter. The outlet here isn't as significant as the Elizabeth River's Hot Ditch, nor does it attract and hold as many fish. But that's an advantage as well as a disadvantage because there's less pressure here, as well.

LRW72 and the rest of the channel flowing behind Goodwin Island is another area you'll find strong currents and a strong striper bite, mostly on fish 24" and below. On the south side at LRW73 croaker will take up residence early in the year and usually be present in this pocket of water until they leave for the ocean in the fall. Slide a little farther down to LRW74 and you'll find the southeastern channel edge drops to 20'. This hole is a good bet for weakfish and croaker, but the better shot here is for flounder. Bounce jigs or minnow/squid combos from the top of the 2' deep point down to 20' and somewhere along that edge, you should find flatfish.

The Poquoson River is another large creek called a river, and doesn't have the depth or water flow to support a major fishery. It should be noted that croaker can be caught throughout the river, but the area is better known for Poquoson Flats. This is another awesome place for speckled trout with puppy drum and some years baby black drum mixed in over grass beds. These flats are more exposed than those in Mobjack, they shift through the years and can be ripped up in large storms and hurricanes. But more seasons than not, they account for a good share of the speckled trout taken on Virginia's Western Shore of the Bay. LRW75 on the north side of the river sometimes has grass and is worth checking out. But the stronger bet is at LRW76. This is the largest section of the Poquoson Flats to reliably hold weedbeds, though no one particular spot on the flats can be identified as a long-term hot spot. As with many of the other grassy areas, every season you'll have to idle into the shallows and look for yourself to see where the grasses are growing, then fish along the edges and in potholes.

The next few rivers heading south—Back River, the James River, the Elizabeth River, and the Lafayatte River—are somewhat less than idyllic, as they are surrounded by the Hampton/Norfolk metropolitan area. There are, however, a few spots well worth noting. The Back is relatively shallow, and similar to the Poquoson in nature. There aren't any significant, deep channel edges but the shallow flats, particularly near the mouth of the river, can be productive for speckled trout and/or reds if you find weedbeds.

The James is a huge river that runs all the way inland to Richmond and beyond. Upriver of Richmond, the James is notable as a smallmouth and muski fishery. From Richmond to the Chickahominy, most of the opportunities focus on channel and blue catfish, perch in the creeks during the spawn, and in some areas, largemouth bass and crappie.

Blue cats are without a doubt the favored fish by anglers of the upper James. In fact, the state record blue cat comes from the James. Interestingly, however, in the Richmond area flatheads hold top billing. From the I-95 bridge in Richmond through the section of the river that boarders Richmond itself, local anglers fish live sunfish on the bottom for flatheads up to 30-plus lb. Slightly farther downriver, in the area of the I-295 bridge, is where blue cat territory starts in earnest. The waters around the bridge itself in the main river, and the deepwater channels at LRW77—an area known as Deep Bottom—are prime blue cat waters. Anglers here usually fish with fresh cut shad or cut eels, set on the bottom, in water 30' or deeper right next to shallower flats. The deep area at LRW78 is another such area; anchor in deep water next to the shallow flats on the inside of the river bend. LRW79, at the mouth of the Appomattox River, is a well-known hot spot for blue cats. Don't worry about competition, though, because from this point down to the Rt 156 bridge there are flats on either side of the river, and the channel between them is all productive water. Many boats can spread out along this stretch, without crowding.

If you want to try night fishing for blue cats, head for LRW80 or 81. Note that these shallow flats have deepwater channels on both sides—the perfect situation when night fishing for catfish. LRW82 and LRW83 in Powell Creek are good areas to try casting for largemouth bass and—particularly during the winter months when the water temperature is in the 40s—crappie. For the bass try poking up each of these feeder creeks in a shallow draft boat. Lily pads, fallen trees, duck blinds, and wood bulkheads will all produce fish. For crappie look for fallen timber and duck blinds. For whatever reason, most of

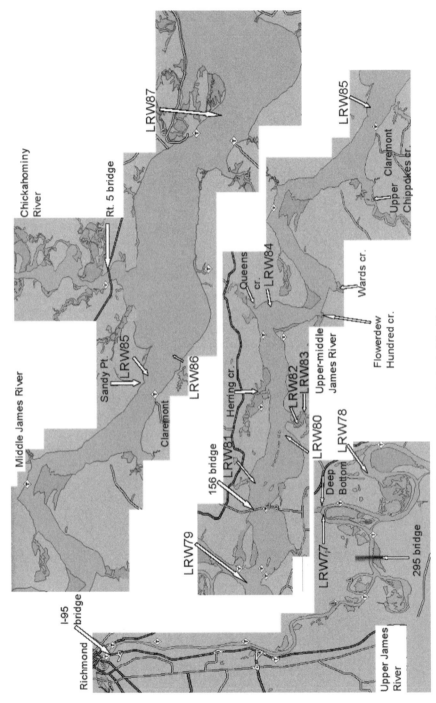

James River. From Richmond all the way to Norfolk, the James River is chock-full of fish.

the crappie caught in the James will come from dead wood cover and as in other tidal creeks and rivers, the fish will usually ball up in large numbers in a few specific spots, instead of being scattered throughout the area. The other nearby creeks, including Flowerdew Hundred, Wards, and Herring, all offer fair bass and crappie fishing. Note that most of the bass in these areas won't be huge; 1–2 lb is average and occasionally a 4–6 pounder will come out jumping.

LRW84, near the mouth of Queen's Creek, is the last major blue cat hot spot. Catfish will be found farther down river, particularly during years of strong freshwater flows, but not in the same numbers. This is also the area in which stripers will become more and more common.

The Chickahominy River, the most significant area tributary to the James, holds more interesting bass and crappie possibilities. Like most of the other tidal bass and crappie rivers, you'll have to try many good looking areas before locating a fish. Yet once you catch one you often stumble into a real honey hole. Piers, duck blinds, wharfs, old wrecks, and farther upriver lily pad beds are the ticket.

The area near Sandy Point at LRW85 is another spot to note, the first in the river for striper anglers. There are numerous wrecks here adjacent to deep water, and they provide good cover that the fish will move up around on high tides. Because there are numerous snags, it's best to fish this area with light jigs or surface baits that aren't apt to become fouled on every other cast.

Early and late in the year, striper anglers will also do well by trolling along the channel edge between LRW86 and LRW87. Most who fish this route regularly troll Stretch-25s and 30s, and bucktails or parachutes dressed with twisters or Sassy Shad tails. In the fall, the same is true of the false channel area between LRW88 and LRW89. Since most of the water in this stretch is about 20', however, smaller, lighter lures are necessary. Most years, 2 oz white or chartreuse bucktails dressed with four-inch Sassy Shad tails rigged behind three to four ounces of weight are the best bet. Some Virginian anglers in this area also like to troll daisy chains of bucktails dressed with twister tails or pork rinds. These daisy chains can consist of 8 to 12 lures rigged in a line, one behind the next, about two feet apart from each other. The rig is commonly weighted with lots of lead—as much as 12-ounces—and trolled along the bottom.

The deep water at LRW90 is the first reliable weakfish area in the James. Most seasons they will move in here during the summer, but won't school until late September or October. Accordingly, night fishing on the edge of the deep water is the best way to target them until the temperatures start falling. Down river at LRW91 and LRW92 croaker can be found starting as early as mid- to late April, and they will remain in this area for most of the season.

From this point down to the Rt 664 bridge, most of the river is relatively shallow. Croaker can be found throughout this stretch, and stripers can be caught by casting to the numerous piers and bulkheads as well as the bridge pilings. Note, though, that this section of the river is rarely thought of as a fishing destination. It's very industrialized, sees a lot of commercial traffic, and is not the most picturesque spot on the Chesapeake. The HRBT (Hampton Roads Bridge Tunnel), however, provides some awesome structure close enough to the open Bay that most salty species can be found swimming by at one time or another. The deep water near its center will fill up with weakfish most seasons, and stripers break water in this area quite often in the fall. Just below the tunnel, at LRW93, there's another stretch of deep water that trout will stack up in.

During the cooler months of the year, the area of the most interest to anglers, however, is in the south branch of the Elizabeth River, feeding into the James near the southern side of the river's mouth. The Hot Ditch, as it's known, is a power plant warm water outlet all the way upriver near the Great Bridge locks that will hold speckled trout, stripers, and some puppy drum throughout most winters. There can be a lot of competition here, particularly on nice weekends in the winter, and catches here are not usually high numbered. Some big fish are caught from the Hot Ditch each winter, however, and in the middle of January it's the only game in town for die-hard spec anglers. Unfortunately, the Hot Ditch is too far upriver to appear on most charts, including those used in this book, ADC charts, and the Maptech chart book. However, directions by road to the nearby launch ramp are included in chapter 4, Reliable Public Launch Ramps. From there, look for the power plant towers and the trench cut in on your left, as you head downriver from Great Bridge locks.

One may ask at this point why there isn't a section of this book addressing the Eastern Shore lower Bay rivers. Simply put, the lower Eastern Shore of the Chesapeake does not have any true tributaries except the Pocomoke, which is addressed in its own section. There are several creeks, including Nassawadox, Hungars, Cherrystone Inlet, and Old Plantation, but none of these provides enough water flow nor depth to be considered tributaries worth focusing on as fishing hot spots. Any and all of these creeks usually will provide light tackle anglers with a shot at small stripers and some speckled trout, but none of them is worthy of making a destination. Thus, they will be covered in the main-stem Bay section.

Lower Bay, Main Stem, Western Zone

The main-stem lower Bay covers about a third of the Bay's overall length, and is significantly wider than the upper Bay and much of the middle Bay. There's a lot of territory to cover here—and a lot of fish to be caught.

Smith Point marks the southern mouth of the Potomac River, and Smith Point light marks the first hot spot in this zone. MLBW1 marks the finger of the underwater point, which comes up to 10' and is surrounded by 25' to 27' to

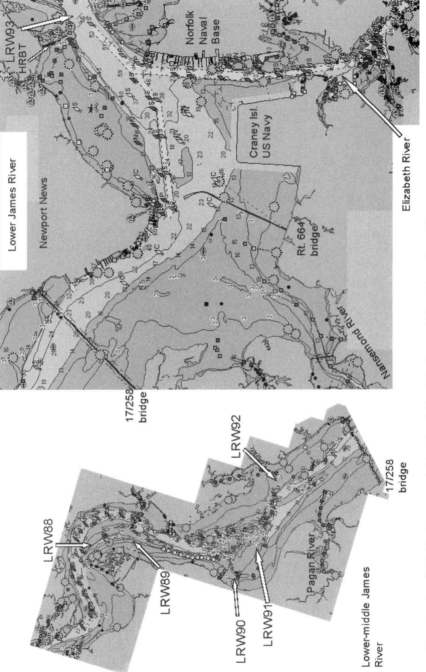

James River (continued). You'll often see naval ships when fishing in the lower-middle and lower James River.

the west and 40'-plus water to the east. Up on top of this point, croaker fishing is often hot from late April or early May through most of the spring. Night fishing up on the same shoal closer to land, at MLBW2, you'll find huge numbers of croaker in the same time frame. If you do a trip here early in the year be sure to also cast out a chunk of menhaden on heavier gear—scattered spring trophy stripers prowl these shallows after sunset. The eastern edge of the point at MLBW3 is a nice edge to fish for flounder on breezy days. It's not the most dramatic edge in the world and usually doesn't hold quite as many fish as some of the lower Bay's sharper drops, but its gradual nature makes it a good place to try for flatties when the drift is a little too quick to effectively fish those steeper edges.

The next point of interest is located just south of the mouth of the Potomac, at the Cabbage Patch. File it under strange but true: there are two well-known areas of the Chesapeake called the "Cabbage Patch," and both are in Virginia waters. This, the more northern of the two patches, is best known as a jigging area for weakfish in the spring and fall, and as a trolling area for stripers earlier and later in the season. In fact, this zone is trolled by many Maryland boats very late in the year, usually during the month of December. Any of the edges around the Cabbage Patch can be productive, but if you're after weakfish, pay particular attention to the edge at MLBW4. The 60' to 120' edge will often hold fish late in the season, usually in 60' to 90' of water.

South of the Cabbage Patch there is a series of wrecks, marked by MLBW5, 6, and 7. Each of these wrecks will attract weakfish, stripers, and croaker. In years of drought, sea bass can also be found on these wrecks, but most are too small to keep.

A couple miles south at MLBW8, there is an excellent flounder drop. The top of this underwater point sits in about 16' of water, with 32' water immediately to the north, south, and east. Jig or drag Fluke Killers dressed with minnow and/or squid along the drop on the south side during an incoming tide, and the north side on an outgoing, to hook up with flatfish.

Just south of this spot lies the mouth of the Great Wicomico River, an excellent spot for intercepting spring croaker and later in the season, spot. Fish the edge at MLBW9 and 10, starting in April for croaker and June for spot. You also have a fair chance of finding breaking stripers and blues in this area, with Spanish mackerel mixed in during the summer months. Another fantastic croaker spot is the drop-off by the red #62 marker, east of the Great Wicomico. Fish the 25' to 60' drop, staying shallower during low light conditions and deeper during periods of bright sunlight. Move slightly north to MLBW11 and you're in a prime weakfish hot spot. This is a sheer drop and it may be tough to fish when the wind is blowing, but jigging spoons and heavy leadheads or drifting chunks of crab baits from May through October will produce good catches. You'll also catch some flounder

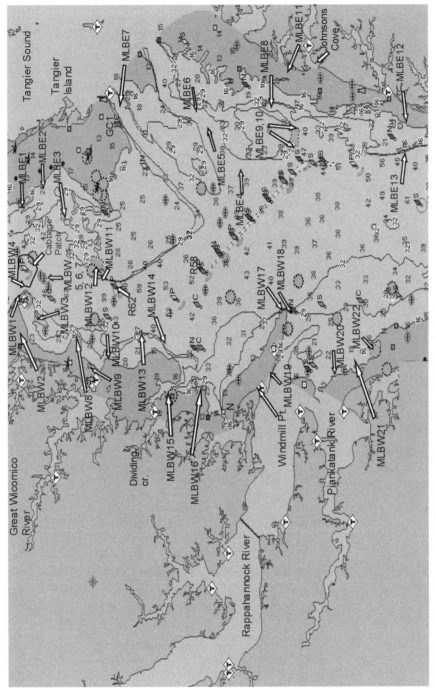

North, Lower Bay. In the northern half of the lower Bay, many oceanic fish begin showing up.

on this edge, usually near the top, and from mid-June through November, small schools of stripers often roam this area.

Just to the north at MLBW12, there is an artificial reef site. This reef does provide some good action, usually on the drift in light winds. Most of the fish caught here are croaker and spot, but weakfish make a showing too, usually for a brief period in the spring and again later in the year. Many of the migratory fish heading north also pop up in this zone at some point during the season. A few black drum, puppy drum, and the oddball cobia—mostly accidental catches—occur most seasons.

Closer to the Western Shore, the edge between MLBW13 and 14 provide a good location for striper and bluefish chummers to set up shop on the western side. The best spot to anchor two years out of three will be right at MLBW13, on the 28' notch surrounded on three sides by deeper water. Some years, however, the fish seem to want to bite in the shallower zone. When this is the case try setting up along the 16' to 25' drop closer to MLBW14. Whenever traveling through or near the deeper water to the east of MLBW14, which ranges from 50' to 90', keep an eye out for birds. Particularly from late September through late November when there's a good chance of spotting stripers and blues on top, with weakfish shadowing the schools down deep. Cast on top to catch the stripers and blues and sink a jigging spoon to or near bottom to catch the trout.

The section of water just outside of Dividing Creek has a very unusual bottom that ranges from 10' to 30' then back to 10' again. As you might expect, this means fish. Croaker move into this area and stay here virtually every season, and weakfish will often move into the deeper sections and hold there through the fall. This area is of more interest, however, to small boat anglers looking for stripers and/or blues in the fall. A couple of excellent edges here are located very close to the Western Shore, providing cover for windy days. In fact, when the wind is out of the west you can almost always still anchor up in this area without taking a beating. The 16' to 25' edge at MLBW15 is a reliable bet most seasons. Drifting along this edge with jigs will also produce flatfish, but they only gather here in strong numbers one year out of three or four. A slightly better bet for flounder is to move south along this drop to the edge at MLBW16. This is a good spot to try on an incoming tide, and since there isn't much water flow from any of the creeks feeding nearby Fleets Bay, the water here usually stays pretty clean on a west wind. Directly south of MLBW16 at the "N" marker, the drop is even deeper. While flounder will be caught here, too, this spot is a better bet for weakfish, particularly when they start running up the Bay in May and early June.

At the mouth of the Rappahannock River lies Windmill Point, which offers more good opportunities for lower Bay anglers. Much of the area around Windmill Point has relatively shallow water, all of which is excellent croaker water. Anywhere you find depths between 10' and 25' is a good bet during daylight, and once the sun drops, the 3' to 5' flat on Windmill Point itself will produce coolers full of croaker. Another unusual attribute of Windmill Point is that this is one of the relatively few spots on the western side of the Bay proper at which you can catch speckled trout. When there's a west wind (or no wind) and the water around the northeastern edge of Fleets Island is clam, try tossing jigs over the shallow flats just off shore. The northern side of the point has a fairly gradual slope, and although the drop-off is rather muted, you will find some flounder hanging around this edge. But on the east side, at MLBW17, there's an excellent drop-off from 18' to 22' then a second drop from 22' to 40'. The close proximity of two distinct drops opens up some interesting multi-species doors: bounce jigs along the first shelf and you've got a good chance of catching flounder, then along the second drop, trout. At MLBW18 the two drops merge, creating an excellent spot to chum for stripers on either an incoming or outgoing tide from June on through the season. East from this spot, in the large expanses of 36' to 40' water, there isn't much structure. However, you'll often find breaking fish in this area from mid-September through the end of the season. Much of the time there will be weakfish shadowing these schools. Late in November and into December, big stripers can also be trolled up in this zone.

On the south side of Windmill Point, another hot spot for both flounder and trout is the edge at MLBW19. Count on finding flatties in the 12' to 30' zone, and trout in the deeper water. Many years, however, the weakfish bite at Butler's Hole (covered in lower Bay, Western Shore tributaries, the Rappahannock) will surpass the action at MLBW19. Because Butler's is also more protected from the wind, it's the spot you'll usually want to check out first when trout are the fish of the day.

A couple miles to the south lies an area of bottom known as the Deep Rock, just off Gwynn Island. Starting in April and continuing through at least August most years, croaker will be found all throughout the Deep Rock zone. In April and May, lunker croaker in the 3 lb range are relatively common some seasons. The drop-offs here aren't spectacular, but the bottom composition certainly attracts gamefish. Setting up drifts between MLBW20 to MLBW21 is a good tactic for locating croaker, trout, and schoolie stripers on jigs or fluke killers baited with crab or bloodworm. There's a state reef at the southern end of the Deep Rock, at MLBW22, that does often hold good numbers of fish including croaker, weakfish, and even some sea bass, but the majority of the fish caught here are usually on the small side.

Wolf Trap is the next area of interest heading south, and it has some of the most varied, jagged bottom in this section of the Bay. Multiple knolls, drops, and troughs range from 10' to 30'. This is an excellent area to eel for stripers in the fall. Another good striper tactic to try is trolling shallow running light tackle—Rat-L-Traps and Stretch 15s work well—back and forth over the ever-changing bottom. From June through November you'll also pick up a lot of bluefish trolling with this method, but the majority for the past few years have been snappers. Some of the deeper holes—MLBW23 and 24 hit 50'—are good places to try jigging for weakfish, or drifting chunks of peeler crab from late April or early May through the season. Thanks to the abruptness of the drops leading into these holes, you'll also encounter good numbers of flatfish on the edges here. If this spot doesn't pan out for weakfish, slide south to the deep water at MLBW25. This spot will often be more productive during the summer months, when the weakfish sometimes ball up in holes. This is also a good area for spring trophy trolling along the Western Shore, usually during May when you may be able to intercept some of the big migratory fish on their way out of the Bay.

New Point Comfort Shoals is another section of bottom in this area that has uneven bottom that attracts fish. The edges at MLBW26 and MLBW27 are good spots to try summer and fall chumming for stripers and blues. This is also a good area to troll through both during the spring trophy striper season and during the fall season. Starting at the deeper section of this edge, a common tactic is to set up a trolling triangle running across to Old Plantation Light, then turning north and heading to Wolf Trap, then heading back down south. As you might expect, croaker can also be taken on New Point Comfort shoals with the best catches coming during the evening hours.

Outside of the mouth of Mobjack there's another stretch of uneven bottom, at MLBW28, which attracts stripers. Particularly in the fall, chumming, eeling, and light tackle trolling will be effective here. Weakfish will move into this area at times during low light conditions, but as a rule of thumb think of this as a striper spot. Just below MLBW28, however, the shoals outside of Plumbtree Bar provide another bayside shot at specs and reds. Spec anglers should pay particular attention to this area late in the year, when the speckled trout begin migrating down the Bay. Shortly after they leave the Piankatank, Mobjack Bay, and other Western Shore areas, the fish can sometimes be intercepted along these shoals in large numbers. Note, however, that the bottom here is unpredictable and can do a number on a spinning prop, so this area is best accessed by shallow draft boats only. Casting and retrieving jigs or bucktails dressed with bull minnow along the bottom on these shoals will also produce flounder much of the season.

A few miles east of Plumbtree, there's an artificial reef called the Back River Reef, which is one of the more productive artificial site in the Bay. Croaker, a few weakfish, schoolie stripers, and small sea bass are caught here regularly. More interesting, however, is the fact that this reef site is the northernmost to attract tautog. The best tog fishing here will take place in mid-spring, when the fish prepare to spawn and move into relatively shallow

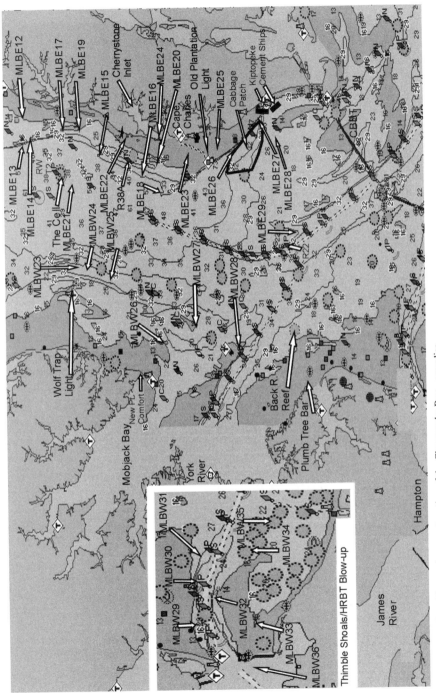

South, Lower Bay. The southernmost section of the Chesapeake Bay—paradise.

water. Spadefish will also show here during some seasons, usually caught on clam bits in a chum line.

Thimble Shoals, just outside of the James River, is one of the best known fishing spots in this part of the Bay. Naturally, that means it's often crowded, not to mention the heavy boat traffic coming and going from Hampton Roads. Remember—since 9/11 you also need to be on the lookout for navy ships and steer clear of them. In this part of the Bay, you'll see them with regularity.

The rocks at Thimble Shoal Light are a good starting point in both spring and fall. As early as March some years, the first croaker show up near the light. Shortly thereafter in early April tog can often be found alongside the rocks. Flounder move in during the same time frame, usually just a week or two after they show up in the seaside bays, and can be caught by bouncing jigs or casting baits along the rocky edges on bottom and along the south-side drop of the shoals. On calm, clear days and often on a west wind, you'll find flatfish right on top of the shoals, too, anywhere in the 12' to 15' zone. Weakfish also move into the Thimble Shoals area some time during April, but they are more commonly caught deeper on the dropping edge on the south side of the shoal than around the rocks. The drops at MLBW29, 30, 31, and 32 are all good areas to look for them. Later in the season during many years, weakfish pack in thick along the bottom of this drop and along the channel edges here as well.

Also look to find flounder and croaker in the spring, and schoolie stripers during the fall at MLBW33. The water is only 20' here but it's surrounded by 12' on three sides. If you can drop anchor in the shallows and position your boat in the deeper water, you have a good shot at chumming up large numbers of stripers with blues mixed in. Some years during the summer or very early in the fall, cobia are also scored here. Two other good spot to set up a fall chum slick for schoolies in this area are the knolls at MLBW34 and MLBW35. Again, you have a shot at hooking cobia on these knolls if the timing is right.

Beginning in October tog will return to the Thimble Shoals area and, depending on the weather, may be caught through the winter. Trolling around and casting to the rocks for stripers is probably the more popular fall fishery, though, and into December and through the winter it will produce linesiders that qualify as lunkers.

The Hampton Roads Bridge Tunnel (HRBT) at the mouth of the James River, is a good bet during a north or south wind that makes fishing the CBBT (Chesapeake Bay Bridge-Tunnel) tough. Again, note that you'll be facing heavy traffic, including navy vessels, in this area. The tunnel area is the section to fish for stripers, and blues, with trolling being the most common tactic. In the fall more than in the spring, weakfish can also be taken in the tunnel area. Because the drop-offs on each side are so sheer, and the depths so great between them, most fish are taken while bait fishing Fluke Killers or bottom rigs with bait and a lot of lead.

The opposite is true of the bridge area, which is very shallow. Since the depths vary between 4' and 15', most of the fish taken from this section of the HRBT are croaker (usually in the evenings, with the best fishing during late April through May) and flounder. Fish for flatties here during clear water and calm weather, in the shallower sections during a flood tide, and in the deeper spots around MLBW36 during a falling or low tide. The pilings will produce stripers, too. Most of the fish taken here will be at sunrise or sunset, when the stripers have moved shallow. If you want to try this area during the heat of summer, night fishing can also be productive for stripers. Liveline peanut bunker or toss out crab chunks in the darkness near lighted water, and there's a good chance it won't sit long before being eaten. Some years weakfish will also move into the shallows here under cover of darkness, and are caught using the same tactics.

Lower Bay, Main Stem, Eastern Zone

The water between Tangier Island and Smith Point holds some of the best fall striper and weakfish territory in the Chesapeake. Since this is such a large, open area, it's also common to locate fish without a flotilla of boats over it—a sometimes impossible chore farther up and farther down the Bay.

MLBE1 (flip back to North, Lower Bay chart), an insignificant-looking drop-off the northern end of Tangier Island, is a great spot to set up a chum line in the fall. Plenty of schoolie stripers and blues are in the area, and most of the competition will be farther south at the Targets. The same is true of MLBE2, although at this edge, the drop is significantly sharper and anchoring over the drop itself can be a challenge when the wind is up. Jigging often allows you to focus on it a little better and will also lead to catches of flounder from May through the fall. Closer to the targets, the drops at and around MLBE3 sees a lot of action more years than not. There is a reason for it: a consistent chumming bite on stripers in the 16" to 28" class. There are also plenty of snapper blues caught in chum lines around here. Finding the hot bite in this area is not hard—most of the time, there will be a good number of boats parked over the fish. Some years trout will also move into this zone despite the fact that it's relatively shallow for their taste, and can be caught by drifting crab or bloodworms on bottom rigs or Fluke Killers.

A few miles south, at MLBE4, the deep hole that drops below 80' will often produce fewer stripers but more weakfish in good sizes and numbers. This doesn't seem to be a particularly hot spring area most seasons but from late September through mid-November, this is an excellent spot to jig or drift baits. The same can be said for the holes at MLBE5 (which also hits 80') and 6 (which reaches over 50'). Note also that the drops at MLBE5 and 6 are less abrupt than at MLBE4. More often than not, MLBE4 is the better bet.

Another tremendous seatrout drop with depths topping 80' can be found near the green can #1, just south of Tangier Island, at MLBE7. This spot is productive most falls but unlike MLBE4, 5, and 6, is also a good bet during the spring when weakfish first move into this area of the Bay, and often remains good through the summer. Baits fished on the shallower half of the drop, between 15' and 35', will also be struck by good numbers of stripers and blues. Trolling along this edge, between the #1 can and the red #58 channel marker, produces stripers and blues in the summer and fall, plus Spanish mackerel during the summer months.

The large open, more or less featureless area spanning from MLBE4 to the red #62 marker (between the Great Wicomico and Tangier Island) down to MLBW17 is all good open-water trophy spring striper trolling. There aren't any specific spots in this stretch that will hold the fish, but the spring trophies are migrating anyway, and they aren't very interested in orienting to structure in the first place. Trolling umbrellas, large spoons, tandem bucktail rigs and parachutes throughout this area is standard "collision fishing" practice. The same can be said of the triangle of water between MLBW18, MLBE13, and MLBE19.

The finger of deep water reaching into the shoal at MLBE8, however, does give the fish something to orient to. And once the stripers school up in mid-May, anchoring at MLBE8 and chumming—particularly on an incoming tide—will produce fish. When the tide drops down, hop over to the edges near MLBE9 and MLBE10. Here the bottom comes up close to 20', and flounder can be caught on the top of this shoal as well as on the top half of this drop-off. During rare years, maybe one in five or six, cobia can also be caught on top of this shoal.

Closer to shore in this area, you're back into the speckled seatrout and red drum territory. Cast into the shallows and around the edges of weedbeds near MLBE11, and in the nearby mouth of Johnson Cove when looking for either species. You'll also find reds and specs on the 3' shoal that sticks out into deeper water, at MLBE12. West of this shoal, at MLBE13, there's a 15' to 30' drop that produces cobia some years and stripers with more regularity for chummers.

Stretching along the main drop from MLBE14 to MLBE18 (refer to South, Lower Bay), the entire edge is a productive area for stripers, blues, flounder, trout, and cobia. When chumming for stripers, blues, or cobia pay particular attention to MLBE15 and 16. These spots are also the prime locations along the edge for catching flounder. Trout can orient anywhere along this drop, and particularly during the summer months many separate, distinct schools will roam up and down this edge through the course of any given day. The best way to fill the cooler with these fish is to stay mobile, and don't drop a line until you've got the boat parked right over the fish. After a drift or two, expect the school to relocate. In the fall they tend to bunch up more and will be easier to stick with. From September through November, you can also expect the trout to be marked by schools of breaking stripers and blues with birds overhead, anywhere in this zone.

While flounder certainly will be caught on this edge, a better bet for a banner catch (particularly on a flood tide) is to move in to the bumps and shoals nearer to shore. MLBE17, 18, 19, and 20 all mark excellent humps and drops, any of which usually produce fish from May through the fall. Croaker can also be taken on these shoals, although the specific location is a little less imperative—many years the area will be riddled with them. Redfish are caught on these humps some seasons, particularly by anglers dragging baits across the shoals. This section of shoals and drops also sees good numbers of working birds over stripers and blues. Note, however, that most of the time these will be smaller fish in the 10" to 15" class. If chasing the birds is in your plan, you're better off moving out to the deeper water and ignoring the inshore flocks.

One of the most famous fishing spots in this area of the Bay is The Cell. This spot is marked by a red #WT2 buoy, and consists of artificial reef added to a hard, bumpy bottom that varies between 35' and 45'. The wreckage here rises to within 22' of the surface, making for some great fish-attracting structure. This is the northernmost spot to reliably find spadefish, which are caught by chummers baiting with clam bits on small hooks during the summer months. Cobia are also caught here many seasons, from mid-June through July and August. Interestingly, The Cell is also responsible for a lot of flounder. Most of the time anglers in this section of the Bay fish significantly shallower for flatfish, with the exception of some of the CBBT channels. But for whatever reason, flounder do like to hold around the edges of the structure here in water as deep as 40'. Seatrout are also caught at The Cell, both in the spring and again in the fall, often holding fairly close to the structure and especially during the last few hours of the day. Stripers hold here, too, and can be caught by jiggers, chummers, and bait anglers. Yup—you guessed it—there are lots of croaker at The Cell most seasons as well.

For all the notoriety The Cell has, interestingly, striper and weakfish can be caught in greater numbers most of the time a short distance away at MLBE21. The drop from 38' to 70' of water is a good spot to intercept weakfish when they first move up the Bay and start feeding in April and May, and the fishing may remain productive through the summer. By September and October, it's usually possible to find large schools of fish hanging on the drop-off, usually in the 40' to 50' neighborhood, but sometimes all the way down in the deeper zones. When late fall turns into winter, this is a favored area to troll for the big December stripers with swimming plugs and parachutes.

Cherrystone reef, right next to the red #38A marker, does not have nearly the reputation of The Cell, but it does have structure reaching all the way up to 16' in 30' of water. Croaker are available here in good numbers from early- to mid-April through the summer, as are sea bass and tautog (usually on the small side), flounder, and blues. Big black drum can also be intercepted here some years, usually during the end of May. Anglers after speckled trout and redfish, however, will want to focus their efforts on the 2' to 5' deep water to the southeast, between MLBE22 and MLBE23. This entire flat can be productive, although it should be noted that a medium to strong westerly breeze will dirty the water and shut down the action quickly. This is one of those times when savvy anglers will move inside Cherrystone Inlet and will fish the grass beds around the edges and shoreline. If that doesn't pan out, reds can also be taken by anchoring along the edge of the channel and casting crab or fresh shrimp baits into the deeper water at MLBE24.

Old Plantation Light, a little farther south along this same edge, marks another great area to fish. The drop here is very sheer, going from 12' to 125' in one area. On the upper levels of this drop you'll find flounder and stripers, with weakfish found in the deeper water. Black drum are also caught in this area with some regularity. Exactly where they will show up along this edge is a crap shoot from year to year—you just have to get out and look for them, or for the boats that have already found the fish—but they will almost always appear somewhere in this vicinity. The deeper water in this zone is another area trollers score on rockfish during the late fall and winter months. Running lures back and forth across this edge is usually successful.

Old Plantation Flats, inside of the lighthouse, varies between 2' and 6' and is another Eastern Shore spec and redfish spot, so long as the wind isn't pumping out of the west. There's a channel at MLBE25 that should be worked over thoroughly by anglers pitching jigs or using bucktails trimmed with crab. Anglers with very shallow draft boats will want to move in near any of the creek mouths along the shore line in this area and cast their lures up into the points. On a high tide it's possible to scootch into the creeks and cast for both specs and reds. Most of the redfish in here will be on the small side, but the same cannot be said of the speckled trout—some good sized fish will come from tight little creeks and holes.

Outside of Plantation lies the second and southern Cabbage Patch. The main structural component here is the western edge of the same deep trench that makes the spots along Plantation so interesting. On the western side, however, it only comes up to 30' or 35' in most areas. Nevertheless, trout can often be found holding at the 35' drop to deeper water at MLBE26. This area is also another deep spot that flounder seem to frequent, and it's not unusual to catch them in 40' of water at the Cabbage Patch. Cobia anglers also focus on the Cabbage Patch some seasons. Most of the action is at the southern end in 27' to 32' of water, and when the fish are in attendance here, there's often a small fleet marking the spot.

The eastern edge of this trough is a lot more distinct and is also an extremely productive area to fish. From MLBE26 to MLBE27, the entire edge is flounder territory from 40' to the top of the ledge, and weakfish territory in the deeper areas. Stripers can pop up in either or both zones. Pay particular attention to the very end of this edge, at MLBE27.

Chumming the shallower water at and around MLBE28, anglers can get into cobia from mid- to late May through July. The fish aren't as concentrated in this area, but neither are the fishermen. Many anglers fish this zone by simply running two to three miles from the Eastern Shore, locating 20' to 28' of water, and depending on the chum to do the rest. Since cobia are pretty mobile creatures, often this is just what it takes to be successful. The 25' water east of the red #22 marker, at MLBE29, is another good bet for cobia. Black drum are also taken here, usually in June, by anglers hunting for them with peeler crab or sea clams. Better known areas for black drum include the buoys #16 and 18, which are described in chapter 3, The CBBT.

Kiptopeke and the Cement Ships guarding its entrance are fascinating to fish. Yes, the breakwater here really is formed by two huge ships that are made of cement. They stick up well out of the water, look like they have been sitting there for about a thousand years and provide lots of structure for all kinds of fish. In my experience, the northern ship is the more productive one. The north end of it lies in 13' of water, while the southern end is in 25'. Any area of the ship can produce stripers when casting lures up the sides and retrieving them quickly along the surface. Casting baited rigs up to and around the ship itself usually results in a quick bite from a small sea bass or croaker. But move just off the ship to MLBE27, and the drop on this edge will usually produce flounder. Casting to the deepest section of this ship will also result in some hook ups with weakfish, but for some reason, during the summer months most of the trout that hold here seem small.

The second ship sits more parallel to shore, in 20' to 25' of water. Again, baited rigs close to the ship often results in small sea bass and croaker, while lures retrieved quickly along the surface are often attacked by stripers and sometimes also blues. Bouncing jigs along the bottom a few feet away from the ships often results in flounder hook-ups. Often when the water temperatures are low, tog can also be found around the cement ships.

Outside of the cement ships, late in the year many anglers troll for stripers. Many of these fish are ocean-run and during the month of December in particular, fish in the 30 lb class and above can be caught in the area using spring trolling tactics.

Small boat anglers may be tempted to launch at Kiptopeke on windy days, and use these ships as protection, in order to fish the Bay on relatively rough days. If you can get there that's fine, but know that the ramp at Kiptopeke is a scary place to launch and retrieve your boat from. The ships really don't provide enough cover and waves often crash right onto the ramp here. On any kind of westerly breeze, the ramp could reasonably be called unusable.

The CBBT (Chesapeake Bay Bridge-Tunnel)

If an angler went to a group of expert marine biologists, engineers, and hard-core fishing addicts, and asked them to build the largest, most awesome fishing reef ever built in the history of man, the Chesapeake Bay Bridge-Tunnel might just be the result. Of course, the CBBT was designed for automobile and truck traffic, not anglers. But this 21 mile chain of causeways, concrete and rock islands, bridges, and tunnels provides us with an astonishing number of fishing opportunities. Crustaceans and plant life encrusts the pilings and riprap; the tidal squeeze at the Bay's mouth creates phenomenal currents; powerful bridge lights attract uncountable colonies of bait in the darkness hours; and alternating channels and shoals provide both deep and shallow water habitat. No matter what saltwater sportfish you're after, there's a good chance you'll find it roaming somewhere around the CBBT.

Before touching on each hot spot along the bridge, it should be noted that any one or any group of piles along the CBBT can be productive on any given day. Sure, start at the known hot spots. But don't hesitate to take a shot at any pile in-between hot spot "A" and hot spot "B." As with the northern Bay Bridge, from season to season, it's just impossible to eliminate or elevate any one specific piling as a "good" fishing spot. One other note of interest: the islands provide areas of protection from the wind and current that are large enough for boats to hide in, but the pilings don't. Since the current is usually humping in this area, in order to effectively and safely fish the pilings it's best to plan on dedicating yourself to captaining the boat while your crew does the fishing.

Starting at the southwest end of the CBBT, the first spot to take note of is the "small boat channel," an area of 30' water surrounded by 20' of water, at CBBT1. The edges of this channel are consistent flounder producers from year to year, beginning in late April and continuing right through the season. In coastal bays and inlets the true doormat fish in the 6 to 10 lb class are caught very early in the spring, but at the CBBT this isn't necessarily true. In fact, many jumbo flatfish are caught here in the heat of summer and into the fall.

The first island of the CBBT—CBBT2—is another consistent producer, but is better known for tog, stripers, blues, and to a lesser extent sea bass. More often than not this spot also provides an excellent early season shot at tog, usually with the best action in early April. By late April or early May the tog will spawn, and during this period, better catches will come from shallower depths. Green and fiddler crabs fished around the rocks are the best bet. By late April the tog thin out as the water warms, but then make a reappearance late in the fall, usually by October, and when weather permits can often be taken during the winter months. Exceptionally large stripers are also caught near the first island of the CBBT, usually during the winter months as the ocean run fish begin to stage for their run up the Chesapeake. Try for these fish along the edges of the deeper water on the southwestern edge of the island, and in areas where the current smacks into the concrete. Black drum are known to make seasonal appearances at the first island, but these fish will usually be caught in the opposite position of where you'll strike it rich on stripers: the downcurrent eddy behind the island. Most of the time there's a lot of competition around the islands of the CBBT, but if you can fish here when there isn't a crowd—that means on weekdays or when it's raining—you may even be able to sight cast to the drum. In the eddies they'll often come up near the surface and laze about. Unfortunately, as soon as boats start roaring up they disappear, so save this tactic for sunrise, sunset, or low-competition days. Redfish and cobia can be found here, too, but their numbers vary radically from season to season and there are usually several areas inside the CBBT where fishing for them is more reliable.

CBBT3 is a wreck that lies between the bridge and the fishing pier on the northern side of the first island. Lore says that this was a barge that collided with the bridge long ago and was left where it sank. In any case, it does add to the fish-attracting structure of the CBBT. While it's not known for attracting any one specific species of fish at any given time, all of the usual suspects can be found here. And since it provides a large area of bottom structure in a consistent depth (as opposed to the plunging rock walls and pilings), it is easier to target sea bass and tautog here than it is at most of the other CBBT areas.

Just after the first island wreck lies the first underwater section of the complex, at CBBT4. The tunnel here goes down more than 60' and lies partially buried on the bottom. Because the tunnel does stick up into the water column, a series of rips often forms over the tunnel. These rips are a good spot to find surface-feeding fish, usually stripers and/or blues. Some years this action begins as early as June, but generally speaking the best topwater action here occurs in the fall with October and November being the prime months. Birds provide the most visible clue to finding the fish's exact location, but in most cases, the feeding predators will be located just downcurrent of visible rips. From June through early September, you may also find Spanish mackerel mixed in with the blues and stripers. In December, trolling through the tunnel area with large swimming plugs, such as Manns Stretch 25s, becomes very effective for capturing late season stripers.

Flounder can also be found along the edges of this channel, but because of the extreme currents, it's all but impossible to target them with common flounder methods. This is where wire-lining for flatfish becomes the most effective technique. By using Monel (soft wire) fishing line partnered with lots of lead, you can slow-troll bucktails dressed with minnow along the edges of the channel without losing touch with the bottom. Unlike wire-lining for

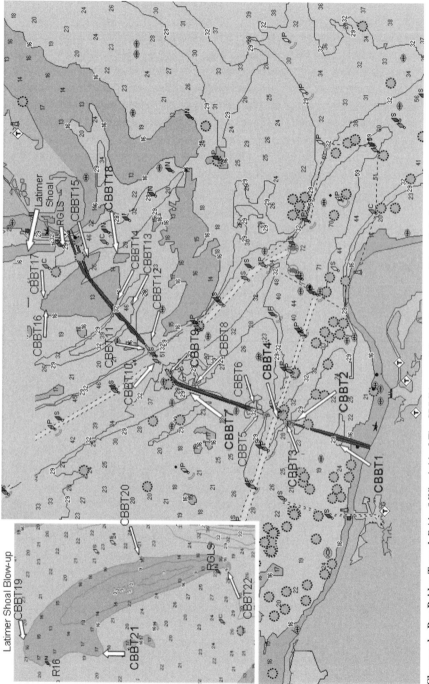

Chesapeake Bay Bridge-Tunnel. Bridge? What bridge? The CBBT is one of the most awesome fish reefs in the world.

stripers, it's not necessary to work the rod. The key factor is simply to make sure your bait stays where it belongs—right on bottom.

The second island of the CBBT (CBBT5) is pretty much the same as the first island, with one small difference: while the maximum depth of the water surrounding the first island is less than 40' deep, there is a pocket of slightly deeper water on the northeast side of the second island at CBBT6 where weakfish often hold in.

Between the second and third islands, there is a long series of pilings—any of which could be holding fish—with little that stands out until you reach the deep water at CBBT7 and CBBT9. The area between these two spots—often known locally as "the bend"—is a good location to search for schooled weakfish from September through late November. Patrol back and forth looking for the telltale caterpillar marks on your fishfinder, and when you find them drop tandem rigs or jigging spoons down to the bottom. In all likelihood there will be a strong current running in this area, so plan on using slightly heavier gear than usual and dropping a lot of weight.

This area is also a good one to patrol in your search for cobia. Many anglers check piling after piling in this area hoping to spot one and sight-cast to it. Tossing a bucktail dressed with a twister tail, a curly tail jig, or a live bait are all effective when sight-casting to these fish.

You'll also note that there's a significant shelf at CBBT8, between CBBT7 and CBBT9. This edge is an excellent flounder spot. Jigging here is tough due to the current and depths unless you use jigs of three to six ounces and have a rod rigged with superline. As a result, wire-lining and drifting Fluke Killers are more common methods used to score flatties here.

Yes, there are stripers in residence at the bend, too. They can be targeted by trolling swimming plugs such as Stretch 25s back and forth behind the pilings, or by casting lures at the pilings themselves. Probably the most popular method of catching stripers here, though, is casting into breaking fish during the fall months.

The third island of the CBBT (CBBT9) differs from the first two because it has significantly deeper water running close by. On the eastern side it drops down below 60' before reaching the edge of the channel, and on the western side, depths come close to 50'. Because of the deeper water, you're more likely to find weakfish close to this one than you are to find them around either of the first two islands. Stripers, blues, drum, and the other usual suspects are also caught here. Unlike the first two islands, the third island is also known for attracting spadefish. In the heat of summer, usually July through the month of August and into September, spadefish will move into this zone. Try anchoring upcurrent of the island, and chum with bits of surf clam. Bait up small hooks with clam bits, and drift them back into the chum slick. Since a ripping CBBT current will scatter the chum and make it tough to keep your baits in the strike zone, these fish are best pursued during a relatively slow tide. Savvy anglers will spend their time fishing for stripers, blues, and weakfish when the current's running hard, and save the clam supply for when the current starts dropping out.

Treat the rips at CBBT10 the same as at CBBT4. Again, the edges of the channel at the tunnel section are good floundering grounds, but you have to get deep and stay deep in a roaring current to score on them. In this zone, wire-lining is just about the only way to do it through much of the tidal cycle. As with CBBT4, there's always a pretty good chance of running into working birds over breaking fish in this area, usually stripers and/or blues. And another similarity is the popular and effective method of catching late season stripers by trolling large swimming plugs across the area.

CBBT11, the fourth island, is the last island of the CBBT chain. It's another good place to chum for spadefish in mid-summer. You'll also find black drum here, usually lazing about in the tidal eddy on the downcurrent side of the island. The other unusual feature here is the awesome edge just southeast of the island, at CBBT12. The 16' to 50' edge provides a shallower area to fish lighter gear for flounder. Try jigging here on the end of the incoming, and the slack high tide. It's also a good place to set up shop for striper chumming in the fall. One caution: this is another area that sometimes becomes inundated with snapper blues, and it may become impossible to catch anything else once they find your chum slick. On the flip side, if it's still early enough in the fall, you could hook into cobia or two here, as well.

Of course, stripers, blues, trout, tautog, and flatfish are also in attendance at the fourth island. Taken as a whole, the third and fourth islands probably account for more fish than the first and second islands, with the possible exception of flounder and tautog some seasons. Bear in mind that each season will be different, and while the first island could be the hot spot one year, the fourth could be the place to be the next year. The downside? On calm days, they also see more traffic. If you have a larger, more capable boat and conditions are rough enough to keep the smaller boats closer to shore, the third/fourth island complex should be in your game plan.

The rest of the CBBT complex itself consists of pilings, any of which could be hot during any particular day, or any particular season. There are, however, several shoals and holes in this area that are extremely important to take note of. The first is the deep water at CBBT13. This trench runs from well above the bridge complex to below it, getting deeper as you head down the Bay. During the spring run of weakfish, this is a good area to search out. Fish could show up here as early as April. In the fall, you'll again find trout holding here, often marked by schools of small blues and/or rockfish with birds working over them. When you locate breaking fish here, try jigging deep directly below them to score on the trout. If you find working fish here during mid-summer, make sure you try ripping a small spoon through the fray—Spanish mackerel will sometimes be mixed in, as well. Late in the winter, this is also a productive area to troll umbrella and tandem rigs for the big stripers, preparing to make their run up the Bay.

The edge at CBBT14 is another good flounder hole, one that is shallow enough that light tackle anglers can go after flatfish with jigs and bucktails. As usual in this area, try to plan your flounder pounding to go along with the end of an incoming or a slack flood tide, as you'll often be forced to abandon this tactic when the current starts rolling again. Wire-liners can work deeper along the edge here, but when the current starts flowing in earnest, even they will have trouble keeping contact with the bottom. This spot is the outer edge of an area generally called the Inner Middle Ground, which is notable for another reason: cobia. The shoals marked at CBBT15, 16, 17, and 18 are all good spots to try setting up a chum slick for cobia, usually from late May or early June through the beginning of September. The best fishing is usually shortly after they show up, when most of the fish will be in pods or small schools. Later in the season, you're more likely to find singles and pairs. In this area you'll also pick up small shark with some regularity when chumming for cobia.

The deep hole to the east of CBBT15 is another good place to patrol for weakfish. Particularly in the fall, they will bunch up deep in this hole and hold along the eastern edge of the Inner Middle Grounds edge until late in November or even into early December. From this point to the red #10 nun marker to the south is a striper trolling zone, particularly late in the year. Spanish mackerel also make a showing in this area during the summer months and can often be caught trolling small spoons at a high rate of speed.

Just to the north of the CBBT lies the area that is probably the most famous in the Chesapeake for cobia, Latimer Shoal. This area is heavily fished at times, but the shoal covers enough territory for anglers to spread out over a large area. Both the eastern edge (anywhere between CBBT19 and CBBT22 with the hump marked CBBT20 the most reliable spot) and several spots along the western edge (at CBBT21 and 22) are productive. This is another area in which you'll catch shark when the cobia aren't biting. Occasionally, perhaps one season out of four, red drum will also stage around Latimer for a period of time. Often it's a week or two in the spring, then again in late summer, but they rarely stick around here for an extended period. The late May/early June is also the time frame during which black drum make a showing in this area. They usually are caught either at the north end of the shoal at the red #16, or towards the northern end of the Inner Middle Grounds between the green #13 marker and the red/green "LS" buoy. As with the redfish, black drum don't hang around for long and a two- to three-week run is all that can be expected before the schools of fish start spreading out.

One final note about the CBBT: this is one of the roughest areas of the Bay. Extremely strong currents can oppose oceanic rollers, the Bay is as wide as 16 miles from shore to shore, and the CBBT complex itself squeezes the currents and causes rips. Small boat anglers must be very careful to pick their days with caution. Even captains of large boats have to use care when deciding whether or not to move in near the bridge islands or pilings. If the conditions make it hazardous for you to fish the CBBT, there's no need to push it—the surrounding areas have plenty of good spots in sheltered water.

Shorebound Angling Hot Spots of the Lower Chesapeake

The lower Chesapeake covers a lot of territory, and there are zillions of roadside pull-offs, beaches, and other areas the public can access to cast from. Here are some of the highlights to get you started catching fish from the banks of the lower Bay.

WESTERN SHORE

• LEESYLVANIA STATE PARK: This park is well up the Potomac, near Woodbridge. It does have a pier with a launching facility and offers access to shoreline angling for bass, catfish, and sometimes stripers as well. Fish the point off to the left of the launch facility, and you can hit fairly deep water with a good cast. Take Neabsco Rd, Rt 610 north, to the park entrance.

• WESTMORELAND STATE PARK: There's a small pier here near a launching facility that allows for shoreline casting. Most of the catch here will be croaker, but stripers, snapper blues, trout, and flounder will also turn up. Take Rt 3 to Rt 347, turn right, and follow the road through the park.

• GREAT WICOMICO FISHING PIER: There's plenty of parking and handicap access at this pier, in the shadow of the Rt 200 bridge over the Great Wicomico. Unfortunately, it closes at dusk so there's no night fishing access. Croaker will be the main catch, along with some stripers and white perch at times.

• WILLIAMS WHARF LANDING: This facility has a fishable section of riverfront along the wharf, where croaker, stripers, snapper blues, flounder, and the occasional trout will be caught. Car-toppers and canoeists can also use this facility. Take Rt 660 until it ends at the East River.

• YORK RIVER STATE PARK: This facility offers access to the York River where there's a good mix of fresh and brackish water. A huge amount of shoreline can be fished, with catfish, croaker, and stripers on the menu. There's a three dollar admission fee that drops to two dollars in the off-season. Taskinas Creek also runs through the park, offering more potential for catfish hunters and perch fishing during the spring run. Take Rt 607 (Croaker Rd) off Rt 64, and stay right when the road makes a Y.

• **CHIPPOKES PLANTATION PARK:** Catfish and perch can be caught from the banks of the Chippokes Creek. Look for a decent showing of perch during the spring run here, which is the best time to visit if you want to keep your fishing rods bent. Adventurous anglers who are willing to hike can also get to the shoreline of the James River, where croaker, stripers, and catfish can be caught. Take Rt 10 to Rt 633 north and follow it into the park.

• **GLOUCESTER POINT BEACH:** This area has no fee, good parking, picnicking areas, a fishing pier, a beach, and restrooms. A wide variety of fish are available, from stripers to croaker to snapper blues to the occasional weakfish and flounder. Unfortunately, the park does not officially open until 10:00 A.M. It is open until 8:00 P.M., so evening angling may be the best way to go here. Take Rt 17 to the bridge over the river and get off on Greate Rd on the north side of the bridge. The park is located at the end of the road.

• **BENNETTS CREEK PARK:** This facility in Suffolk has ramps as well as a fishing pier. It's pretty far up the river, however, and you may not want to eat catfish and other bottom dwellers coming from this area. Croaker, stripers, and eels will also be caught here. Take Shoulders Hill Rd to the end.

• **LYNNHAVEN BEACH:** This facility has ramps and car-topper access, but bank anglers will be interested in it for the stretch of beachfront on the Bay. Stick with the channel area to the north during full light, but during low light, try casting from the beach into the shallow Bay areas, where stripers and croaker will move up to feed. On weekends, you may have to walk a ways to get away from sunbathers and swimmers. Restrooms are available, and there's no fee if you aren't launching a boat. Take the Lesner Bridge to Piedmont Circle.

EASTERN SHORE

• **KIPTOPEKE:** Just inside the cement ships, the 24-hour access fishing pier here provides action on croaker, stripers, blues, spot, flounder, and the occasional trout or sea bass. The pier is lighted, so night fishing is a possibility here. Parking is ample and restrooms are available nearby. There's a $3 daily fee or a $20 yearly permit can be purchased. Surf anglers can also walk down to the beach area here and cast into the Bay suds from the sand. Take Rt 13 to Rt 704 and follow the signs to the park.

• **THE CBBT/SEA GULL ISLAND:** The southernmost island of the CBBT chain has a huge 625' long handicap-accessible public fishing pier that provides action on just about every fish to swim in the lower Bay. Shark, spadefish, drum, and other big game that usually requires boat access to catch will be taken here with regularity. The pier is lighted for night fishing, and there's plenty of parking, restrooms, cleaning stations, a restaurant and even a gift shop. Even though this facility is huge, it will become crowded on weekends in the summer, so serious anglers who want to stake out a good spot should plan to arrive early. The pier is free, but you'll have to pay the $12 CBBT toll to get there. Take Rt 13 to the CBBT and get off at Seagull Island.

RELIABLE PUBLIC LAUNCH RAMPS

Please note that only public ramps are included in this guide, and this is by no means a complete listing. There are many private ramps at marinas along the shores of the Chesapeake and many other public ones as well, but some are unreliable at best. Launch fees, operation hours, and accessibility change as the seasons change, and nothing is worse than arriving at a boat ramp in the pre-dawn hours, only to find a chain across it. Whenever you plan to use a private ramp, you should call the day before to verify accessibility. Ramps included here are listed from north to south along the Western Shore, then along the Eastern Shore. You can also obtain the map "Guide to Maryland Piers and Boat Ramps" from the Maryland DNR by calling 1-800-FINS. Beware, however, as I have attempted to use some of the ramps listed in it and found them non-existent or unusable several times. Virginia anglers can find links to boat ramp listings via the VMRC (Virginia Marine Resources Commission) Web site. The ADC Chesapeake Bay Chartbook (www.adcmap. com, available in most boating stores) lists over 200 ramps and marina facilities, both public and private, with phone numbers when applicable, for facilities in both Maryland and Virginia. Regardless of the information source they discovered it in, anglers should never attempt to use any ramp for the first time without checking it out the day before, speaking to someone with current local knowledge, or asking at a nearby tackle shop.

Because of the ever-changing nature of ramp accessibility and usability, the only ramps included in this guide are those that have been used or spot-checked shortly before this printing. They should serve you well.

Western Shore Public Ramps

MARYLAND

• **TYDINGS PARK RAMP:** Located in Havre de Grace, at the end of Union Ave, this ramp provides access to the Susquehanna Flats. The ramp is small and shouldn't be used by boats over 18' or so. A $5 permit is necessary and can be purchased on the spot; before and after hours there's a drop-box with envelopes for the fee. Call 410-939-0015 for information.

• GUNPOWDER STATE PARK: This ramp provides access to Dundee Creek and the Gunpowder. This is a relatively large ramp with several launch slots, and can be used by most trailerable boats. It's open year-round and has bathrooms. Take Eastern Ave to Grace's Quarter Rd and turn right. Take the next right, and the road dead-ends at the ramp.

• ROCKY POINT PARK: This ramp feeds Back River and provides good access to Hart-Miller Islands and the surrounding waters. There are two ramps, both of which can accommodate relatively large boats, and the facility is open year-round. Take Rt 702 off of Eastern Ave, go right at Barrison Pt Rd and right again at Rocky Pt Rd.

• FT ARMISTEAD PARK: On the western side of the Patapsco River, at the base of the Francis Scott Key bridge, this ramp can be used by all sized boats with no fee necessary. This is the normal launching point for anglers fishing the nearby power plant in the winter and is busy during the summer months with anglers and pleasure boaters. The pier was destroyed during hurricane Isabelle, but by the time of this printing its repair should be complete. This facility is closed from midnight to 6:00 A.M.; no fee, no bathrooms. Getting here is confusing, as Rt 695 roars right by but does not offer easy access. Instead, take Ft Smallwood Rd to Glidden Rd, which ends at the park.

• BROEING PARK: This ramp is another one for winter anglers; it offers easy access to the Middle Branch, and the channel in front of the hospital that is popular with cold weather Baltimore anglers. The facility is fine but you will not want to stick around here after dark, as the locals are not always friendly. The ramp is located on the south side of the Hanover St bridge in Baltimore City. Don't forget to lock your car.

• SANDY POINT STATE PARK: From Baltimore to Sandy Point there is a complete absence of public ramps. Luckily, Sandy Point, at the western base of the Chesapeake Bay Bridges, is an awesome facility. One of the biggest access points on the east coast, there are 22 launch slots all with deep water and piers. The facility is open 24/7 but be sure to bring lots of single bills with you in the pre-dawn areas, because you'll have to pay the fees by loading dollar bills into a machine. Bathrooms, and (in-season) boat rentals, snacks, drinks, and fuel are all available here. The DNR has a large facility with several police boats, right next to the ramps, so be sure to obey the 6-mph speed limit. To get to Sandy Point take Rt 50 east heading towards the Chesapeake Bay Bridges. Then take the last exit before the bridge, marked Sandy Point State Park, and follow the signs to the boat ramp.

• TRUXTON PARK: This ramp feeds into Spa Creek, off the Severn River, in Annapolis. The single ramp is in good condition and has a pier, but parking is very limited and I wouldn't plan on launching here after 6:00 or 7:00 A.M. on a weekend. Take Bay Ridge Ave to Hilltop Lane, then turn right from Hilltop onto Primrose Rd.

• JACKSON'S LANDING: This ramp provides access to the upper Patuxent, but is best for use with boats that can be lifted and launched manually. It would be hard to get anything over 14' or so in here, and most people use this facility for canoes, kayaks, jon boats, and the like. Just south of the Rt 301/Rt 4 junction, take Mt Calvert Rd to the end.

• SOLOMON'S ISLAND: This ramp is close enough to the Bay that a huge number of anglers use this access point to fish in both the lower Patuxent and the main-stem Chesapeake. It is a large facility with a huge parking lot that still becomes overcrowded on nice weekends. They charge five dollars to launch but there is no drop-box for pre-dawn launching. The dock worker writes down license plates when he arrives and will want payment as you leave at the end of the day. There are four launch slots, all of which have piers and deep water, and there are restrooms. Because of the crowds, it's best to arrive here early in the day or expect delays. To get there, simply take Rt 4 to the bridge over the Patuxent; the ramp is located under the bridge on the north side of the river, just before Solomon's Island.

• SMALLWOOD STATE PARK: Anglers headed for Mattawoman Creek, the middle Potomac, and/or the D.C. fishing areas will want to use this ramp, which has a half-dozen slots and good parking. This ramp is also a good location for hitting the many other creeks along this stretch of the Potomac for bass, catfish, and perch. To get there, take Rt 224 to Sweeden Pt Rd, turn left, and follow it to the ramp. For more information, you can call the state park at 301-743-7613.

• FRIENDSHIP LANDING: Use this ramp to launch in Nanjemoy Creek, and to access the lower-middle Potomac. It is large enough for boats up to 18' and has deep water, but the pier is a fishing pier with a rail that you must clamber over, and it is not set up well for older people or physically challenged people. It's open year round, no fee, no restroom. To get here take Friendship Landing Rd off Rt 425.

• PT LOOKOUT STATE PARK: This ramp has several slots and there's plenty of parking, but a lot of people launch here and you should come early or prepare to have a wait at the ramp. They also rent boats and have a minor-league bait and snack shop, both of which are seasonal operations and should not be depended upon. The launch facility has good piers and deep water, able to accommodate most boats, and there are restrooms.

VIRGINIA

• **COLONIAL BEACH:** This ramp accesses the Potomac River, about half way between D.C. and the Chesapeake. It's a double ramp, located in the town of Colonial Beach, on Rt 1156. Take Rt 205 into town, and when the road Y's, follow it to the right. The ramps will be on your right side.

• **SALUDA:** Small boats can use this single ramp to access the Rappahannock River, one and a half miles north of Saluda. Rt 618 ends at the facility. Boats 16' and under are best suited for this area. Take Rt 17 to Saluda, and Rt 618 splits off to the north.

• **MATTAPONI RIVER:** The town of West Point has a double-ramp facility that can handle boats suitable for the Mattaponi and upper York Rivers, right where the Mattaponi and Pamunkey join. The ramps are easily located, in the shadow of the Rt 33 bridge. Just take Rt 33 into town, and look on the northwestern side of the bridge in West Point.

• **WARE RIVER:** This single ramp can handle boats up to 19' or so, in the headwaters of the Ware River. It's located at the end of Rt 621, off of Rt 17 near Warehouse. There aren't any facilities here, but it's not a long run down the Ware to Mobjack Bay.

• **DEEP BOTTOM:** Use this double-ramp to access Deep Bottom on the James River. The ramps are located in Henrico at the end of Deep Bottom Rd, just off Kingsland Rd. The facility can handle boats appropriate for this stretch of the river, and there's plenty of parking, but this is a very popular area for catfish anglers so you should expect to wait in line to launch if you arrive on the late side.

• **NEWPORT NEWS:** In Huntington Park, the Newport News facility offers access to the lower James with a relatively short run to the Bay and the HRBT (Hampton Roads Bridge-Tunnel). It has six ramps that will handle most trailerable boats, and plenty of parking. Expect it to be busy but sufficient on weekends; arrive early to avoid backups. The facility is easy to find, as it's in the shadow of the James River Bridge, Rt 258, on the northwest side.

• **GREAT BRIDGE LOCKS PARK:** This ramp is used by anglers accessing the Hot Ditch and the Elizabeth River. There's no fee, and there is plenty of parking, but it's still a good idea to arrive early on sunny winter weekends when competition may be stiff. Take Battlefield Blvd to Locks Rd west, which ends at the park.

• **LYNNHAVEN BOAT RAMP:** This facility has four ramps that can handle boats of just about any sizes. It provides excellent access to the CBBT and the mouth of the Bay. Get there early during summer weekends to avoid waits, but there is plenty of parking and you should have no trouble finding a space.

There are also restrooms and changing areas. Launch fees are $5. Located under the Lesner Bridge on Piedmont Circle in Virginia Beach.

Eastern Shore Public Ramps

MARYLAND

• **ELK NECK STATE PARK:** Use this ramp to access the northern reaches of the Bay and the flats. Take Turkey Pt Rd to Thackery Point. There are restrooms, but they're only open seasonally. No permit is required.

• **CRUMPTON:** This ramp is good for relatively small boats and bass boats accessing the upper Chester River. A Queen Anne county permit is required and can be purchased at local tackle shops. Take Rt 290 to First Street and follow the sign to the ramp. There aren't any facilities, including bathrooms.

• **KENT NARROWS:** This double-ramp, located in the shadow of the new Kent Narrows Bridge, offers good access for boats of all sizes. A county permit is required and is not cheap—$25 for Maryland residents for the season or $10 for a single launch. The permit can be bought at local tackle shops. Take Rt 50 to the Kent Narrows Bridge, exit at the base of the bridge, and turn onto Main St that takes you over the old Kent Narrows Bridge. The ramp is at the base of the old bridge.

• **TUCKAHOE RIVER:** Go to Hillsboro and take Main St, turn left onto Maple Ave to access this small, single ramp. There are no facilities here and boats over 14' will not be able to use the ramp on a low tide. This one is best for canoes, car-toppers, and small aluminum boats.

• **MARTINAK STATE PARK:** This ramp accesses the upper Choptank and Watts Creek. It's a large ramp with a good pier and can accommodate most trailerable boats. Take Rt 404 to Denton, turn right at the brown sign for Martinak State Park, turn left at the park entrance 200 yards down the road, and follow the signs to the ramp.

• **WYE LANDING:** Boats up to 18' can use this facility, which also has seasonal boat rentals and a tackle shop, to access the Wye River. Follow Rt 662 to Wye Landing Lane, which ends at the boat ramp. During duck hunting season, the area should be avoided by anglers.

• **MADISON:** There is a little-used, old ramp on the side of the road in Madison, just past Church Creek that can be used to access the Little Choptank. Parking is very limited, but the ramp gets very little action. It's useable for boats up to 18'. No fee, no facilities. Just drive down Rt 16 and look along the right side of the road after passing through Church Creek.

• **HONGA RIVER:** This ramp can accommodate boats up to about 19'. When leaving the ramp area, be sure to drive right at the marker outside the creek as there's shallow water on either side. This ramp gives you good access to the Honga and the Chesapeake, if you run downriver then cut under the Hooper Island cut. There's plenty of parking, and a porta-pottie that should be avoided unless absolutely necessary. No fee or permit is necessary. Take Rt 335 to Hooper Island; the ramp is right alongside the road on the right, just before the bridge.

• **COULBOURN CREEK RAMP:** This is a large ramp and can take most trailerable boats, providing access to the big Annemessex River. There's good parking but on sunny weekends it's a good idea to arrive early, as the lot will occasionally fill to capacity. No fees, no facilities. Take Rt 413 towards Crisfield, turn right onto Charles Cannon Rd, then left onto Coulbourn Creek Rd.

• **CRISFIELD:** In the town of Crisfield there is a double-ramp with lots of parking. It sees a lot of action during the season, however, and you should arrive early or expect to wait before launching. Overflow parking along the road is okay. The ramps can take almost any size boat, and there is no fee. There are bathrooms and a fish cleaning station. Be advised that the bugs in this area are astonishingly fierce, and when using this ramp at sunset you will need bug repellent or you will regret ever being here. Follow Rt 413 into town, take the left at the Y just before the downtown area at Norris Harbor Drive. The road will take a 90-degree dogleg to the right, and the ramp is about ¼ mile down, on the right.

VIRGINIA

• **HARBORTOWN RAMP:** This double ramp can accommodate most Bay-worthy boats and provides easy Bay access near Pungoteague. Take 180 all the way to the end, and it dead-ends at the ramps.

• **CAPE CHARLES:** This facility has a quad-ramp that can handle most boats. It's located in Cape Charles, on the right off Rt 1103. This facility provides the closest access to the open Bay and the Old Plantation Light area.

• **KIPTOPEKE:** This is a large ramp that can handle most boats, but because of the exposure to the Bay, it can be very difficult to use. Only plan on launching here when there is an easterly breeze or little to no wind. On a west wind, it's at its worst. There is plenty of parking, and restrooms are available. It offers direct access to the Cement Ships, the Cabbage Patch and Latimer Shoal. Park fees are $3. Take Rt 13 to Rt 704 and follow the signs to the park.

Part II:
Tactics
and Tackle

CHUMMING

Chumming is one of the most popular forms of fishing on the Bay, and there's one simple reason: it works. Chumming will allow you to draw the fish right up to your boat, and at times you'll even be able to spot stripers and blues swirling behind your transom. The downside? It's messy and menhaden chum is smelly stuff. In fact, your better half may take serious offense to the smell on your clothes when you drop them in the laundry bin. Hey—it's a small price to pay for a hot bite.

The idea behind chumming is pretty simple: put ground bait fish into the water, to attract game fish. In the case of stripers, blues, and cobia, the fish most commonly chummed for in the Chesapeake, menhaden are the baitfish used. Stripers are by far and away the fish most commonly targeted by chummers, and this chapter is, therefore, dedicated to them. Chumming specifically for blues and cobia will be addressed separately, at the end of the chapter.

We should recognize the fact that there are some people out there who argue that chumming is not a good or "sporting" way to fish. One argument is that it conditions the fish to feed in certain areas (where people chum often). There's probably a kernel of truth to this theory; plenty of seasons we've seen large schools of fish remain in a specific area while chummers were present then disappear when the food supply was cut off, usually the result of a long stretch of rough weather that keeps all the chummers in port for an extended period of time. However, I am not convinced that this is a bad thing. Most of the fish in these large schools are undersized, and although they may be caught and released several times through the season, they are receiving a free meal ticket for all their troubles. No one can say for sure whether this is more or less harmful than a complete absence of chummers would be, but in either case, the fish get a benefit here, too.

The second argument usually heard against chumming: It's too easy, and thus is not sporting. Yet I've never met an angler who found it necessary to make it more difficult to catch fish. Plenty of chumming days are spent waiting, not catching, and during the spring trophy season it is in fact harder to take fish on chum than it is to catch them by trolling. So much for argument number two.

Chum Types

Just about every bait and tackle shop along the shores of the Chesapeake carries chum. Most offer it in one of three forms: frozen in a plastic bucket, frozen in a log wrapped in plastic and sealed in a net bag (these are often provided by Mikes' Bait, a commercial supplier to tackle shops), and frozen in a plastic bag. The plastic bucket is the easiest and least messy form of chum to use. Simply cut a few holes in the bucket, tie a rope to it, and hang it over the side. As the chum melts it will wash out of the holes, and provide a steady flow for two to four hours of fishing, depending on sea conditions and the size of the holes you cut in the bucket. On rough days, cut smaller holes or lengthen the line the bucket hangs from to extend your supply. On calm days, it may be necessary to grab the rope and shake it now and again, to keep the chum flowing steadily.

Keeping the flow steady is a key to chumming successfully. A heavy but interrupted chum slick will attract fish intermittently, while a meager but consistent flow will attract fish and hold them—sometimes for hours at a time. To attain this steady flow, it is usually necessary to start the day by setting a chum bucket on the deck to thaw as you run to the fishing grounds. When you arrive, cut three quarter-sized holes in the bottom of the bucket, three on the top and six along the sides. On rough days cut fewer or smaller holes, and on calm days make them larger or more numerous. The more your boat rocks and rolls with the wave action, the more the chum bucket will be jerked and shaken, releasing chum and encouraging melt-off. About 10 minutes after hanging the bucket over the side, watch it to be sure you're getting a sufficient flow. If your chum hasn't softened enough to run out yet, pull the top off of the bucket and rake a bait knife across the frozen contents to speed the process.

Tying on the bucket sounds simple enough, but I've learned from painful experience that you must tie the rope through both the top and the side of the bucket. Tie it to the top only, and the bucket may pull free and float away, leaving you with nothing but the top attached. Tie it to the bucket itself and the top may pop off when a big wave jerks the bucket, and your chum will float right out. On rough days, you should make the top double-secure by pushing a swivel clip through the top, then the side, and clipping it shut. What's the proper amount of rope to hang it with? Again, it depends to some degree on just how rough it is. On a glassy day you'll want to put out just enough rope to keep the bucket in the water, so that when your boat rocks on even the smallest waves it gets jerked partially out of the water. Keep an eye on it and if the flow seems lethargic, give the rope a few tugs every minute or two. On rough days you'll want to let out enough rope that the bucket stays submerged as your boat bounces, so the constant jerking doesn't wash away your chum in an hour. Remember to start with small holes in the bucket in rough weather; if it's not flowing quickly enough you can always cut more or larger holes, but if you cut too many and you're blasting through the chum supply, you can't close those holes back up.

Plastic-wrapped net-bag logs are another common form of chum found at Chesapeake bait and tackle shops. The usual way to rig them is to slide the frozen log out of the net bag, remove the plastic wrap, and slide it back into the net. (This will make a mess, as the mesh usually catches on the log and rips tiny bits free.) Then you can tie a rope to the net, and dangle it over the side. Don't use this method—trust me, sooner or later you will be watching your chum log float away. The net bags that come with these logs are not strong enough to handle the stress in any kind of seas and will rip where the rope is tied. It's a much better move to slide the log into a sturdy nylon chum bag (they're available at all the tackle shops, too). And, since the store-bought chum bags are larger than the net that comes with the log, it's usually not as messy to prep.

At stores that grind their own chum you may find the chum packaged in a plain plastic bag. While store-ground chum is usually fresher than the commercially supplied type, buying it in this form requires you to have a chum bag of your own. Again, you'll find this messier than the bucket method. Often the chum freezes over folds and bulges in the plastic bag, and you'll have to rip it out in shreds—making even more of a mess—or risk having it thaw out and release plastic bits into the Bay.

Very few stores carry fresh-ground chum, which is usually mixed with water and spooned over the side. While fresh-ground may attract more fish, in my experience the difference is negligible. Spooning the chum over the side requires constant attention and stopping to land or fight a fish can be enough to ruin the chum lines' consistency, so this is not going to be the favored method for most anglers.

If you've ever been chumming on a charter boat you're probably thinking right now, "But they ground chum on the spot on the charter, and charter boats use the most effective methods. If they ladled fresh ground fish on the charter, isn't that the best way to do it?" In the case of charters, yes, they usually do choose ladling fresh ground juice over hanging a frozen log or bucket. But charters also hold a few advantages over pleasure anglers when it comes to this method—they have two people aboard, the captain and mate, who pay constant attention to ensure the flow remains uninterrupted, and they spoon out massive amounts of chum using this method—often an entire bushel of menhaden in a day. It's both expensive and impractical for sport anglers to work with this amount of chum, and at some point the volume hits a diminishing return. Spooning out ten times as much chum may pull a few more fish in, but by no means does it attract ten times as many fish.

Of course, if you can find a supply of fresh menhaden, you have a grinder and the desire, you can grind it on the spot. Hand grinders can be purchased for about $150, (check out the Mr. Chummer by Fish-Ng Accessories, www.fish-ng.com) but using them is time consuming and a workout. In fact, I have suffered from chum-grinders' elbow on more than one occasion. Electric grinders are much easier to use, but are expensive and there aren't many suppliers of them. Chum Master makes several models that cost about $650 (www.chummaster.com). Both hand and electric grinders will turn your boat into a massive chum-mess, and extend cleanup time quite a bit. One other option is to use a device like the Chum Churn ($125 or so) that is essentially a PVC tube fitted with cutting blades. When you shake the tube violently, the blades chop up whatever is inside, which then oozes out of slits cut in the PVC. The device works well, but sometimes gets stuck on large fish heads. And after using one for about a month, the lower cap fell off as I shook it, allowing the blades to sink to the bottom of the Bay. Note that I had a prototype for a test-unit, and I would hope they've made some design changes since then, but buy one at your own risk. You could make a similar chum chopper easily enough, if you're handy with PVC, a welding torch, and a saw.

Chumming the Water Column

During the fall season most of the schoolies will be up near the surface, and that's where you'll want your chum. If you want to try for larger fish, however, or if you're chumming for spring trophies, you're going to have to use a few tricks to get chum down deep where the larger fish are lurking. Note—it is true that the majority of spring trophies caught trolling are hooked in the upper water column, nowhere near the bottom. Yet every spring trophy I know of caught on chum came from a bait set dead on the bottom. I have no reasonable explanation for this strange contradiction, but have tried fishing chum baits at mid-depth and the surface during the spring trophy season time and time again, without ever getting a strike. I can't tell you why it is, but the fact remains: spring trophies caught on baits while chumming come from the bottom, period.

There are several ways to get your chum deep. Weighting a regular chum bucket is not one of them. The frozen chum possesses quite a bit of buoyancy, and you'd need a pound of lead to start it sinking. If there's any kind of current, that will pick it right back up and pull it behind the boat, higher and higher as the current increases. Luckily, many tackle shops carry small mesh cages with weighted bottoms. You'll have to chop your frozen chum into small pieces to fit it into these cages but the effort is worthwhile; they sink much better than a bucket and by adding six to 10 ounces of lead you can get one to stay on bottom in a two knot current, in 50' of water. Unfortunately these bait cages deteriorate quickly and are only good for a season or two, but they only cost $6 or $7, and a new one can be purchased each spring without breaking the bank.

Sand balls are another way to sink chum, but they are a bit more work-intensive. You'll need the chum thawed ahead of time to use sand balls, and you'll need to carry a bucket of sand on the boat. When you're ready to fish, put some sand in one hand, place a golf ball sized lump of chum on top, get some more sand, and mold it into a ball around the chum. Pack it firmly, then drop it over the side. The sand will weight it down enough to fall quite deep before it all disburses.

The third method of sinking chum is to place a handful into a brown paper bag, put your hook through the bag a couple of times, and lower your rig to the bottom. When it hits, a few strong tugs will rip the bag free of the hook, allowing it to open and the chum to drift out. As with sand balls, this is labor intensive and messy.

The fourth and least-often seen method of sinking chum is to attach a tiny chum pot or a film canister with holes poked in it to your rig, usually where it attaches to the main line. The pot or canister is, of course, stuffed with chum, and releases it close to your bait. This method is effective and isn't as messy or as much work as sand balls or the bag method. On the downside, the tiny chum container will usually run out pretty quickly. To keep it actively disbursing chum you'll be forced to reel up your line and re-fill the canister every 15 minutes or so.

I strongly recommend using the weighted chum cage method when you want to keep your chum deep. It's simpler, easier, and less messy than the other options. However, there's one caution: when you hook into a large, uncontrollable fish, make sure someone pulls the chum pot immediately. Otherwise, you risk tangling your fishing line around the chum cage line— and that spells disaster.

Thickening the Chum Slick

There are several methods savvy Bay anglers use to "thicken" their chum slicks, and draw in more fish. One common way to enhance a surface slick is to add a menhaden oil drip bag into the mix. The drip bag, similar to the common IV bag seen in hospitals, will allow tiny drops of menhaden oil to dribble out at a slow, constant rate. During the summer and fall seasons when stripers and blues are schooled and feeding in the upper water column, this gives your chum slick an effective boost. In the spring season, and when putting your baits down deep in search of a lunker, the drip bag will have little or no effect because the oil it releases floats and disburses on the surface, only.

Dropping chunks is another way to turn your chum slick into a super slick. Chunks are commonly thumbnail-sized bits of sliced menhaden, a handful of which are tossed overboard every few minutes. Since these chunks are larger than the ground bits in your chum slick, they sink and drift at a different rate and will expand the influence of your chum slick. Tossing chunks is particularly effective when the current is very strong, and your chum doesn't have time to sink much before it's whisked away. To get the best effect out of chunks, be sure to vary the part of the boat you toss them from. Put one handful over the port side; the next over the starboard side; toss the next batch up near the bow, and so on.

Artificial chum is also used by some anglers on the Bay. There are several varieties including Glory Hole and Team Berley (both are available through Outdoor World, www.basspro.com) as well as oils such as Menhaden Milk. All seem to have some limited value; none are an effective full-time replacement for ground menhaden. My favorite of the bunch is Team Berley. It doesn't seem to attract any more fish than the other chums do, but it does put stripers into a feeding mood when they might not otherwise be in one. While testing this product for review in *Boating Magazine* I found that the window of tide during which spring trophy stripers would take menhaden baits on bottom was extended by about 25% when Team Berley was mixed into the chum line. When predicted feeding time (more on this later) was from 1:00 to 2:30 P.M., for example, the fish would start hitting at 12:45 P.M. and wouldn't stop until 2:45 P.M. According to the manufacturer Team Berley has enzymes cooked into the chum logs that trigger a feeding response from many sportfish. I can't speak to the accuracy of the claim, but the stuff does seem to work for this specific purpose.

Spring Trophy Chumming for Striped Bass

Ask virtually any charter captain, inveterate angler or commercial hook-and-liner on the Chesapeake Bay, and they'll all tell you the same thing: you can't chum for early spring trophies. Traditional theory holds that the spring fish aren't attracted to chum, and trolling is the only way to take them until mid- or late May. I take delight in proving this false by taking anglers chumming for trophies on opening day every spring, usually with great success.

I absolutely positively guarantee you that if you put in your time you can and will catch stripers chumming in the early spring. Big fish, too, usually in the 36" to 44" class. Larger cows do not seem to be caught with this method, but neither do throw-backs—better than 90% of the hook-ups using this style of fishing will turn out to be keeper fish. It is just as true that on most days, trollers will catch higher numbers of fish. Many days they will have double the catch, although they will also be catching a much higher ratio of undersized fish.

While spring trophies do seem to respond to chum, they do not stay in a chum line the way schooled fish will. However, I've experimented with fishing baits without chum, and the number of strikes definitely declines. These fish seem to act sort of like a married man who sees a gorgeous woman—he'll hesitate and look, then continue on his way. Same goes for the trophy fish. You might get them interested in your chum slick for a minute or two, but you won't be able to hold them at the boat as you can with schoolies.

So: if trollers catch more fish, why bother chumming? For many anglers, the answer is simply to troll through June. But some anglers do not get excited by spring trolling. Heavy tackle, large lures (particularly umbrella rigs) and line weights, and the constant forward motion of the boat means that reeling in a 40" fish can feel like cranking up a cinder block. Once the fish is hooked there just isn't much going on in the way of a fight. Catching the same fish on light tackle—say, 12 lb test on a medium/light spinning rod, with one ounce of weight—requires skill, luck, and technique. When you boat a fish after a 20-minute fight during which you were the one who was out-gunned, not the fish, it's much more of a thrill.

What about those who say that chumming is harmful because you gut-hook more fish than you would while trolling? While this is true, and spring chumming should only be practiced by anglers who plan to harvest fish, there is an environmental upside: spring trophies taken on chum rarely have roe. I cannot explain the scientific reason why, but less than one in 10 trophies taken chumming over the mud has roe, while many of the trophies taken trolling have roe. Maybe it's because post-spawn fish feed in such a way that they take menhaden baits off the bottom more often than pre-spawn fish, or perhaps males and females follow a slightly different migratory pattern. Whatever the reason might be, check the fish you catch yourself, and you'll find that it's true. One more plus side—since you catch fewer throw-backs, there's less danger of accidentally harming a fish that you'll be releasing. And let's not forget that (at least with current regulations, which do not seem likely to change any time soon) you can only keep one fish per person per day, anyway. It's not like you're trying to catch a dozen keeper fish. So you're not really giving up all that much by opting to chum, versus trolling, and this is a "clean" way to fish while creating a minimum of negative impact on the fish stocks.

If you do opt to chum for spring stripers, you will be struck by how very different it is than chumming for schoolie fish. Baiting up, for starters. As mentioned earlier, the trophies you hook will come from baits set dead on the bottom. Jigged baits go untouched. Drifted baits are ignored. Motion on your line is not good, contrary to common fishing theory. Make sure that at all times, your baits are sitting dead on the mud. The chum pot should also be kissing the bottom, hung just a foot or two above mud so the motion of the boat helps dissipate the chum. Baits should be large, either chunks or fillets almost as big as your fist. The baits will seem very large in comparison to the hook used for a spring trophy chumming rig (see chapter 12, Standard Bay Rigs), but don't worry—these fish have very large mouths, and can inhale baits this size in one gulp, often without even noticing that little hook. When using a fillet, put the hook in through the meat side and out through the skin side, so the hook point is exposed. When using a chunk, go in through one side of the back section and out the other, making sure your hook penetrates skin going both in and out of the bait. You'll note that the shank of the hook is pretty exposed baiting up with this method. Hide it by cutting some dime-sized chunks of menhaden, and threading them up the shank before you put on the main bait. Better yet, one of my favorite tricks is to thread the menhaden's guts onto the shank (make sure the hook penetrates the hard gizzard, or the guts will wash away fairly quickly).

Next comes one of the most important parts of chumming for trophies: hold your rod over the side, allow the bait to sink for a few inches, then quickly drag it through the water. If it shows any tendency to spin, pull it off the hook and re-bait it. Expect that half of the fillets and one quarter of the chunks you bait up with will be spinners. It can get very frustrating when you bait up once, twice, even a third time, and your bait still spins. But don't shrug and drop it to the bottom. Even when using the highest quality ball-bearing swivels, a spinning chum bait will twist your line and often makes a tangle.

Quality of baits can be categorized as follows: Fresh is best, frozen is okay, and refrozen or frozen over a month ago is practically hopeless. Unlike the chum itself, the baits' condition is very important. Fresh menhaden will out-fish the frozen stuff any day of the week. Unfortunately, it's hard to find a reliable supply of fresh menhaden. You'll have to check out each and every shop within a reasonable drive, and pray that one of them will carry fresh menhaden. (Anglers' on Rt 50 near Annapolis is the only one in the entire Baltimore/Washington metropolitan area I know of that regularly carries fresh menhaden.)

Let's assume you can't find fresh menhaden, because most anglers won't be able to. Those that can locate such a shop are still likely to walk in one day and find out they're out of fresh. So, what next? Go for frozen menhaden. It should be packaged in a plastic bag, preferably the Zip-Lock type. There should be little air in the bag, and there should not be much frost on the menhaden. Stay away from those packaged on those yellow or blue foam plastic trays, similar to the trays meats are packaged with in the grocery store. These are mass-packed by a commercial bait house, and are usually months old by the time you pull them out of the bait shops' freezer. Crushed or smashed menhaden, and worst of all yellow sections of meat and fins, are bad. (Even in deep freeze menhaden will rot, particularly if there is poor air flow around the bulk packages of bait. The yellowing flesh indicates such rot, and you won't like the nasty smell as it thaws—neither will the fish.)

Thawed baits that were previously frozen are not as good as frozen ones, because it's nearly impossible to cut them without smushing the meat, tearing the skin or otherwise ruining the bait. Frozen, thawed, then refrozen baits are the worst; they usually show some rot, the meat turns to mush the moment it starts to thaw, and the skin is so delicate you can rip it just by staring really hard.

Once you've baited up with a quality chunk of menhaden and dropped to the bottom, you need to decide if you're going to fish with the rod in hand, or in the holder. Rods in holders should be left on freespool with the clicker on or should be rigged with a hair trigger so that fish can take line freely. Held rods should be kept in freespool (or open bailer) at all times, with a finger keeping the line from spilling out. The moment you detect the slightest sign of a bite, drop the tip and feed the fish line. While you will sometimes get that freight-train strike, even the biggest trophies often slurp in a menhaden bait so gently that you can barely detect it. Allow these fish plenty of time to take that bait—between five and ten seconds of uninterrupted eating before you tighten up the line and attempt a hook-set is appropriate. As stated earlier, you'll gut-hook a lot of fish, which, since virtually all hook-ups will be keepers, is just fine when you're taking your one per day. But remember, if you plan on catch-and-release fishing, this is not an appropriate method. If you limit out when chumming for spring trophies, quit fishing or change tactics! This holds true even when fishing with circle hooks; I recognize the fact that this runs counter to everything we read and hear, but from what I've seen, circle hooks will still end up in the fishes' guts with regularity (maybe half as often as with J hooks) when chumming for spring stripers.

One fascinating aspect of chumming for spring trophies is the fact that their feeding habits run like clockwork, according to the tide. A decade of graphing each and every trophy caught chumming on my boat and my fathers' boat, and whenever possible friends' boats, has shown a regularity that will allow you to predict when the stripers will hit (if they hit), each and every day. I use a computer program called "Tides and Currents" (available for about $100 in any good boating supply store; it is also included on many electronic cartography chips and may already be available on your chartplotter) to track this data by putting the tide in a bar-graph form, and plotting each fish caught. What I found is that 80% of the trophies came during the last three bars of the tide, which represents the last hour and a half of the tidal flow. The incoming tide holds a slight advantage over the outgoing, but both are productive. 10% came during a dead slack tide, and with only two exceptions, these fish were taken in a single season (1998). The remaining 10% were what I call "sun bites" that came during sunup or sunset, transitional periods of low light that—I'm sure you already know—are two of the hottest times to fish any day of the year. When the sun bite and the tide bite coincide, you have the best case scenario for loading the boat with chum-caught trophies.

Determining when the hot period will be is easy. Just put your tide program into the bar-graph format and locate the peak tide. Then highlight the last three bars back. The approximate time can be matched to the bars by looking along the bottom of the graph, and you've got your hot period determined. That's it. Remember, though, that these tide programs, like all tide charts, are "prediction" based. The actual peak of the tide can change as a result of winds, currents, pressure systems, or in the case of the upper Bay, a large release of water from Conowingo Dam. In fact, when chumming for stripers on the upper Bay water releases from the dam have a pretty major impact on the effectiveness of this tactic as well as others. It can turn the water muddy in a flash, delay or speed tide timing, increase the outgoing tidal flow, and decrease the incoming tidal flow. Unfortunately, there's not really much we can do about it, short of running farther south to fish. Luckily, the days that are seriously affected each spring can usually be counted on one hand.

If the stripers will only feed during these relatively brief periods of the tide, what do you do the rest of the time? Either switch to trolling, or chase the tide. The day before you fish, determine the hot times at a series of spots running north to south (on an outgoing tide) or south to north (on an incoming tide). Start at the southernmost or northernmost spot, fish through the hot period, then pull the anchor and run up to the next spot. You should be able to catch up to and pass the period of tide that produces fish, re-anchor, and catch the hot tidal period for a while longer. When the prime time passes, pull up and run again, and so on. Using this run-and-gun tactic, you can usually hit three good spots for three hot tidal periods in a single day—unless you limit out first, of course.

Location is a key factor when it comes to chumming. Although locating your boat in the strike zone is important when chumming for spring trophies, it's not nearly as difficult or tedious to find exactly the right spot as it can be when fishing for schooled fish. This is because the places you'll want to chum are large featureless areas, not pinpoint structures. You've probably heard before that these spring fish are migrating into the Bay to spawn, then they migrate back out of the Bay. These fish are, for the most part, in travel mode. You don't want or need to be anchored directly over structure because these fish are not stopping and orienting to it. Instead, you want to anchor over mud flats. I've found that many of the spring trophies caught at this time of year have crushed manoes clam shells in their bellies. I cannot swear that manoes live in the mud at the depths you'll be chumming at, but either they do or, the fish you catch using this method are moving over the mud flats from an area where they eat manoes. Either way, you'll want a mud flat ranging from 28' to 46' deep. Yes, this is a very large range. However, you'll trim it down some when you arrive over the flat you choose to fish. Most of these flats, particularly the one west of Love Point and the one east of Thomas Point, have very slow, gradual slopes. In both cases, you'll need to travel a good half-mile to get a 10' drop.

When preparing to locate your spot for chumming a mud flat, slow to a hunting speed of 6 or 8 knots when you reach a depth of 28'. Then keep a close eye on the fishfinder as you putt along into the high 40s. Yes, it will take a while to do so, so make sure you build an extra hour or so into your planned setup time before the period of hot tide begins. What you're looking for is the area of depth that has the most baitfish. You'll see scattered pods of bait and an occasional large mark, but don't expect the fishfinder screen to blank out on massive schools of fish. More likely, you'll notice that a particular range varying 5' or so seems to have more marks than the surrounding depths. This is where you'll want to anchor up. Make sure that on the first few trips of the spring you search all of the potential depth ranges thoroughly, and by your third trip or so you'll know just what depth to start fishing at. Bear in mind that the hot depth zone will vary from week to week, as the water warms up. If you only fish on weekends, plan on searching the range before you set up each and every trip.

Chumming Schoolies

Chumming for average size stripers in the late spring, summer, and fall is an entirely different ball game than chumming for trophies in the spring. Baits, for starters, should be scaled down to fillets or chunks the size of a matchbook. As when chumming for trophies, it is beneficial to cover the shank of the hook with a couple of small chunks of meat. Again, menhaden guts are effective for this purpose. Also as with spring chumming, you should check each and every bait for spinning before letting it out. Fresh menhaden are still better than frozen, but bait quality is a lot less imperative when chumming for schoolies since you tend to get shots at a much higher number of fish.

Anchoring over structure and boat positioning are far more important than they are during spring trophy season. Fish are usually holding tight to structure, although some years they will camp out over mud flats for a week here and a week there. To effectively chum these fish, you'll want to find a hump, ledge, trough, or bar and anchor on the upcurrent edge. This way, the tide will sweep your chum line over and around the structure. If, for example, you have a hump that is 20' at the top and is surrounded by 30', then you'll want to motor upcurrent of the hump, drop anchor, set it, and let out line until your boat sits in 26' to 23' of water, over the upward-sloping bottom.

In some cases chumming for schoolies will put you in competition with a large number of boats, all putting out their own chum lines. Particularly at popular spots within shooting distance of major metropolitan areas, things can get a bit tight. At the Hill, for example, you may see 200 boats all anchored up close together, with trollers meandering through the pack (which most chummers consider a very impolite thing to do, by the way). There are a few ways to deal with this type of situation. First off, you can simply go somewhere else. If that's not an acceptable option, make sure you leave the dock before sunrise; few anglers will arrive before 7:00 A.M., and the bulk of the

pack usually rolls in between 8:00 A.M. and 8:30 A.M. If you're forced into join-
ing an already-present pack of chummers, make sure you set up downcurrent
of the pack. This will enable you to take advantage of the tail end of the packs'
chum, and sometimes, you can anchor downcurrent of a large pack and catch
fish without even releasing your own chum.

Unlike chumming for spring trophies, with the schooled fish you will often
catch more fish at or near the surface. Putting a chum pot on bottom is not absolutely necessary, although it is still advantageous simply because you're covering more of the water column with chum. Getting the fish to bite near the
surface can be accomplished with the simple "set-and-sit" method. This is how
most people chum, and it does work: They set out a line with little or no weight,
30' to 50' back, right on the surface. A second line goes out with ½ oz of weight
and is set the same distance back just below surface. A third line gets an ounce
and hangs at mid-depth, and a forth line is rigged with enough weight to stay at
or near the bottom. All four rods are placed in holders, and the anglers sit while
they wait for a strike. This is simple and somewhat effective but very lazy fishing tactics. If you want to boost your catch rate by a good 25%, use these two
tricks: Number one: do not set your surface line. Instead, put it in freespool and
dangle the bait right next to the chum bucket. Now give a few tugs on the
bucket's rope, so a nice cloud of chum flows out. At the same time, release all
tension on your surface bait and allow it to drift back and sink naturally, in that
cloud of chum. Strip line from your reel and keep everything slack, so the bait is
not pulled out of the chum cloud by tension from the line. Watch the slack line
as your bait moves back, and when you see the line jerk or suddenly change direction, set the hook. If nothing strikes after you've drifted the bait back 100' or
so, reel in and start over. Any day of the week you'll catch a lot more fish using
this method than you will with a rod in the holder.

Trick number two: as you already know, larger fish will often come from
baits set on bottom. You should also know that in order to effectively fish the
bottom you'll need weight, and if you set a rod untended in the holder, you
won't be able to feed fish line upon the initial bite. Fish that strike the bottom
line are therefore likely to feel that weight and dump the bait. You can fix this
problem, however, at least whenever the current is moving. Use an egg sinker,
larger than necessary to hold bottom. I like to use at least three ounces for this
purpose, and usually four is better. Set it on bottom, then let out line as you
sweep your rod tip forward. Keeping minimum tension on the line, let your tip
go back slowly. The current will pull on your bait, and take line out through
the egg sinker. (This is why you want an oversized weight; smaller sinkers
will get pushed back by the current.) Repeat the process two or three times until you have let 10' to 15' of line out through the egg sinker.

When a fish takes a chumming bait it is usually swimming into the current. Since it will be swimming towards your weight when it grabs the bait, it

will continue swimming for several seconds before feeling any unusual resistance, thanks to that length of extra line out beyond your egg sinker. This will give it a moment or two to eat and get that bait all the way into its mouth; as long as your reel is set to freespool (clicker on) or on a hair trigger, if you get this extra line out beyond your weight your hook-up rate will soar.

There are a few other peculiarities to chumming every Bay angler should know about. The most important is to use monofilament, not superline or braid, when chumming. Superlines are great for some situations, but chumming is not one of them. For some reason superlines change the sink rate and seem to cut the water better and sink faster than monofilament. They also have greatly increased sensitivity, and although this means you feel the fish bite sooner than you would with mono, it means they feel you sooner, too.

Casting chum rigs is another bad move—there's no better way to quickly get your bait far away from the chum line (and the fish) than casting your rig away from the boat. Using lures is another no-no. You will get the occasional strike, but fish in a menhaden chum slick usually want to eat more menhaden, not go chasing after some alternative fish zipping around in the chum.

What about using razor clams, or other popular non-menhaden baits? This works sometimes, but rarely if ever will your catch rate actually increase. Often razors will not be as effective; sometimes they will be as effective, but never has anyone proven them to be more effective than a nice, fresh chunk of menhaden. Note—in years past anglers used to chum with manoes clams, razor clams, and sometimes grass shrimp. Will these techniques work today? I'm sure the easy answer is yes. However, in today's world they are simply cost prohibitive. You'd have to spend $150 to get enough manoes or shrimp to keep a chum line going all day.

As usual, there's a glaring exception to the rule: live baits do often out-fish cut menhaden in a chum line. Three to five inch menhaden, spot and white perch are all good live baits; when using perch clip the sharp dorsal spines off to increase their effectiveness. On a dead or very slow tide, clip off one pectoral fin of any live baitfish to make it swim erratically. (In a strong current, clipping a fin will cause the fish to die more quickly, as it can't swim into the moving water effectively.) To fill the livewell with perch or spot you usually will need to bait a bottom rig with very small hooks and baits, and catch them the day before you go after the bigger fish. Menhaden can be caught in a cast net. Go up to brightly lighted piers or bridges in four to ten feet of water just before sunrise, and you should have no problem gathering a dozen or so in a couple of good casts from August through October. Later in the year casting in 10' to 15' of water on points and bars in the rivers produces livies, but they will be much harder to find in large numbers. Also take note that when bluefish are present in large numbers, using live baits is pretty much impossible, as they will bite the fish in half much of the time.

Chumming for Cobia

Cobia chumming really isn't all that different from chumming for stripers or blues, but there are a few tactics you'll want to change. First off, as with spring stripers, put your chum and your baits down low. You should always keep out a line or two higher in the water column, but the majority of feeding a cobia does is near the bottom. Yes, you will sometimes spot cobia right on the surface; these fish are usually not feeding actively and it can be pure torture to cast to them time and time again, only to watch them ignore your lure or bait. Speaking of bait—with cobia, live baits are much more effective than cut baits. (If you're forced to use cut baits for cobe so be it but make sure they are fresh and fist-sized). Spot, small bluefish, and menhaden are all good choices, but the king of cobia baits is live eels. Rig them just as you would for striper eeling, and set them out on a hair trigger or freespool with the clicker on. Give the cobia a good five-count before setting the hook. There are some other peculiarities to cobia, but these will be covered in part III: chapter 17, Cobia.

The other difference you'll need to note when chumming for cobia is boat location. Cobia tend to travel around in small pods, and these pods tend to be found in the same general vicinity. There's no way to predict, year to year, just where the hottest zones will be for cobia. You'll need to ask around at tackle shops and keep an eye on fishing reports to track the current cobia hot spots. And don't worry quite as much about anchoring right on the edges of sharp drops and humps. More often than not cobia will be found near shoals and ledges (Latimer Shoal and the Cabbage Patch are the two most famous for cobia fishing) and often the better catches will come from on top of these shoals in the 15' to 25' range, as opposed to the dropping edges.

Chumming at rockpiles, such as at the CBBT (Chesapeake Bay Bridge-Tunnel), can also be effective for cobia although most anglers fishing for cobia here will be sight-casting to them. Again, remember that cobia on the surface are not active feeders. Usually they need to be teased into eating with a wriggling eel or multiple casts of a jig. But if you spot some near a rockpile and they won't respond to surface casting, it may justify an attempt at chumming there—later in the day after the tide has switched, and the cobia have headed back down deep. Also take note that cobia can sometimes be sighted under large markers, flotsam, and sea turtles. For some reason, cobia following sea turtles often seem to be in more of a feeding mood than those found under static items. I have heard (but cannot confirm) the theory that cobia follow the turtles to snatch stunned baitfish from the tentacles of jellyfish, which the sea turtles are feeding on. It sounds reasonable, and in any case, usually the fish you spot under turtles will bite.

Chumming for Blues

This type of chumming does not require a lot attention to details. Find a drop or a hump, put some chum over the side, and if blues are in the area they will usually flock to your baits. One big difference between bluefish and striper or cobia chumming: you'll need to use wire leader. This stuff used to be a pain in the neck, but recent advances in wire leaders have made life a bit easier. Tyger leaders (www.tygerleader.com) are made of micro-braided stainless steel coated in nylon, and you can actually tie knots in them just like mono. American Fishing Wire Titanium Tooth Proof is also knotable, though a little less so.

When chumming for blues, forget about using live bait for two reasons: number one, it's simply not necessary. Blues are eating machines, and they won't hesitate to take a chunk of bait. Secondly, when you do use live baits, bluefish have an uncanny ability to bite the front or back half of the fish off, and leave you with a head or a tail.

One more note about chumming for blues: don't bother with bottom lines. They will not produce larger fish, as blues of all sizes will zoom up and down through the water column eating everything they can find, anyway.

TROLLING

Trolling is undoubtedly one of the most effective ways to catch large numbers of fish on the Chesapeake Bay. The concept is simple—drive your boat at a low rate of speed, while trailing multiple lures. In practice, however, trolling is actually pretty complex. There are many variables to keep track of—many of which change with a shift in the wind or tide—and many different styles of trolling. We'll first divide them into light tackle trolling and heavy tackle trolling.

Light Tackle Trolling

Let's look at light tackle trolling first, because it's a lot simpler than heavy tackle trolling. Mainly, this is because you won't be dealing with vast water depths when trolling light gear. It simply can't be accomplished, because of the extreme weights necessary to overcome your line's drag through the water. In general think of light tackle trolling as taking place in 30' or less of water, with the one exception being when fish are breaking water, since in this scenario they can be caught right on the surface.

Most light tackle trolling takes place in Bay tributaries, again because of the depth restrictions. It's a great tactic to use when the wind blows too strongly to get out on the open Bay, and you're limited to protected water. Any spinning or conventional tackle rated between 8 and 20 lb is just fine for this type of fishing.

Boat speed should be minimal for light tackle trolling. Even when you're towing a 3" plug, 4 mph will put a lot of bend into a light or light/medium action spinning rod. Idle speed will be best for most boats, and those that have a minimum speed greater than 4 mph will have to slow themselves down. This can be accomplished by tying a 5 gallon bucket to a mooring line, cleating it off in the stern, and dragging it behind the boat. You can also shift the boat in and out of gear, but this will take a toll on your transmission.

Lures used for light tackle trolling run across the spectrum. Generally speaking, diving or swimming plugs are a good bet because they'll get below the surface with no added weight. Rat-L-Traps and similar plugs, Manns'

Stretch 12 or Stretch 15s, Rapala Husky Jerks, and similar lipped plugs are all good choices for trolling in Chesapeake tributaries for stripers, blues, and weakfish. In my experience, Rat-L-Traps prove to be the most reliable producers. If your gear is heavy enough to add weight or to pull a heavy leadhead, bucktails dressed with a pork rind or twister tail are also effective trolling baits. When pulling these or similar lures, however, you need to be sure you have sufficient weight and are moving slow enough to keep the lure down near the bottom.

Most of the time you won't need to use heavy leaders when trolling these lures with light gear. You can tie the lure directly to the main line, or tie to a swivel clip and clip on the lure. One exception: when lots of snapper blues are around, you'll have some bite-offs trolling without leaders. A 6" or 12" trace of wire may discourage a few stripers from striking, but will be necessary.

Since most light tackle trolling takes place in tributaries, and because you'll keep moving the whole time, you'll need to identify large areas of structure rather than pinpoint bumps or holes. Usually, the main river channel edges are the ticket. You'll also find that long edges that parallel the main-stem Bay shoreline and river mouths are good areas to try trolling along.

A common spread for this type of trolling is usually between four and six lines. Two lines with lures that dive to similar depths are placed on either side of the boat, then two more that dive a bit deeper or a bit shallower are placed on either side. Avoid running two lines with lures that run at similar depths on the same side of the boat, or you'll spend a lot of time dealing with tangles. Many light reels don't hold the amount of line that you'd usually want to set out when trolling. As a result, lure distance behind the boat will often be dictated by line capacity. Let out line until half of the spool is gone, then set the rod into the holder. Drags should be set light; the stress of being pulled through the water will stretch your line, and when a fish hits, a tight drag can lead to break-offs. As a rule of thumb, you'll want to set your drags loose enough so that (once the lure is deployed) when you sweep the rod quickly from stern to bow, the drag just barely clicks.

The most exciting opportunity for light tackle trolling comes when the fish are on the surface, breaking water in a feeding frenzy. Many anglers will motor up to the school and cast and retrieve their lures. This is usually fine, and some would consider it more fun than trolling around the school. It also allows for the possibility of jigging your lures below the breaking fish to find trout. However, as often as not the school of breaking fish will get spooked and disappear right about when you reach casting distance, only to pop up a few hundred yards away five minutes later. Usually in this situation you'll only get in one or two effective casts before being forced to move and chase the school again. This is the time to start trolling those casting lures.

Any lure you would throw to the breaking fish—bucktails, swimming plugs, feather jigs, or spoons—can be trolled slowly around the breaking fish. Just cast as far as possible behind the boat, let out line for another 10 seconds for good measure, then circle the breaking fish. Don't drive right through the school, because this is a sure-fire way to push down the fish and end the feeding frenzy. Instead try to keep your boat on the fringes of the fray. This is also a good situation to break out a heavy rod or two, rig up with several ounces of weight, and drag a line down 25' or 30' deep—that's often where the lunkers will be hiding when schoolies are busting the surface.

Heavy Tackle Trolling

Like chumming, heavy tackle trolling needs to be divided into two main categories by season: spring trolling and summer/fall trolling. As the vast majority of trolling that takes place in the Chesapeake targets striped bass, again the information offered here will be mostly targeted to that species. Specific tactics and changes in the basic trolling techniques for other species commonly trolled for (Spanish mackerel, bluefish, and flounder) will be covered in the chapters addressing those species.

Spring trolling is sometimes described as "collision fishing." This is a pretty good way to think of it. You won't be trolling along structure or breaks, water depths will vary greatly, and fish will for the most part be scattered. There is one common factor, however, in the location of the fish being caught: they will come from the upper section of the water column, most from 15' to 35'. Water depths these fish are found in range from 35' to over 100' and they can be caught just about anywhere in the main-stem Bay where you find these depths. The spring fish are migrating in and out of the Bay and into the tributaries to spawn, with the vast majority doing so in the Susquehanna. As mentioned earlier, they really aren't interested in finding a good structural habitat and feeding. You can't plan on where they will be, so you simply troll around until one of your lures collides with one of those fish.

To effectively target the trophies, you want to pull a spread of at least six lines so you can cover the top 35' of water with lures, with two running 15' down, two running 20' to 25' down, and two running 30' to 35' down. Capable anglers will drag 8 lines, really ambitious ones pull 10, and most charters and others working on a professional level pull 12 or 14. Bottom line: the more you can saturate the productive depths with lures, the more likely you are to have a fish run into one.

Lures used for spring trolling are most commonly variations of large bucktails dressed with plastic shad or twister tails, including parachutes and gang rigs known as umbrella rigs. Some anglers, particularly those in the southern reaches of the Bay, like to also use very large swimming plugs like the Manns' Stretch 25 or Stretch 30. These big lures and gang rigs are large, heavy, and feel like a ton of bricks on the end of the line—with or without a fish attached. This, plus the fact that you'll be weighting some down with additional lead, means that they require very stout tackle, 40 lb to 50 lb class line, conventional reels, and broomstick-stiff rods are the norm.

Whether you're pulling umbrellas, bucktails, or any other lure, one of your main goals must be to know where your lures are. As a general rule of thumb, use the "Rule of Fives." At 5 mph, with 50 lb test line, 5 oz of weight, and 50' of line out, your lure will run at about 5'. So, if you have a tandem rig with two 5 oz bucktails attached, let out 100' of line and your lure will be running at about 20'. This rule goes out the window when you're pulling gang lures that have increased water resistance, or lipped lures that dig down through the water column. And naturally, current, wind, lure size, and sea conditions will all conspire to prove this rule untrue the rest of the time. Part of being a good angler is recognizing this fact and constantly adjusting your lines to make up for a combination of these factors. If, for instance, you're facing a 2½ mph current and your GPS tells you you're doing 5 mph, that means your lures are being hit by the amount of water pressure that a 7½ mph current would produce. Your rigs, expected to be at 20', are now running 15'. Take note of this fact and drop speed, or let out another 50' of line, to get your lures where they belong.

Your spread of trolling lines should be staggered to minimize tangling. A trick some anglers use to maximize their spread is the use of side-planer boards. These are attached to a heavy line and cleated to the boat; as they are dragged through the water, they run out to the side, allowing the angler to run a rigger clip out on the planer line, and get another pair of lures (one on each side) into the spread. Unless you're a real pro, I do not recommend planer boards. They are cumbersome, they flip over often in rough seas, and they cause tangles. They will account for a few extra bites, but usually not enough to be worth all the trouble. Unfortunately, outriggers aren't very effective for this purpose, either, because the amount of weight on spring trolling rigs is too much for outrigger clips to hold. If you tighten them down far enough to keep a grip on 10 oz of lead being dragged along at 5 mph, then half the time they won't release even when a 20 lb striper hits.

The common spring recreational trolling rig should consist of at least two umbrellas, one set 100' and one set 150' behind the boat. The next two lines should be tandem rigs, differing by at least 2 oz in total weight so they run at slightly different depths. The remaining two lines should be Stretches, twin-hook spreader bars like the Billy Bar, or a mix. If you can get out additional lines, umbrellas are your best meat-gathering implement. When you're limited to a small spread stick with the basic colors—chartreuse and white. Yellow and pink are good too and if you can get out additional lines, experiment with new colors, but time and experience will prove that chartreuse and white account for the lion's share of the fish.

Note that I've used the 5 mph speed as an example several times when referring to spring trolling. In fact this is on the fast side, particularly early in the season, but is good to use as an example because overall it's a pretty good average speed. You'll have to make a judgment as to specific boat speed each time you fish, because you'll want to vary it according to conditions. Early on when water temperatures might be in the mid-40s go as slow as you can stand it; 3 mph is not too slow. When the water hits the upper 40s, 4 mph is good. In the 50s, 4 to 5 mph is appropriate. In the summer months the 6 mph range is not too fast, especially if you want to also have a shot at attracting Spanish mackerel that like a bait moving quickly through the water.

Remember that these speeds refer to speed through the water, not speed over ground. If you're facing a stiff current and you open up the throttles a bit to increase speed into the appropriate range, your lures will act as though they are being pulled at the combined speed of boat and current. Hint: if you're not really comfortable deciding how much you need to adjust your engine rpm and boat speed to match the conditions, troll across the current or across the seas, whichever is a stronger influence on your boat at the given moment. This will negate the effect as much as possible.

So—you know what to tow, when to tow it, and what the spread should look like. Specific rigs will be covered in chapter 12, Standard Bay Rigs. The big question that remains: where to troll in the springtime. In part I, many hot trolling areas are specifically mentioned. But as a general rule of thumb, remember that you can take trophies by trolling across any section of the main-stem Bay that has deep water, with the best areas usually being in or near the old Susquehanna riverbed, forming the deep channel that runs down the eastern side of the Bay. Some years the mud flats to the west will be hotter, but as a rule, stripers use the channel as a migration super-highway. When trolling over the deep water, stick with an east/west pattern as opposed to a north/south one. This will allow you to present your lures over more greatly varied depths and bottom types. And, since the currents run north/south in most areas, it will also negate the effect of current somewhat.

This rule goes out the window with summer and fall trolling. Yes, you will still take stripers trolling in these areas with these rigs. But you'll catch a whole lot more fish if you completely restyle your trolling methods.

There are three big differences between spring trolling and trolling at other times of the year: location, lure size, and placement in the water column. Location changes because as the water warms and the fish school, they will begin to locate on structure. No longer are you collision fishing, now you're pinpoint fishing. Bumps and humps, sharp drops, and oyster bars are where you'll find large concentrations of stripers. Instead of meandering over open water, concentrate on these bottom features.

Lure size should be dropped significantly. In the spring your large parachutes and bucktails are imitating the fat spawning-stock herring and early season menhaden. But later in the year these fish have, for the most part, departed from the Bay. Anchovies, juvenile menhaden and other small fish make up the majority of the game fish's diets. Accordingly, you should be towing bucktails dressed with twister tails or Sassy Shads in the 4 inch range. Spoons should also be downsized. And at these times of year, trolling hoses also become very effective. Color is a crap-shoot; the most effective color can change from week to week, much less season to season, but always remember that old Chesapeake Bay adage: if it ain't chartreuse, it ain't no use. This overstates the case a bit, but there's a kernel of truth to be found here. Again, refer to chapter 12, Standard Bay Rigs, for more detailed information on what to pull behind the boat in the summer and fall.

Placement in the water column is also going to be different than in the spring months. No longer are you looking to keep your lures in the top of the water column, only. It's always a good idea to run your lures at staggered depths and leave a line or two running shallow, but particularly in the fall, you're going to want those lures close to the bottom—sometimes, so close that you can bounce your weight off of it.

Bottom-bouncing is a time-honored method of fishing in the Chesapeake Bay, and it's a lot more interesting than the usual troll-and-yawn. With this type of trolling anglers actually work the fishing rods, constantly letting out and retrieving line to keep the bait right on the bottom even as the depth changes. A special rig is used for this purpose—yet another reason to refer to chapter 12, Standard Bay Rigs. This type of trolling also requires a lot of communication between the captain and anglers, since the captain is the only one who can see the depth finder and will be able to give the anglers a few seconds of advance warning before adjustments become necessary.

This tactic starts with the boat moving forward at a speed of three to four mph, headed for some form of structure which is (hopefully) holding fish. The angler lets down line until he feels the weight bump on bottom, then holds the line five or ten seconds, then drops again. It may take a third drop to get that weight dragging in sand. The angler should then quickly sweep the rod tip forward (yanking the weight and lure off the bottom), then let it drop back towards the stern—maintaining minimum tension—until he feels the weight hit again. As soon as contact is established, the next sweep of the rod begins. If, after several sweeps forward and drops back the angler doesn't feel the weight bounce on bottom, he should let out additional line. If he feels the weight drag on bottom during the sweeps forward, or if the weight makes contact before the tip has dropped back all the way, he should take in some line.

As the boat passes over a hump or ridge, the captain should call a warning to the anglers to let them know of the upcoming depth change. Let's say you're trolling over Belvedere Shoals, towards a 16' hump surrounded by 24'. As the depth finder shows the edge of the shoal under the boat, the captain should call out "the bottom's coming up eight feet." The anglers will then know that the moment their weight starts dragging, they need to crank in line to make up for the depth difference. When they have their lines set and start bouncing over the top of the hump is often the moment of truth; since there's such a long leader behind the weight it takes a moment longer for the bucktail to hit the edge of the hump, and this is where the fish usually strike. As the boat passes off the edge of the hump and water depth shoots back down to 24' the captain should again call out a warning, and the anglers must be prepared to let out line as soon as the weight loses contact with the bottom. If this sounds work-intensive and a little tough for beginners to master, that's because it is. Bottom-bouncing is also significantly more effective than just dragging lines behind your boat, and it's not unreasonable to hope for double the catch if you bottom-bounce competently in an area rich with stripers.

Oddly, this is also a popular way to catch flounder, particularly in the lower Bay. The same bucktails will work, although the use of minnow as a dressing is a bit more prevalent. (Before the advent of plastic twister tails, large bull minnow were traditionally used to dress bucktails when bouncing for stripers, too.) Also, the action imparted by bouncing is not nearly as imperative when trolling for flounder. Yes, it is beneficial, but the real important aspect when trolling for flounder is to keep that lure right over the bottom, and bouncing your weight ensures that you accomplish this goal. It also sends up puffs of mud, which some anglers believe helps the fish hone in on the location and travel direction of your lure.

Some other notes on bottom-bouncing: Monel (wire) line is the best to use for this form of trolling, as it will get down and stay down faster than mono. Be prepared to lose some rigs; whenever you're fishing this close to bottom, you're bound to have some snags. And always rig up with small bucktails in the three to five inch range, dressed with twister tails or (for the traditionalist) bullhead minnow or pork rind. Since it is imperative to maintain bottom contact with this type of trolling—and lots of lead will tire the anglers working the rods—it's a tactic best used in water 40' or shallower.

LIGHT TACKLE CASTING

This is one of the most enjoyable ways of fishing the Chesapeake. The use of light tackle is easy on the arms, and it forces the angler to use finesse, rather than brute strength, to catch the fish. Pin-point casting accuracy, the ability to understand how turning the reel crank relates to lure speed, and the ability to feel the slightest bumps and nudges on the line all combine to make skill as much of a factor as luck.

For the purposes of this book, we'll consider conventional or spinning gear in the 6 to 14 lb range as "light." Rod length should be kept relatively short—6'6" is about as long a rod as you'll want—because when more than one angler casts from the confines of one boat, mid-air snagging, rod collisions, and rod collisions with such items as VHF antennas or outriggers becomes a major problem. In fact, it's best to remove any obstructions from your boat, if possible, before light tackle casting.

Choosing lure size is a bit more complex. Base it not on the size of the fish you're targeting, but on the depth and current of the water you're fishing. If you're casting to points, riprap, and pier pilings for stripers, for example, most of the water you'll be working in will be under 10'. A ¼ oz leadhead jig is all it will take to maintain contact with the bottom, and you'll be able to work the jig as slowly as you please. If, however, you're casting for speckled trout in a 20' deep tidal cut with a two-knot current, a ¼ oz leadhead is worthless. In this situation you'll need at least an ounce to even reach bottom. And doing so is often key—no matter what type of situation you're fishing in, during one part of the tidal cycle or another the fish will probably be feeding at or near bottom.

Of course, you can avoid this whole issue by casting topwater or diving plugs. At times, this is an effective way to take fish. But in more cases than not, a leadhead jig dressed with a plastic tail is the better choice. These jigs have many advantages over plugs: you can change the size, color, and swimming action of the lure body in seconds, you can control lure depth more completely and more easily, and you have the option of vertical jigging if your fishfinder suddenly shows a hole or a school of fish directly under the boat.

Increasingly Chesapeake anglers have also been discovering the application of largemouth bass style spinnerbaits to salt and brackish water fishing.

They are effective for stripers and speckled trout, and on occasion even redfish will strike a spinnerbait. The downside is pretty much the same as it is for plugs and light spoons; it's harder to quickly switch bodies, work these baits deep, and they can't be jigged vertically. In addition, you have to be careful as to what type of spinnerbait you cast, since the vast majority of them are made for freshwater only. The swivels, spinners, and hooks tend to rust out very quickly.

One of the most important aspects of light tackle casting is boat positioning. The captain must learn how to position the boat so that every angler onboard has an unobstructed shot at productive water. They must be close enough to hit the target, but far enough away that the fish aren't spooked. Several tools can be employed to help you more effectively captain the boat when light tackle casting. The first is a grappling anchor. It should be rigged on a relatively short rode—30' is usually enough—with a 5' shot of chain. Coil the rope in the bottom of a 5 gallon bucket, then drop the chain on top. Hold the anchor upside-down, and insert the shaft into the bucket. The tines will sit over the edge of the bucket, and the whole affair is contained where it's easy to access but won't chip your boats' fiberglass. Unlike most situations, this is the one case in which you'll want to let the anchor out from the stern. This allows you to put the forward casting deck (the most desirable casting platform, on most boats) into prime position. Just be sure that there aren't any seas hitting the stern, including boat wakes that could easily swamp a stern-anchored boat.

Another useful tool is a metal rod or a push pole. This can be used to slowly push the boat into position, then it can be shoved into mud or sand bottoms and tied to the boat to "stake it out." An electric trolling motor can also be used to effectively position the boat, but be sure it's a saltwater model or it will corrode after the first trip. When casting in long tidal cuts, along channel edges or in other places where a drift is desirable, a drift sock can also help you position the boat properly. A good one can be expected to slow the speed of your drift by a little less than half, and you can also control the angle your boat sits into the wind by placing it on cleats in different positions.

Of all the above, my choice by far is the electric motor. It allows you to sneak up on the fish, can be used to constantly change boat position, can hold you in the current or wind, and can also be used to slowly move to other nearby spots without alerting the fish of your presence. Of course, electric motors only have so much oomph. Even today's top of the line electrics only reach about three horsepower, and don't help much if you're fishing from a 2,000 lb, 25' long boat.

This brings us to boat choice, which is a lot more limited for this type of fishing than any other type you're likely to encounter on the Bay, except for fly fishing. For light tackle casting on the Chesapeake, nothing beats a small center console. Something in the 18' range with a flat forward casting deck, an aft cockpit and a console to hold onto in the middle, allows maximum fishability with minimum draft, so you can get into shallows and small cuts where many other anglers can't access. A boat of this size can also be controlled with an electric motor in the 70 lb thrust range, which goes for about $350 in a saltwater version.

Another aspect of light tackle casting that cannot be ignored is retrieval techniques. First, remember a couple of general rules: the warmer the water is, the faster the fish expect their prey to swim, and second, erratic is good.

Whether you're casting to the rocks around Thomas Point Light or the riprap islands of the CBBT, in mid-summer you're going to want a fast retrieve. In fact, you'll discover situations in which cranking the lure back to the boat as fast as you can reel will catch more fish than any other retrieval technique. But if it's late November and the water temps are hovering around 48°F, you'll need to force yourself to slow down the retrieve. In both cases, a smooth, steady retrieve is usually not going to produce nearly as many strikes as an erratic one. Use jiggles and jerks of your rod tip to make your lures look like injured baitfish. Occasionally stop the retrieve completely for a second, then continue as before. And when your lure is being retrieved across the bottom, hop it up and down instead of bringing along on an even flight path.

How will you know whether to work your lure along the bottom, at mid-depth, or on the surface? The most effective retrieve will usually change with the tide. Stripers, speckled trout, red drum (in the southern Bay), and flounder are among the most commonly sought-after fish in the shallows, and all will vary their feeding patterns according to the tide. Naturally, if you want to take flounder in the shallows you'll need to keep your lure within a foot or two of bottom, but at times stripers and specs will be feeding higher in the water column. It would be nice to say that you should always fish deep on an incoming tide and shallow on an outgoing, or vice-versa. But the fact of the matter is that the fish often establish a pattern one way or the other, which might last for one day or an entire season. (There are a few exceptions that are site-specific and are mentioned in part I). Usually, there's just no way to know for sure until you actually start casting. That's why you should always vary your retrieval technique until you discover what's working. Stick with it until you notice a drop in the bites, and look around: has the tide changed? Lighting conditions? Has a front moved through? Try different techniques again, until you find another that works.

We should also mention the fact that light tackle casting is a form of fishing that is very vulnerable to the effects of light conditions, since it often takes place in shallow water. Once the sun is high in the sky you're unlikely to get strikes in the shallows from specs, stripers, and reds, but when it's cloudy, large predatory fish may remain in two feet of water all day long. For this reason savvy anglers will often target fish in the shallows at daybreak, then move out into the open, deeper waters of the Bay during the day and try the shallows again at sunset. But when it comes to flounder, don't forget that the opposite is true. Expect them to bite in the shallows best at mid-day in full sun.

VERTICAL JIGGING

This is another technique that forces an angler to employ skill and finesse, as well as offering the opportunity to use light tackle. Vertical jigging can be effective in a tributary river, on the open Bay, or in just about any part of the Chesapeake with 12' or more of water. It can be used to capture stripers, blues, weakfish, flounder, croaker, black sea bass, and yellow and white perch. Better yet, it offers you the opportunity to catch a mix of these species, without ever rerigging or changing places.

Just about any size gear can be used to jig vertically, as long as it matches the size of the lures you're using. As a general rule of thumb start light and work your way to heavy as necessary. In 20' of water with no current, for example, you can jig a 6 lb class setup with a ½ oz jig or spoon. This is an exciting way to fish, since you'll feel every sniff, twitch, and slam a fish gives your lure. But when you move out into 50' of water and a breeze is blowing, you'd better have a 14 lb class rig at the ready along with a 3 oz jig, or you'll never reach the fish. Bottom line: every time I leave the dock with the intention of vertical jigging, I have at least three rods and reels aboard for every angler: a light, a medium/light, and a medium/heavy.

The actual jigging motion itself is pretty simple and doesn't vary much whether you're jigging shad darts for perch or big spoons for stripers. Start with the lure either on bottom or at the lowest depth that you want to fish, and your rod tip inches from the water's surface. Quickly sweep the rod tip up to an 11 o'clock position, then drop it back down to the water. You should make the dropping part of this motion quickly enough to allow the lure to fall freely, but slowly enough to maintain minimum tension on the line so you're ready for a quick hook-set. Occasionally a fish will strike as you sweep the rod tip up, usually resulting in a solid hook-up. But nine times out of ten, the fish will slam the lure as it's falling. If you're not paying close attention, you may think the lure has hit bottom or you might not notice anything unusual at all. Pay close attention to where the bottom is, where your lure is, and if it stops falling before you think it should bring the rod up sharply for a hook-set. Don't worry if you miss a hookup or two. This is a common problem with vertical jigging, especially when you're going for weakfish—the easily-ripped membranes in their mouth are what earns them their name.

One exception to this standard jigging technique occurs when you're jigging for weakfish in particular. For whatever reason, in certain conditions seatrout want a jig that is just hanging there. When you're jigging for them and not having much luck, try setting the jig about three feet off bottom, and let it hang. This technique, called "dead-sticking" will occasionally out-fish active jigging two to one.

One other factor to take into consideration when gearing up for jigging is rod action. This is a situation in which a rod with a soft tip (slow action) gives you an advantage. A flexible tip allows you to keep a slight bend in the rod and tension on your line as you drop the tip, allowing the lure to sink, without affecting the lure's freefall. If your rod has a stiff, fast action tip you'll either have to let the line fall slack to get a natural drop, or keep a lot of tension on the line and ruin the free-falling action of your lure. (If you're stuck with this situation, let the lure fall on slack line. Then watch the line as it slips down into the water. Instead of feeling for the hit, watch for it—when your line stops or jerks suddenly, go for the hook-set.)

When vertical jigging, whether you're trying to get on top of a car-sized hole filled with yellow perch or an acre-long mass of weakfish, boat positioning is one of the most important variables. As with light tackle casting, electric motors and drift socks can be of use, but anchors aren't much help because most of the time you'll need to keep moving to vertically jig effectively. That's not a disadvantage, though; it's a big point in your favor.

The example of fishing for weakfish in Tangier Sound illustrates my meaning. For many years through the '70s and '80s, the boats plying Tangier Sound were spoiled. Huge masses of seatrout moved into the sound and held along the deep drop-offs and channels. Captains became accustomed to running out to these edges, dropping anchor, and hauling up awesome catches day after day. But in the early '90s the trout numbers dropped. By the mid-90s, catches that would have been scoffed at in earlier years were suddenly a "run" of fish. I was more or less an outsider to the Tangier locals, spending most of my time fishing farther north—and this was a key advantage that allowed me to out-fish the locals on a couple of occasions, much to my own surprise.

Farther up the Bay we were used to dealing with smaller, more mobile schools of trout. We jigged on them for a pass or two, lost the school, had to relocate them, and so on. So when we went out into the Tangier, we never even considered anchoring. Instead, we located a pod of fish, made a drift or two, then kept moving. This mobility meant that we never sat in the same spot, waiting for fish—we went and hunted them down. Meanwhile, the local captains found their favorite spot, dropped the hook, and rarely moved. It may have worked in years past, but when the massive schools turned into small pods, it was not the most productive way to fish.

This advantage of mobility is one of the best reasons to try vertical jigging. You can hit a spot fast and hard, move on, find fish, lose them, find them again, and keep on hunting until your rods are bent.

Another advantage provided by vertical jigging: it allows you to present your lure at the exact depth you choose. In fact, on most modern fishfinders of moderate quality, you'll be able to spot your lure rising and falling as you jig your rod. When you spot fish suspended at a specific depth it's easy to place your offering there, and it's easy to change the depth you're targeting in the blink of an eye. This is part of why you can target several different species of fish at the same time. Let's look at another example: You're at the drop from 15' to 70', at red #84 off Poplar Island in the middle Chesapeake. Starting in 15', you bounce your jig off the bottom and catch several flounder. As your boat passes the shelf and the bottom drops to 35', you spot a school of fish holding at 25'. You reel up so your jig is 10' above the bottom and catch striped bass. At the bottom of the slope your fishfinder shows a lot of bait at 50', with a string of larger marks hugging the bottom beneath it. You drop your jig down deep and hook into weakfish after weakfish. This scenario isn't a fantasy, it's a reality we've experienced on my boat many times—all because we spend a lot of time vertical jigging. Chumming, trolling, and most other forms of fishing aren't nearly as versatile and don't allow you to shift gears to target different fish nearly as quickly and easily.

Lure choice for vertical jigging depends on what type of fish you're trying to catch but will be dictated by current and wind speed. As usual, more movement requires more weight. As with light tackle casting, leadheads are a good choice because they allow you to modify your offering very quickly. However, they will only take you so far; even in a mild current, you need 3 or 4 ounces to keep your line down deep, and leadheads of this size aren't usually the best choice. Luckily, you have several options. One is to use a tandem jigging rig, as described in chapter 12, Standard Bay Rigs. This allows you to super-size your lure weight. You can still offer the fish a small lure by rigging it on the top of the tandem and using a large jigging spoon on another very heavy offering on the bottom of the tandem. They're only hitting the small lure, in deep water? Tie a tandem with two lures and a third line on the bottom, to which you add a regular bank sinker of whatever size is necessary to get your lures to the depth of choice. Note that at some point, you may have to up-size the rest of your gear to match the weight of the lures and leads.

Whatever type of lure you're using, vertical jigging requires a lot of action. Unless dead-sticking is the approach that is working, keep that lure moving at all times. When jigging for flounder, try using the most violent upward sweep of the rod you can muster, but stop at 9 o'clock or 10 o'clock instead of eleven. This will keep your lure closer to the bottom, more of the time. One more note about jigging for flounder—for some reason they seem to prefer simple white paddle-type jig tails over twister tails or Fin-S type tails in the Chesapeake Bay. I have no idea why, but experience will bear out this fact. You'll notice that it does not hold true when jigging for flounder in other places, such as the barrier island coastal bays. With most other types of fish, lure type and action of choice on any particular day is much more variable. So start off with easily modified baits, like leadheads with re-movable rubber tails, and change color and body type often until you find the productive combination.

LIVE BAITING

When targeting a specific type of fish in a specific place or hot spot, most of the time, live baiting is going to fill the cooler more quickly than any other method of fishing. Live baiting is not, however, simply fishing with live bait—there's more to it than that. In fact, for the discussion of this technique we're going to stick with just three kinds of live baits: live eels, live spot and/or perch, and live menhaden. Yeah, okay, grass shrimp, bullhead minnow, and even bloodworms could be called live bait. But in most cases when you fish with these baits you'll be drifting bottom rigs or Fluke Killer rigs, which is not even similar to the technique called live baiting.

First off, bait types: eels, spot, white perch, and menhaden are all good for stripers and blues. Scratch perch from the list and the remaining baits are also good for cobia. Spot and menhaden of the proper sizes are awesome baits for flounder and weakfish. Note that both flounder and weakfish make good live baits themselves, but cannot be legally used as baits since minimum size limits are larger than maximum bait sizes.

Eeling for stripers is sort of a world unto its own, one that was discussed a little in part I. The basics are pretty simple: you drag an eel right across the bottom while drifting over underwater humps or ledges where striped bass gather. But, there's a lot more to being a successful eeler than that. First and most important is picking your spot—use part I to help with that. Secondly, you must realize that tidal influence is just as important when eeling as it is with any other form of fishing. You could drag eels right past a hundred stripers and they won't touch the baits for hours, then at the moment the tide becomes favorable, you can't keep them off the hook. Which part of the tidal cycle is best? That will vary somewhat from season to season, but as a rule of thumb, try to do your eeling during the change of tide. The last hour of a tide, the slack water, and the first half hour of the next tide are usually the best periods.

Eels require special treatment. This isn't to prevent die-offs—they're tough as nails. The problem is that it's nearly impossible to get a lively, wriggling eel onto your hook. They're just too slimy and too wiggly to hold onto. But you can make it a whole lot easier. Place your eels in a gallon-sized Tupperware box, with a tiny bit of water in the bottom. Not too much—you want the eels to be moist, but if the water covers the eels completely they may suffocate, strange as that may sound. Store the Tupperware box in your cooler. This will keep the eels contained and cold, and since eels are cold blooded, they'll fall into a hibernation-like state and won't struggle when you put them on the hook. A matter of seconds after being dunked into the Bay, however, they'll wake up and become as spunky as ever.

Even though stowing them in the cooler will make eels lethargic, they'll still be impossible to hold in your bare hand. Bring along a towel or a pair of leather work gloves, for handling the eels. Grasp the eel just behind it's head, and insert your hook in through the lower jaw then out through the upper jaw.

Now you're ready to fish—but as soon as you've drifted over your favorite hump, you'll need to reel in the now-active eel and restrain it somehow, as you motor back up to the hot spot. Never leave the eel hanging—it will ball itself up around the hook and rig, creating a huge mess. Instead, place rods in gunwale holders and individual eels in small buckets or tubs while you make the run. Never, ever place two rigged eels in the same bucket, unless you enjoy cutting apart knots and rerigging lines.

It's imperative to keep the eel on the bottom as you drift. That does mean you're likely to snag bottom sometimes, particularly as you drift the uphill edge of a shoal or lump. You play, you pay—it's unavoidable. Jigging or otherwise giving the eel action is completely unnecessary and may in fact work against you; just drop it to the bottom and let the eel do its thing.

When a striper takes the eel, he'll suck it in, hesitate, then suck it in deeper. On your end of the line, this will feel like a short series of three to five thumps, over a period of three to five seconds. Set the hook on the first thump, and you'll never catch a fish. Instead, on the first definitive thump release all tension and start a slow five-count. Then tighten up and set the hook home. Assuming you wait the proper amount of time, the hook will usually be set way back in the stripers' throat, where it's tough to get out without doing any damage. (Try and set the hook earlier to get it in the jaw, and you'll end up missing fish after fish.) So as you might expect, eeling is a method of harvest fishing, not catch-and-release. This is the main reason why eels are illegal to use in Maryland's portion of the Chesapeake during the spring trophy season. However, on the bright side, you'll rarely catch a striper under 24" on an eel. So during the summer and fall seasons, if you get a hook-up on an eel it's a sure bet the fish will be legal.

Eeling for cobia at the CBBT and eeling for stripers at the Bay bridges are tactics that are a bit more specialized. Often at the CBBT, anglers will be sight fishing. While it's true that (as mentioned earlier) cobia on the surface are not usually active feeders, it's just as true that they have a hard time turning down a wiggling eel, no matter how full their bellies may be. Sight casting in and of itself is pretty self-explanatory. However, there are a few points to keep in mind. First, stay as far from the fish as possible. Inch to within casting distance from behind or from the side of the fish—never head on—and force yourself and your crew to throw harder and longer to avoid spooking the fish. Secondly, don't throw the eels right at the cobia. These fish are not used to being attacked by their food, and if an eel drops from above right onto the fish's head, it will spook. Instead, shoot for a point five to ten feet in front of the fish, and off to the far side. This will allow you to retrieve your eel in front of the fish. If you're a good enough caster you can toss an eel with no additional weight, which is the best way to do it. As soon as the fish takes the eel go into freespool, give it a three count to allow the fish to get the eel fully into its mouth, then set the hook and hold on tight.

Eeling at the Chesapeake Bay Bridge is a highly specialized form of fishing, one that has been mastered by few. I don't pretend to be an expert at this form of fishing, and those captains that are experts at it are few, far between, and tight-lipped. The basics are covered in part I, chapter 2, under Fishing the Bay Bridges, but to really become good at eeling the bridge, plan on putting in some serious time.

Live baiting with spot, menhaden, and white perch is a whole different ball game. Menhaden is probably the most effective live bait, although spot will run a close second, and when these baits are in short supply you can often do well with perch.

Menhaden are not only the most effective, they're also the easiest baitfish to catch. Yes, catch. While you can buy live eels in the bait shops, perch, spot, and menhaden are a different story. There are a few bait shops that do carry live spot, but there aren't many and the vast majority of Bay anglers will have to rely on themselves if they want to fish live bait.

Menhaden can be taken in one of two ways: with a cast net or by snagging. Cast netting works well for catching "peanuts" in the 3 to 6 inch range, while snagging usually works better for producing menhaden in the 6 to 10 inch range. You'll get larger ones, too, but they're too big to fish live.

Peanuts can be found in virtually all the creeks and rivers on the Bay from May through November, but most will be too small to fish with until mid-August at the earliest. Mid-September through October is when you'll catch those prime five and six inch baits, and although they are still catchable in November, it gets harder and harder to locate the schools as they move out into deeper water.

It's easiest to locate the peanuts by leaving the dock well before sunrise, and going from lighted pier to lighted pier. The brighter the lights, the more likely you'll find menhaden. Make one good cast on a large school, and you can pull in several dozen baits. It's imperative that you don't overfill the livewell or the majority of your menhaden will go belly-up. Overcrowding is the number one reason for die-offs and while it's true that menhaden are delicate baits no matter how much room they have, if you have a gallon of livewell capacity for each individual fish along with good water flow, they will live through an entire day of fishing. If your livewell has a screened outlet be sure to check it every few hours; peanuts lose many of their tiny scales in a livewell, and they will clog up screens pretty quickly.

Live baiting with menhaden can be effective in several situations. The first and best is when you sight a school of menhaden on the surface, and occasionally see a predator ripping through them. You've probably experienced this at one time or another. It may be a couple or even just a single large fish hunting in the school, and troll, cast or jig as you may, you get no strikes—a very frustrating situation. This fish is hunting live menhaden; that's what it's focused on, and that's what it wants. With live peanuts in the well, now you've got a shot at this fish. Use a standard live bait rig, unweighted, tied directly to your main line. Make sure you're using thin hooks, because thick ones will sometimes split the jaws on peanuts. (Gamakatsu makes a good thin live bait hook; 2/0 is about the right size for peanut bunker in the six inch size range.)

Insert the hook up through the lower jaw and out through the upper jaw. Motor within casting distance of the school, and flip your livie right into it. Often, your bait hitting the water will spook the school, and cause a commotion. This is a good thing, as it attracts the attention of that lone predator. Keep your line in freespool, and when you feel a take allow the fish to eat for a five-count before setting the hook.

If you need to reposition the boat, or if there is any other reason to remove your bait from the water, be sure to drop it into a bucket or the livewell. Never dangle it or drag it through the water next to the boat, because if you do a hooked peanut bunker will die very quickly. No matter how careful you are you'll still only get 10 to 20 minutes out of most baits, or a half-dozen or so casts.

Another situation that is prime for live-baiting peanuts is night fishing along lightlines. Lightlines, where powerful artificial lights over a bridge or bulkhead cast a shadow line across the water, are an excellent place to catch striped bass and weakfish. In fact, weakfish feed so strongly at night that in some areas, anglers fish for them primarily after dark. Bluefish will also attack at night, and in the southern reaches of the Bay sea bass will also make a showing.

Live baiting at night is simple: just place a menhaden on the same type of rig, toss it five or ten feet beyond the lightline, and allow it to swim at will. Leave your reel in freespool so the menhaden can travel wherever he wants, a tactic called live-lining. When a fish takes the bait your line will zip off at a noticeably faster rate; wait five seconds and put on the heat. You can sometimes predict the strike by keeping a close watch on your rod tip and slack line, because when the menhaden sees a predator coming at him he will absolutely freak out. If there's the slightest amount of tension on your line, the rod tip will usually quiver vigorously, and if the line is laying slack on the water's surface, you'll see it jerk then go slack, jerk then go slack, three or four times in quick succession. If you see either of these clues, pick up your rod and get ready.

Chumming is another good situation in which to live bait with menhaden, spot, or white perch, particularly when you're bunched into a fleet of boats. The live baits definitely get struck more often than chunks. Live-lining in this situation is usually only effective if the tide is fairly mellow, however, as most live baits will tire quickly when there's a hook in their mouth and a current to fight. An egg sinker, a torpedo weight, or a rubber core can be used to put a little lead above the leader, and for baits being set all the way down on the bottom, egg sinkers hold an advantage since they allow you to feed the fish line without it feeling the added tension from your weight. Note that if there are blues in your chum slick, it's wasted effort to drop in livies—they'll be chopped in half in a matter of seconds.

Live spot are particularly useful when hunting doormat flounder. Flatties of 5 lb and up are suckers for six-inch spot, and flounder of all size will also inhale peanut bunker with vigor. But spot live longer in the livewell and on the hook, and for whatever reason, they really seem to attract big, fat flounder. When fishing for doormats, the spot can be rigged the same as peanuts (with enough weight to hold bottom, of course), but the live bait hook should be swapped out for a Kahle or octopus style hook. Their longer shanks will reduce bite-offs, which can occur thanks to the flounders' sharp set of dentures.

Cobia are also partial to live spot, although in my experience they will take an eel before a finned fish any day of the week. Of course, before you can live bait with spot you have to fill the livewell with them. This can be accomplished with a few tiny piece of bloodworm and a top and bottom rig with #8 hooks. Drift with the rig over oyster shell bottom, and wait for jackhammer-like strikes.

As a bait the usefulness of white perch is pretty much limited to stripers and blues. Blues, of course, will chomp on just about anything that moves. Stripers seem partial to white perch in fairly specific conditions, however. In areas where there are naturally lots of small perch but no menhaden—rocky riprapped shorelines in the late summer through fall, for example—perch will excel as live baits. Biologists tell us that in years of low menhaden numbers, stripers fall back to perch as a mainstay, so this makes perfect sense.

No matter what type of baitfish you're live baiting with, there are a few tricks you can use to make your fishing time a bit more effective. When your bait won't be fighting a strong current, take a pair of scissors and cut off one pectoral fin. It'll struggle and swim in circles, attracting predators looking for a easy meal. And when there are schools of large fish in the area, you can often draw them right up to the transom of your boat by live-bait chumming. This is a pretty simple but gruesome technique, usually used with peanut bunker that are too small to bait with. Grab a handful of them, lean over the side of your boat, and throw them into the hullsides. The half-stunned fish will pinwheel and stagger in the water, presenting an easy to catch meal to any predator swimming near by.

Another trick you can use is to "direct" your bait up or down in the water column, assuming the current is slack enough for the baitfish to swim against it. Hooking through the jaws, the most common technique, will make it hard for the fish to swim down. As a result, after a dive or two they will usually remain fairly close to the surface and swim more or less horizontally. Hooking a bait in the back, in one side and out the other just aft of the dorsal fin, however, will encourage the fish to dive down deeper. Note that this will not work when the line is weighted with more than a half-ounce or so, because the baitfish won't be able to pull the lead around and will end up tail-first in the current—a very unnatural presentation.

Of course, you can cast, drop, and drift live baits pretty much anywhere there are predators at pretty much any time, and expect some degree of success. The situations described in this section are merely those in which live baiting will far outcatch other methods of fishing, on most days in most conditions. Since it takes a lot of time and effort to catch live baits and keep them alive, most anglers won't want to use them on a regular basis when it's not necessary.

DRIFTING BAITS

Drift fishing really is as easy as it sounds: drop the lines over the side and let your boat drift along with the wind and current. But there are some tricks and tactics you can use to help turn drift fishing into drift catching. Baits, rigs, and lures used while drift fishing will hinge entirely upon what species of fish you're after, and what technique you're using. Eeling for stripers over a set of shoals, jigging for seatrout in a deep hole, and dragging Fluke Killers across a bar for flounder are all forms of drift fishing, for example. But one thing they all have in common is that boat positioning is paramount to success.

One of the most important jobs the captain has when drift fishing is to know exactly how his or her boat will drift in the given conditions. Wind, current, sea state, and the boat itself will all conspire to make the boat drift differently and at different speeds in different conditions. How do you learn how your specific boat drifts? There's no substitute for experience. To gain that experience, you'll just have to fish more—sorry.

There are a couple of tactics you can use to identify how your boat drifts, and respond accordingly. Before considering these methods, though, you should know that as a general rule of thumb outboard-powered boats tend to drift with their stern into the seas and inboards tend to drift beam to the seas. A glaring exception is single-screw outboard-powered powercats that also tend to drift beam to the seas.

The simplest way to identify drift is to always carry and use a float marker. This is a good idea anyway since it will allow you to visually orient to an underwater feature. Toss it over the side when you locate the lump, hole, or bar you want to drift over, then shift into neutral and identify your drift pattern. Then move your boat updrift from the marker, and see if you can predict when and on which side you'll pass the marker again.

A more complex—and more effective—way to keep track of and set up properly for drift is to learn how to use your GPS in trackplotter mode. All but the cheapest units have a trackplotting mode these days. If you don't have a GPS, get one before you pull out of the dock again. It's an invaluable safety feature, and an invaluable fishing feature. Not only will it help you figure out drift, it'll allow you to troll the same exact open water spot over and over without losing track of the position, return time and again to the exact spots you catch fish at, and head for new fishing spots with no significant margin of error. But back to the track feature: it draws a line on either a clean display or, on better units, overlaid on a chart. The line goes wherever you go. Turn a circle, make a zigzag, or abruptly change direction and you'll see it onscreen. The beauty of this feature is that the moment you put your boat into neutral, you can push "go" and in a few minutes, just by looking at that little GPS display screen, know exactly what direction and speed your boat's drifting in. You won't think it, you won't guess it, you will know.

Another important item all drift fishing anglers must know about is the drift sock, also called a drift anchor or a drogue. This is a large canvas cone that is dragged through the water to slow the boat's drift speed. (In a pinch, a 5 gallon bucket will work, too, though to a lesser degree.) With small, light boats that are pushed over the surface easily and quickly by the wind, a drift sock can turn unfishable conditions into a banner day. They are available at any good boating supply store or tackle shop, and the packaging is usually stamped with the size of the boat that corresponds with the size of the specific drift sock. When you purchase a drift sock, go one size up; it'll magnify the effect, and when you get a nice, slow drift over a tight pod of fish, you won't regret it.

Two more little tips to help you become a better drift fisherman: when you pull up to do a drift, crank the wheel hard-over and always place the side of the boat you want to fish from into the wind. If you leave the boat's bow into the wind it might blow around in either direction, and you will have to wait until it does so to get your lines into the water, or risk having the boat drift over them. Secondly, if the boat isn't drifting the way you'd like, try cranking the wheel or rudder until it's pointed the opposite way, or until it's centered. Some boats respond so well to this tactic that you can actually steer the drift, and encourage the boat to move a great deal in one direction or another.

NIGHT FISHING

Night fishing on the Chesapeake Bay can be a fantastic experience: green bioluminescent glowing from the prop wash, dead winds, and little competition are a few of the fringe benefits. Oh, yes, and did I forget to mention awesome catches? During the months of May and June for croaker, then July for stripers, then August and September for stripers and trout, night time is the right time. In fact, when water temps soar and the fish fall into dog-day doldrums, the night bite is often the only decent bite you'll have.

To try night fishing on the Bay, you'll need some special equipment. Flashlights, obviously. But don't get the hand-held variety. You'll need your hands for tying knots and baiting hooks, so the type that clips to your hat brim (Pelican Lights, available at Bass Pro Shops for about $15) or headlamps that you wear like a hat (Petzel and Survival Systems both make good ones that run between $30 and $50 and are available at REI or Bass Pro Shops) are the way to go. You'll also need to get a set of night lights for your boat—the more light you can put on the water, the more bait you'll attract, and the more bait you attract, the more big fish you'll catch. White halogens work well; for years I used a set attached to a broomstick, which I dropped into a rodholder and aimed at the water. But in recent years green fluorescent lights like the Hydro Glow ($200, www.meltontackle.com) have been developed, and they are truly amazing. The two foot long tube will throw a halo of green light 30' around the boat, and menhaden are attracted to it just like moths to a porch light. In fact, I've watched schools of menhaden numbering in the thousands circle around the Hydro Glow in a swarm so thick, they blocked the light until the green glow was a mere sliver. Whenever you put one of these lights over the side also keep a net handy, because they attract crabs, too. Some nights, you'll go home with as many crabs as fish, if you want. Note to offshore guys: these lights are just as effective at attracting squid in blue water.

Some anglers also use small lights that attach directly to their lines, usually at the line-to-leader swivel, or clip a cylume light stick on as you would when swordfishing in the Atlantic canyons. I'm not convinced that helps much, although this may be because their effect is dampened by the overwhelming light of a unit like the Hydro Glow.

It should also be mentioned that there are knockoffs on the market at this point. Bass Pro Shops has their own version of green night lights, as do a couple of other companies. While I'm sure they work well, I can't vouch for them as I haven't tried them personally and haven't looked back since experiencing the effects of the Hydro Glow.

Don't forget that lights like this are strictly for attracting bait, and in turn, larger predators like trout and stripers. If you're night fishing for croaker in deep water with bottom rigs and cut bait, don't expect them to do you any good.

Another tool all night anglers need is a good handheld spotlight. You shouldn't cruise with it on because it will destroy your night vision. But a strong spotlight is invaluable when you're trying to find channel markers and other landmarks.

Okay—you've got the gear you need, the sun's getting low on the horizon, and you're psyched to hook into some serious scale. What next? That depends on whether you'll be chasing croaker, stripers, or trout, so we'll address each in turn.

Night Fishing for Croaker

Croaker unquestionably bite better at night than they do during the day. They also tend to move into shallower water in the evenings, making it possible to pursue them with lighter gear and less weight. This also gives shoreline and pier anglers a good shot at them. In any case, these fish are strictly bottom feeders, and you need to make absolutely sure that your baits are dead on the bottom. Simple top and bottom rigs are most commonly used for croaker, but any rig that keeps your bait where it belongs will do the trick.

Bloodworms, cut squid, clam snouts, and grass shrimp are all good croaker baits, with bloodworms topping the list. Rig up for croaker with small hooks; #6 is the best choice because croaker have small, downward-pointing mouths like spot, redfish, and other bottom feeders. Don't let this fact mislead you into believing that croaker are small, weak fish. You'll catch them up to 3 lb in the Bay, and they will fight as hard as any other finned fish.

When night fishing for croaker, you'll want to stick to relatively shallow oyster bar bottom. In some areas, extremely shallow (two or three foot depths) muddy bottoms will also attract croaker, particularly just after dusk. In fact, this is the best type of bottom for shoreline and pier anglers to find. Note, however, that this bite usually peters out about an hour after dark and often doesn't pick up again unless the conditions are just right—specifically, a strong incoming tide combined with a clear, moon-lit night.

Boat anglers can get in on this bite by putting into the shallows. Whatever the platform you fish from is, croaker fishing is as simple as fishing gets: bait up a top and bottom rig, cast it out, sit your rod in a holder or lean it against a rail, and watch the tip for a bite. When the bait is taken set the hook immediately, and reel it in.

Boat anglers do have more varied opportunities to chase the croaker throughout the night. Oyster bars in the 8' to 12' range are usually prime spots, as are channels of this depth that run close to shore. Marsh cuts with strong current also attract croaker, although fishing them will require more lead on the end of your rig.

Night Fishing for Trout

During the dog days of August and early September, trout often seem to suffer from extreme lockjaw. You can spot schools of them on your fishfinder right where you caught them a few weeks ago—and where you'll catch them a month later—but they won't take a bait or lure no matter how long you wiggle it in front of them. There's only one way to get these fish to bite: night fishing.

You can night fish for trout in the open Bay, but usually this isn't your best bet during this time frame and through September. The trout haven't schooled in open water yet, and you'll be searching for scattered fish. Stick to the tributary rivers from the Bay Bridge south, however, and you'll find plenty of fish. Generally speaking, when it comes to weakfish, the farther south you are, the more you'll find in the tributary channels and holes.

Try to set up before it gets dark. This is safer, and it will give you some time to locate an area holding fish before it's time to bait up. Points at river mouths and points in the rivers with sharp drops and shell bottoms, channel edges, and bridges with lightlines are all good places to look for trout. Once you've found a good spot, drop anchor and set out your night lights. Keep a cast net handy, as you'll usually be able to fill the livewell with menhaden soon after dark, when they flock to your lights. Both trout and rockfish will hit live-lined peanuts quite aggressively. Don't count on them as your main bait, however. When trout fishing at night, it is absolutely make-or-break important to have fresh soft crab on the cutting board. Maybe it's the potent scent, maybe it's just what trout like the most, but in any case, soft crab cannot be beat when night fishing for seatrout, period. Frozen crab, peelers, and fresh shrimp will work, too, but not as well as fresh softies.

When night fishing for trout in the rivers, where current is usually minimal, downsize your rod and reel to light tackle (8 lb gear is about right) and you can get away with using just a half-ounce or so of weight. Stick with egg sinkers rigged in front of your swivel and leader, so you can let the trout run with the bait for a few seconds before setting the hook. Interestingly, if your hooks are small enough you'll also catch a lot of eels fishing this way, and in some areas, catfish as well.

If you're fishing at or near a strongly lighted bridge or pier, you can also try throwing lures. Four-inch root beer, black, purple, and chartreuse twister tails retrieved slowly and steadily along the lightline are often productive. In the lower Bay, this will also produce speckled trout. When fishing from a boat with lights, however, artificials rarely seem to produce. Casting in this situation is also a bad idea. Remember—the fish are being brought to your boat by your lights. Casting usually accomplishes nothing except to move your bait farther away from the light and the fish.

Night Fishing for Stripers

The techniques described for trout also work well for stripers, and in most Bay tributaries it will be rare to go home without picking up a keeper rock or two or more, mixed in with your trout. There is, however, a specific method of targeting the stripers which is very deadly. As usual, location is key—you'll need to find a well-lighted bridge with relatively deep water in the channel (at least 12' or 15') and a decent current. You'll also need to fill your livewell with live peanut bunker.

Boat positioning is key when hunting stripers at a bridge's lightline. In most Bay tributaries you'll want to anchor upcurrent (or upwind, if there is little or no current) within easy casting distance of the lightline where it crosses over the deepest part of the channel under the bridge. If you're at a bridge over very deep water, such as the Rt 2 bridge over the Patuxent River, instead of looking for the intersection with the channel, find the area where the depth transitions from 20' to 12'. Essentially what you're looking for is close access to water over 10' with a lightline that crosses into a shallower zone, because stripers will frequent these intersections during both cycles of the tide. If you set up in a spot surrounded only by shallow water, you're not likely to have much success on a low tide, and if you set up in a spot surrounded only by deep water, you're not likely to have much success during a flood tide—so try to find a lightline that has the best of both worlds.

Once you've pinpointed this intersection and you know where you want to place your bait, motor away and drop anchor just within casting distance. Rig up a direct line to leader connection, without any swivels or weights. Cast towards that magic intersection, and live-line your baits. Leave reels in freespool or rig them with a hair trigger, so the stripers can run with the bait without feeling any tension and give them a slow five-count before setting the hook.

Night fishing for stripers in the main-stem Bay is quite a bit different, as you'll have to contend with more current and wind. Night chumming is probably the most effective way to go about it on the open Bay, but don't leave home without those night lights—even in open water you'll see throngs of baitfish and crabs, attracted by the green glow. Baiting and rigging remains essentially the same as during daylight with this style of fishing, as does location. Do bear in mind, however, that you'll tend to find the stripers in shallower areas during the night. Deepwater haunts that are productive in daylight, such as the 35' edge of The Hill, aren't usually the winning choice in the dark. Instead, move up over humps and ridges that rise to at least 20'; 10' or 15' is even better.

Other good night fishing spots for stripers include major points that jut out into the Bay. At areas such as Point Lookout, a great evening/nightfishing plan of attack is to rig with casting gear and toss jigs to the riprap as the sun sets. When it's fully dark, move out to 15' or so deep water, set up your lights, and fish cut baits. When the menhaden move in on the lights throw the cast net and then live-line peanuts.

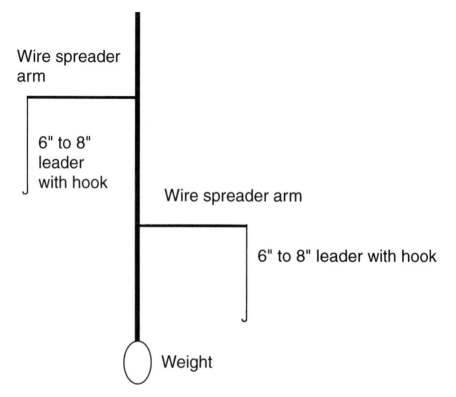

Wire spreader arm

6" to 8" leader with hook

Wire spreader arm

6" to 8" leader with hook

Weight

The top and bottom rig is an old standby that's effective on most bottom fish.

STANDARD BAY RIGS

No matter where you fish on the Bay, these ten rigs will come in handy. Many anglers alter them slightly to fit their style of fishing, and you shouldn't hesitate to customize them, either.

Top and Bottom Rig

This is perhaps the most commonly used panfish rig on the Chesapeake. The wire arms hold the hooks and leaders apart to prevent tangles, and with a clip on the bottom and a swivel on the top, these rigs are easily weighted and attached to your main line. Use them drifting, at anchor or cast them from shore when targeting croaker, spot, and perch. Weakfish, small stripers, flounder, blowfish, sea mullet, and many other small bottom feeders will also be caught on top and bottom rigs. Bait with bloodworm, soft or peeler crab, bull minnow, grass shrimp, or squid strips. When fishing with them, the only important thing to keep in mind is that the weight should maintain contact with the bottom at all times.

Russell's No-Tangle Bottom Rig

This variation of the top and bottom rig allows you to upsize the leader and hooks to target larger fish, without seriously increasing the risk of tangles. The beads will spin around the main line of the rig, so the leaders and hooks don't snag and tangle it. It's effective for weakfish, sea bass, stripers, and flounder. Bait with the same baits as a top and bottom rig, just use larger chunks. Fish it the same ways, while maintaining contact with the bottom. Russell's rig is not made commercially or sold in any stores, so you'll have to make them yourself. You can use any wire or heavy mono material for the main body of the rig and prepare the spinning beads as shown in the illustration. The rig is named for its inventor, Russell Sindler, an Ocean City angler who passed on a few years back, after sharing his innovation with the fishing world.

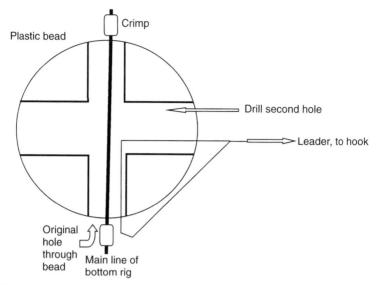

Russell Sindler came up with this modification of the top and bottom rig.

Fluke Killer/Trout Scout

Another popular, commonly used rig, the Fluke Killer (also sold under the name Trout Scout) is most effective for weakfish and flounder. The beads and spinners forward of the hook add fish-attracting sound and vibration to your bait, while the bucktail hair skirt increases profile and contrast. A variation on this theme is the Spin-N-Glow, which replaces the spinner blade with a propeller-style spinner. Most of the variations of this rig work well, and most serious anglers are well-stocked with different colors of this rig. (Start with chartreuse or white; in dim water go to yellow; in low light try purple or blue.)

For weakfish, it's best to bait a Fluke Killer with soft or peeler crab. For flounder, most people use either squid strips, bull minnow, or a combination of both. Of course, with these baits on the hook, you'll also catch stripers, sea

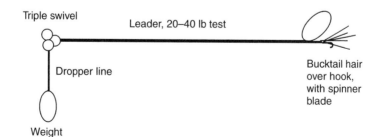

The Fluke Killer is just that—a killer.

bass, and blues. The best way to fish this rig is on the drift; the advantages of the beads, spinners, and hair skirt are negated when the rig sits at rest. It should be weighted sufficiently to bounce the weight along the bottom as you drift. Maintain constant contact with the bottom for flounder, and intermittent contact when using it for seatrout.

Standard Chumming Rig

Despite its simplicity, the standard chumming rig has a million variations available hanging from the tackle shop wall. You're best served by ignoring all of them. Store bought chumming rigs are generally made with overly thick leaders and cheap hooks. Those that come with swivels usually have the worst, cheapest swivels available. Plus, chumming rigs in the tackle store are usually far overpriced. Instead, make your own—it's so easy! Tie a spider hitch into one end. That will leave you with a loop to clip your swivel onto. Pull out 4 to 5 feet of leader (30–40 lb test fluorocarbon for stripers; 50–80 lb test for cobia; 30 lb test with a 1' wire trace tied to the end for bluefish,) and tie your hook on the other end with an improved clinch. Use a 5/0 to 7/0 for stripers and blues, and a 7/0 to 8/0 for cobia.

Of course, the standard chumming rig is used most often while at anchor, with chum going over the side. It can be floated near the surface (blues, stripers from early summer through the fall, and cobia), weighted slightly with a rubber-core sinker or a torpedo weight (blues, stripers from early summer through the fall, and cobia), or sunk to the bottom with an egg sinker rigged on the main line, above the swivel (spring trophy stripers, cobia). Most of the time, when weighted this rig is best left at rest, be it on the bottom or suspended mid-depth. When it is floating weight-free, however, you'll catch the most fish by freespooling the rig, allowing it to sink back and away from the boat in the current along with the chum bits.

4' to 6' of 30–40 lb test leader

Swivel or loop

Run main line
through egg sinker
before tying on
swivel or loop.

This rig is incredibly simple and incredibly effective.

Live-Lining Rig

The common live-lining rig is simply a chumming rig with the hook swapped out for a short-shank version. The live bait should be hooked through the jaws—in through the lower jaw and out through the upper jaw—if you want the fish to swim at or near the surface. When you want the bait to swim down towards the bottom, hook it through the back just behind the dorsal fin (unless you are drifting; back hooked baits will not drift naturally). When a live bait rig is weighted it should be done with an egg sinker, so the fish can take the bait without feeling the extra weight of the lead. Live baits can be used in a large variety of situations, for which you'll have to weight accordingly depending on the current conditions. Remember that the short-shank hook is easy for toothy fish to bite off. If there are lots of blues or mackerel around, add a short wire trace.

Umbrellas and Spreaders

Umbrellas and spreaders—primarily used for spring trophy stripers, but effective on stripers year-round—are sold both rigged and unrigged. If you have the unrigged variety—or if you have a break-off—you'll have to know how to rig these lures. Fortunately, it's as not as complex as it looks: for your hooked lure, cut a two to three foot section of 50–80 lb test leader, tie one end on the umbrella or (either side of the) spreader, and tie a large parachute or bucktail to the other end. For lures on spreaders (such as Billy Bars), use a 12–18" section of leader. On both rigs, the hookless teasers can be secured by attaching swivel clips to the loops in the frame. Then run the clips through the plastic body of the shad tail and push them shut.

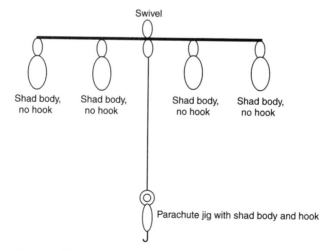

Umbrellas are a bear to reel in, but they do catch fish.

Tandem Trolling Rig

Another simple one, but a rig you'll need to know since they aren't usually seen in tackle shops. Tie an 8' section of 50–80 lb leader on a triple swivel. On the end of this line, tie the heavier of your two bucktail or parachute lures. Make the second section 14' to 16', tie it to the second eye of the triple swivel, and attach to its end the lighter of your two lures. To stow this rig, cut a 6" section off a pool noodle, push the hook of the lighter bucktail into the foam, and wrap it up.

Tandem rigs can be trolled for stripers at any time of the year, but they really shine during the spring trophy season. Usually, bucktails and/or parachutes between 6 and 12 oz are used.

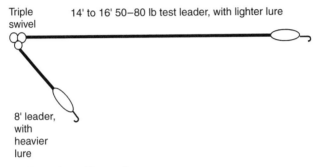

Tandem rigs are another spring trolling staple.

Bottom-Bouncing Trolling Rig

For this classic upper Bay rock-catching rig, you'll need another triple swivel. Tie a 4' section of 20 lb test to a bank sinker (usually 6–10 oz is necessary to maintain contact when bouncing in 20' to 30' of water with Monel line) and attach that to one of the swivel eyes. Use 50–80 lb test for the running leader, which should be 18–20' long, and tie a 1–3 oz bucktail on the end. (Using

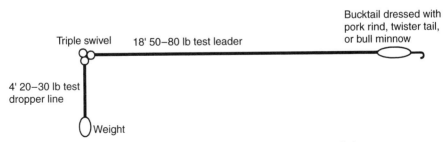

Bottom bouncing is an old tactic that works as well today as it did for your grandfather.

lighter leader for the weight allows it to break before the main line if it snags bottom, so you don't lose the whole rig.) The third swivel eye attaches to the swivel on your main line.

Although you will take blues and the occasional trout or flounder while bottom bouncing, this rig is primarily for stripers. It should be trolled slowly as the rod is swept forward, then dropped back, so the weight bounces on the bottom on the end of the drop-back, as described in the chapter on trolling.

Tandem Jigging Rig

Think of this as a miniature tandem trolling rig, with one important difference: the heaver lure goes on the longer leader, instead of the shorter one. Make the short leader 6–8" long, and the long leader about 4'. Usually this rig works best with a very light lure up top—maybe a ¼ oz or ½ oz feather jig or tube jig—and a 3 or 4 oz jigging spoon or leadhead jig on the long leader. This rig should always be used while on the drift, and is most effective when jigging deep for trout under breaking fish, for large stripers holding under

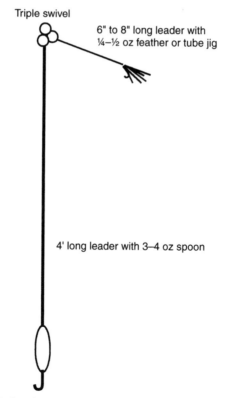

Triple swivel

6" to 8" long leader with
¼–½ oz feather or tube jig

4' long leader with 3–4 oz spoon

Jig this type of tandem rig deep for trout and stripers.

schools of small fish breaking water, or for stripers holding at mid-depth. Give it lots of action for the stripers. Weakfish may like it better moving fast or slow, depending on the conditions and their mood.

Feather Jigging Rig

This is an extremely versatile rig, as it can be jigged, dead-sticked, or trolled. The feather jigging rig differs from many others in that the triple swivel has a clip on one eye, on which you attach a bank sinker ranging from 1–6 oz, depending on tackle size and water depth. The leader—30 lb test is usually plenty—should be about 4' long, and a 3 or 4" feather jig is tied to the end. This rig can be used either for drift fishing over edges and/or bumps.

Whether drifting or casting at structure, feather jig rigs should be allowed to sink to the bottom, then reeled up while the rod tip is rhythmically pumped. The motion should continue until the rig breaks water, as stripers will often follow it to the surface before hitting. When dead-sticked in deep water, weakfish also respond well to feather jig rigs. And when light tackle trolling, a feather jig rig can be bounced on or near the bottom to take stripers of varying sizes. Note, though, that a single bluefish will shred a feather jig. When they are around in large numbers it's best to switch to a more hearty lure.

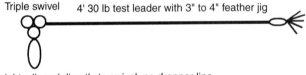

Triple swivel   4' 30 lb test leader with 3" to 4" feather jig

Weight, clipped directly to swivel, no dropper line

The feather jigging rig works for casting and retrieving, and light tackle trolling as well.

Part III:
Chesapeake Bay and
Tributary Sportfish

Black drum: Some people say they aren't pretty, but we disagree.

BLACK DRUM

Black drum give anglers in the lower and middle Bay the possibility of catching fish in the 100 lb range, an opportunity that can only be matched by cobia. Pound for pound they may not be the world's greatest fighters, but what they lack in will they make up for in brute strength. Black drum can grow extremely large, and the world record caught in nearby Delaware hit 113 lb 1 oz, although the Maryland record (103 lb 8 oz) and Virginia's (111 lb) come pretty close to that mark.

Their reputation as poor eating fare is a little overemphasized, but since it has surely accounted for a lot of released fish, it's not a bad thing, either. If you keep and fillet a black, you will usually find worms in the meat. They are quite obvious and rather large, so they are easily cut out of the fillets, and in any case won't survive in humans. But, they are a bit of a gross-out for a lot of folks.

Another black drum trait that is overemphasized is their poor eyesight. Many anglers believe that blacks hardly use sight at all, and it is true that they have unusually well-developed senses of smell and vibration detection. However, studies by marine biologists in Florida have proven that, at least down south, black drum do use their sight extensively when feeding.

In the middle Bay and in much of the lower Bay, soft and peeler crab are accepted as the best black drum baits. Some anglers far to the south also believe strongly in the use of chowder clams when fishing for big blacks. Regardless of the specific bait you choose, black drum are notorious for spitting baits. They have sensitive mouths and if they feel tension or excessive weight on the line, are said to spit the hook. For this reason, just about everyone fishing for black drum uses a fishfinder rig. Despite this fact, it's interesting to note that Chuck Harrison, an expert angler in the Hampton Roads area of the lower Bay and a writer for *The Fisherman* magazine, regularly catches black drum near the islands of the CBBT on spoons. And just as interesting, I have seen outdoors writer Rocky Calia hook into black drum on plastic worms worked slowly over the bottom.

Fishing for black drum requires a little more heft than most Bay fish. Conventional gear in the 30–40 lb class range is appropriate. Oversized spinning gear rigged with superline will also do the trick. Unfortunately, the nature of drum fishing dictates that there will often be a lot of competition on hand. Some of these competitors, particularly charter captains who act as though they own the whole Bay, will not hesitate to drive their boat right over your line as you fight a fish, if they think it will allow them to get on top of the school of fish. This problem is notably more prevalent in the middle Bay, during the Stone Rock drum run. If you use heavier gear in this situation, you may be able to horse the fish in before a charter has the chance to cut you off. For those who think I sound bitter, here's why: in the past six years I've had five black drum cut-offs caused by knowing, uncaring, and belligerent charter captains in the Stone Rock region. I've had exactly zero from recreational boats.

Part of the problem here is that this is close quarters combat fishing. Anywhere from 20 to 100 boats may be milling around, looking for the school. When one hooks up, it becomes a rat race to see who can get closest quickest and get a hook-up. This occurs because black drum tend to travel in pods or schools packed in tight against each other. Hundreds of fish can be swimming in an area the size of just three or four boats. So rushing in and piling on when you see another fish caught is, unfortunately, effective.

Of course, it's not the only effective way to get on drum. Anyone with a quality depth finder can hunt up a pod of fish away from the pack. Usually when the drum run, they will follow a contour or series of contours with drop-offs ranging from 12' to 30'. It's rare to find a school actively feeding much deeper than this, and most often the action comes in 20' to 26' on the downslope of an edge. Black drum are easy to spot since they provide such a huge target. Even in 20' of water, when you drive over a school of fish it looks on your fishfinder like they take up half of the water column between the bottom and the water's surface. They appear as huge triangles, sometimes just off and sometimes attached to the bottom.

To get on these fish, meander upcurrent or upwind (whichever is stronger) along a potentially productive edge. When you see the big triangular marks near bottom—they'll be solid red on color machines—immediately shift out of gear and cut the wheel one way or the other, allowing the boat to come to a stop ASAP with the beam into the wind. Get your baits over the side as quickly as possible and keep them on bottom until you've drifted back over the marks.

This is one drift fishing situation in which dropping a marker buoy is not a great idea. First off, drum usually only stay in the same spot long enough to get in one or two productive drifts before the fish move around. Secondly, if any other drum anglers are close enough to see that marker, they'll come over and drop lines. Within five minutes, you'll have a pack on your tail. So on second thought maybe it can be helpful to drop a marker—it may help cut down on the competition, if you drop it where you don't plan on fishing. Here are ten tips that'll make you a more effective drummer.

1. When you feel a solid hit, don't give the fish a terribly long time to eat. A three count is plenty and a five-count is simply too long. Let the fish play with the bait for that much time and there's a fair chance it will feel tension or weight on the line at some point, and drop the bait.

2. These are big fish, and they want a big meal. To make a single drum bait, cut a soft or peeler crab down the middle and use the whole half-crab. Fishing clams? Thread several big, gooey ones onto your hook.

3. Always net a black drum, never gaff it. These big fish have very thick, strong scales that are between the size of a quarter and a half-dollar. They're thicker and tougher than your thumb nail. Gaff shots will sometimes bounce right off of them, so you're a lot better off using a net. Note, though, that you need a really large net—a standard hoop won't cut the mustard, and a three-footer is the minimum diameter net you want onboard. You're on a buddies' boat, and his net isn't big enough? Get the biggest spoon or bucktail in your tacklebox, duct-tape it to a scrub brush handle, and when the fish is tired out and up close, slip the hook into the soft meat in the middle of its lower jaw.

4. Stay in hunting mode when you're after black drum, until you're positive you've located fish. You can drift around with lines down all day, but you'll never catch drum until you locate them and drop baits right on top of their heads.

5. If you're new to chasing drum and want to cheat a bit, go to the Stone Rock during the peak of the drum run. (It usually starts somewhere between the second week of May and the second week of June and lasts for anywhere between a week and a month. On-again, off-again action is common.) Get close to the pack of boats, prep your baits and rigs, then sit back and watch with a pair of binoculars. Don't enter the fray until you see a couple of bent rods, then move in slowly and park the boat just upwind or upcurrent of the boat with the hooked fish. Don't run over hooked fish! Give the boat with the bent rods plenty of room! Keep a close eye on the fishfinder, and soon you'll know what a school of drum looks like.

6. In close quarters chasing big drum is a good idea, not to catch the fish more quickly but to keep your boat close to the fish, thereby protecting the line. If someone's in the way, don't be afraid to yell (politely) and ask them to back off. Most recreational boats will happily do so.

7. Keep a jigging rod or a spinner with a Trout Scout handy. After you catch some black drum work the area for trout and stripers.

You'll often find a few fish of these species playing cleanup behind the drum.

8. Drum can move large distances in short time periods. One day they can be in spot A and the next be in spot B, 10 or 20 miles away. If you return to a place that proved hot the day before, but you see absolutely nothing, don't hesitate to expand your search area. Remember to focus on the hunting, not the fishing. You must get right over these fish to make dropping baits worthwhile. If you're not spending 80–90% of your day searching with the lines dry, you're probably not searching hard enough.

9. Remember drum's enhanced ability to smell. Make sure your hands are clean, free of fuel or other contaminants, and treat your baits with care. Keep them in the cooler until used, and never leave them in direct sunlight. It's not a bad idea to wash your hands in the Bay before handling baits.

10. If you plan to fish for drum during the main spring run at any of the famous locations, Stone Rock, the CBBT, etc., you should upsize your tackle to facilitate a quick fight. Remember, in the hot spots during the runs, it's often close-quarters fishing with lots of competition. Otherwise, there's a good chance someone will cross your line, drive over it, or even snag your fish by accident.

BLACK SEA BASS AND TAUTOG

Like tog, black sea bass are regular customers in the lower Bay only, though they do range into the Tangier Sound some seasons. Also like tog, the bigger sea bass are usually caught in the ocean, not the Bay. Both Maryland (8 lb) and Virginia (10 lb) records come from the ocean, and the IGFA record (10 lb 4 oz) was caught off Virginia Beach. As a result of their larger size and numbers in the nearby ocean, few anglers target sea bass in the Bay and they are usually a coincidental catch. During the summer months, however, there can be decent bass bites on wrecks and rockpiles for fish in the 1–3 lb range. Once water temperatures cool below about 60°F, most of the sea bass migrate out of the Chesapeake and head for deeper ocean waters.

Black sea bass are an excellent eating fish, with firm, white meat. Interestingly, sea bass are hermaphrodites—they begin life as females, then change to males as they grow older. They are voracious predators that will eat just about anything from squid to fish. Because it stays on the hook well and works as well as anything else, squid is usually the favored bass bait. Since bass have very large jaws and suck a bait straight down without hesitation, they are relatively easy to catch once located. Like spot and croaker, this trait makes sea bass an excellent target when you have kids onboard and need fast, constant action. Although bass bites will ebb and flow with the tide, they will feed to some degree during almost any tidal cycle, adding to their reputation as a cooperative fish.

Another interesting quirk of the sea bass is its appearance when mature and well fed. Large, healthy fish will develop a hump on their forehead, just behind their eyes. These fish are nicknamed "humpbacks" or "humpies" and usually weigh 5 lb or better. Here are the tricks that will help you sink your hooks into a humpie.

1. Big sea bass are aggressive and will often beat the smaller fish to the bait, so the largest fish holding on any one wreck or rockpile are usually caught early in the game. Accordingly, when you catch small fish after small fish without any larger ones mixed in, after a half hour or so it's reasonable to expect that there are only small ones in that area and you may want to consider moving on to a new location.

Black sea bass frequent the lower reaches of the Bay and tend to be caught around structure.

2. Because they have large mouths and feed voraciously, sea bass are one of the wreckfishes in the mid-Atlantic region that can be targeted effectively with artificials. Jigging spoons, soft plastics on heavy leadheads, and large bucktails are all effective. Conventional wisdom calls for tipping such lures with a squid strip or a slice of fish, but this isn't entirely necessary and there are days when screw tail plastics out-fish cut bait by a wide margin.

3. Like tautog, sea bass like to stick close to structure. To target them effectively you need to anchor directly over the structure the fish are holding on, or repeatedly drift over it. Anchoring over a small wreck or rockpile may be challenging, but it will result in fewer snags than drifting. Savvy anglers will locate a good spot with their fishfinder, and drop a float marker on it. Then they will take the time to anchor so the boat holds right next to the float, and the structure is directly below.

4. Watch the gill plates on sea bass. They're every bit as sharp as those found on croaker, and will result in nasty cuts if you're not careful. Children should not be allowed to handle sea bass. Their dorsal fins can stick you as well, but always look out for those gill plates.

5. Sea bass seem to be more apt to blow their air bladder when reeled up quickly than many other fish. In fact, if you fish near other boats and everyone is catching small sea bass in water deeper than 30', you will often see numerous released fish floating by in the throes of death. When you get into a large number of undersized bass, the best move is to relocate. When you feel a small fish on the line, reel it in very slowly to give it a chance to adjust to the pressure changes, and there's a better chance it will survive.

6. Sea bass like a little flash. Even when fishing a bait like crab chunks or squid strips, you'll increase your catch by using hooks dressed with beads and spinners. When dropping jigging spoons, choose those with a bright silver finish.

7. It's best to use breakaway weights when sea bass fishing. Because of the need to fish close in to structure, sea bass anglers encounter a lot of snags and lost rigs. When you set up your top-and-bottom rigs—the standard for sea bass—tie a short length of light leader between the bottom of the rig and your sinker. This way, if the weight becomes wedged in the wreck or rocks it will break off before the entire rig does.

8. Small moves can mean a lot when you're fishing for a species that holds so tightly to structure, and shifting your boat a few yards will sometimes change the action completely. While anchored over structure in a strong current, it's possible to shift the position of

your boat without re-anchoring. If you've fished a specific spot for a while and it seems that the best fishing is over, crank your steering wheel all the way to one side or the other. In a stiff current this can move the boat as much as 15 or 20 yards, which will give you virgin territory to try. If the results are unsatisfactory—or fast action becomes slow again—crank the wheel all the way in the other direction and try again. For an even greater change run your anchor line off of a spring cleat (sea conditions permitting). Although this may hold your beam to the sea, increasing the rocking and rolling of your boat, it will change your position even more than cranking the wheel hard over does.

9. Although sea bass do stick close to cover, they tend to hover a few feet above it. If you're fishing in an area with tons of snags, try pulling your line up a couple of feet after you've located the bottom. Your bites may drop a hair, but for the most part the action will continue and you shouldn't lose as many rigs or lures.

10. Although sea bass and tautog are more or less sedentary, you can draw them into catching range with an unusual method of chumming. The day before you go fishing, you'll need to go to a seafood store or crab house, and ask them if they will give you (or if you can purchase for a reduced amount) their day's die-offs. Most are more than willing to point you to the bushels of dead crabs. So long as they haven't gone rancid in the sun, die-offs work just fine for this tactic.

Smash a few crabs, and put them into a wire basket or a mesh bag with lots of weight. Usually, at least 2 lb is needed, because you want that chum to sit directly under the boat, right next to your lines. Every half hour or so add another smashed crab, and you will draw hungry bass into striking distance. (This tactic also works well for weakfish, spot, and croaker. Even flounder pop up sometimes when fishing with die-off crab chum.)

Tautog, also called blackfish or tog, are usually caught in the same places as sea bass. Often, they're caught with the same baits and rigs; however, anglers targeting them specifically will use crustacean baits as opposed to squid. Without a doubt, tog are one of the strangest looking fish found in the Bay. Their large, tough, puffy lips look like they are always puckered up for a kiss, but those large puffy lips are also the key to understanding how to catch these fish.

Tog tend to test potential food with their lips, before taking it into their mouths. If the bait passes muster, they then take it in their huge front buckteeth. These teeth are designed to crack open the shellfish tog enjoy eating.

But set the hook at this stage, and you'll miss the fish—they have a second set of teeth, set back in their throat that actually "chews" their food.

Speaking of food, tautog are excellent eating fish. No wonder when you consider their diet, which consists almost exclusively of shellfish. Mussels, crabs, clams and the like are favored foods, with green crabs ranking as the top bait choice.

Although the largest tog in the record book hit 25 lb, catching one in this size range in the Chesapeake is a long shot. The largest recorded tog from Maryland hit 19 lb and Virginia's record is 24 lb, but both of these record setting fish were caught off the coast in the open ocean, not in the Bay. Most caught inside the mouth of the Bay will be between 1 and 3 lb, with an occasional fish up to 10 lb. Tog will move in and out of the Bay seasonally, but it's important to watch for fish with white, saddle-like markings down the middle of the fish in the spring months. These marks indicate a pre-spawn female that should be immediately released unharmed. Tog are relatively slow growing fish and localities can be fished out rather easily. But when the time is right to put a tog or two in the cooler, use these tricks.

1. When a tog first picks up a bait, you'll feel a peck. Remember—the fish hasn't really eaten your bait yet, he's just testing it at this point. Wait until the peck is followed up with a tug, before setting the hook.

2. Tog hold very close to the structure they are oriented to, much more so than sea bass and other wreck fish commonly caught mixed in with the tog. This gives anglers two concerns: first, to hook the fish you must be anchored or drift directly over the wreck or structure you are fishing, or you don't have much chance. Second, the moment you have a tog solidly hooked, you should crank as quickly as possible to drag it away from the structure. Otherwise, there's a good possibility of becoming entangled in it.

3. Tog should be targeted with heavier gear than one would normally use for fish of this size. Again, the object is to drag the fish away from structure as quickly as possible. Going to line in at least the 20 lb class, matched up with leaders in the 40 lb class, will allow you to crank down on the drag and pressure the fish hard for those first few imperative seconds of the fight.

4. Another way to keep the fish from tangling the structure is to use superline that allows you to yank the fish up off the bottom with no line stretch. Superline has a second advantage in that it also will help you distinguish between that initial tap and the real tug. Unfortunately, there is a downside. Hook the bottom with superline and you'll have a tough time breaking it off. In fact, a 26' boat can be held in place as though it were anchored by an angler with 30 lb

test superline. Too much pressure placed on the rod in such a situation will result in a broken rod. And if you try wrapping it around your hand to break it free, there's a good chance you'll end up with a nasty cut. Keep a pair of snippers handy whenever you fish with this stuff, or use a wooden dowel to wrap the line around before attempting to pressure it.

5. Green crabs are the most popular tog bait, but don't overlook mussels. This is especially true when fishing in or around rockpiles and riprap, where mussels naturally grow. Sure, crabs work in these areas, too. But at times a ball of shelled mussels will attract the fish more quickly and be eaten by the tog with less hesitation. Plus, in many areas mussels can be bought or harvested by hand in large numbers, at low or no cost.

6. When fishing for tog, you're going to end up snagged some of the time no matter what you do. These fish are just too good at swimming into holes and crevices when they feel the sting of a hook. When this happens, don't yank and pull on the line. Instead, slack it completely. Sometimes the fish will mistake the lack of pressure for freedom and will swim out of the wreckage for you.

7. Use thick, Virginia-style hooks when fishing for tog. Remember, these fish have a tough mouth. Thin, wiry hooks just don't have the penetrating power to get through the tough hide and are apt to bend before puncturing the fish's mouth. Think thumbtack, not needle.

8. When removing the hook from a tog, watch out for those buck teeth—they can do some damage! Always carry a pair of forceps with you and if you don't have any onboard, cut your line close to the hook, leave it in place, and re-rig instead of risking a nasty bite.

9. Don't be discouraged if you start catching large numbers of small tog. Unlike many schooling fish, large and small tautog will often be mixed in the same area. Just because you catch a bunch of small ones, don't assume there aren't any larger tog nearby and move on.

10. Many anglers like to fish wrecks and structure with hooks that are dressed with spinners, beads, or bucktail skirts. While these are effective for attracting other gamefish, when it comes to tog, they are a detriment. A simple, plain old baited hook will out-fish one dressed up with all the goodies virtually every time.

BLUEFISH

Blues may not be as popular among anglers as stripers are, but they are certainly more vicious. In fact, they will continue to slash through schools of bait even after they have eaten so much that they are constantly regurgitating shredded baitfish; this violent nature has earned them the nickname "Chesapeake Piranha." Of more interest to anglers, blues fight with the same violence and vigor. They provide spectacular jumps, and they don't tire until they've fought to a near-death state. They also are dangerous—let one get too close to a finger or a toe, and you'll have a very nasty cut to deal with thanks to the bluefish's razor-sharp chompers.

Bluefish are known by several different names, according to their size. Small fish up to a pound are called snappers, and these are by far the most common size blues in the Bay. From 1–3 lb blues are commonly called tailors. And large, 15 lb or better blues are known as choppers. Choppers are more commonly caught in the ocean than the Bay, which is a more or less recent development. Back in the '80s when stripers were in short supply, bluefish invaded the Bay in great numbers and very large fish did sometimes pop up. These days it's rare to get a 10 lb blue north of the Potomac, and the real choppers are caught almost exclusively in blue water.

Why this shift? Anglers, scientists, and fisheries managers have been arguing about this for years. It may have something to do with increased competition due to the striped bass resurgence, or it could be the result of the decline of menhaden numbers in the Bay. Climatic changes could also be to blame. In any case, although the angling opportunities for very large blues are not what they used to be from Love Point to the CBBT, there are huge numbers of snappers and tailors to provide great angling action.

Bluefish are unusual in that they are found nearly worldwide. They grow to be 20–30 lb, and the world record, caught off Hatteras, NC, was 31 lb Maryland's state record is 23 lb 8 oz, and Virginia's is 25 lb 4 oz. Blues will feed on anything. All finfish—including other blues—clams, crabs, eels, you name it. If you put it on a hook, a bluefish might eat it.

Catching bluefish is probably easier than catching any other Bay sportfish, because as well as their desire to eat whatever is at hand, they're almost

Teeth and temperament have earned the bluefish the nickname "Chesapeake Piranha."

always willing to bite regardless of the time of day or tidal cycle. In fact, more blues are probably caught by accident than on purpose, by anglers targeting other species. If you want to catch blues in specific—or if you're tired of losing lots of hooks because of their sometimes overwhelming presence—you will need to add a trace of wire leader to your hook or lure. Not only will blues bite right through monofilament, they'll also bite the hairs off your bucktails, scrape the paint off your plugs, and shred the teasers off trout scout rigs. If you have a favorite striper lure and the blues have moved in, you're best off saving the lure for another day. Use these bluefish-specific tips to hook up with more of these feisty, voracious predators.

1. Blues will be found feeding at or near the surface more often than most other Bay sportfish. As a result, if you want to catch them in a chum line or under working birds, focus your effort on surface baits.

2. Bluefish love to chop baitfish right in half. This makes live-lining for them almost impossible, as they constantly take the tail-end off of your livies. Instead, cut the head and tail off of your live bait, toss them over the side for chum, and put the middle of the peanut on your hook.

3. Blues don't slurp, nibble, or inspect baits—they kill and eat them with the utmost urgency. Accordingly, when you feel one strike set the hook immediately.

4. Blues love flashy lures. Troll a spoon next to a bucktail, and bluefish will hit the spoon twice as often. Whenever choosing a lure to be trolled, jigged, or cast to bluefish, pick out something that shines.

5. Bluefish have a good sense for feeling or hearing vibrations in the water. As a result, lures such as Rat-L-Traps that put out constant vibrations are very effective on them. It is downright dangerous, however, to catch blues on plugs with multiple gang hooks. It's nearly impossible to get the trebles out of their snapping jaws, and the blues' tendency to go absolutely crazy while being held means that the second set of trebles will often end up in the anglers' hand or finger. Before casting a plug like this to a school of breaking blues, swap out the trebles for single hooks.

6. Smaller bluefish are much better eating than large ones. Although it's not as much of a thrill to catch a 3 pounder as it is to catch a 10 pounder, the 3 lb fish actually tastes a whole lot better—so don't feel bad about taking home the smaller ones and throwing the choppers back.

7. Chumming at night with a set of night lights out will bring swarms of bluefish to your boat. Don't try this if you're hoping to catch stripers or trout when it seems they're being overwhelmed by the blues.

8. Blues are jumpers, and fish in the air have a much better chance of shaking out a hook than those in the water do. When fighting a bluefish it's best to keep your tip low and off to the side, which will discourage jumping. If the fish does make it into the air, reel like a madman to keep maximum tension on the line.

9. If you jig for trout under working birds or breaking fish, you'll often encounter blues, too. Occasionally, you'll be reeling in a fish, feel a sudden tug, and pull up the front end of an undersized trout, dripping blood. When this happens lower the half-trout back into the water immediately, and let it sink of three or four feet. Often the marauding bluefish will still be right under the boat, looking for the other half of his meal.

10. When the tails to your plastic baits keep getting bitten off, you'll know there are blues in the area. Swap the plastics for a spoon to put them in the cooler.

CATFISH

There are many species of catfish inhabiting the Bay and its tributaries, but most that anglers will encounter with regularity are channel and blue cats. Both are considered good eating, and although both may be caught in some of the same areas, it's easy to distinguish between the two because channel cats have a peppering of spots along their sides and tail.

Channel cats are usually considered more of a "sport" fish than blues, if for no other reason than because they will occasionally strike lures. Commonly, most other catfish hit only dead baits. Channel cats, which are found throughout the country, have been known to grow quite large and the IGFA recorded one in excess of 58 lb.

Blue cats can grow even larger—the record stands at 116 lb, caught in Arkansas. Blues are not a native to the Chesapeake, but come from middle America. They were introduced in Virginia, thrived, and now constitute a significant recreationally caught food fish in lower Chesapeake tributaries.

Bull cats are also common in the Bay region. They are easily identified by their rounded tails, yellowish appearance, and smaller size. Bulls rarely grow beyond 3 lb, and most caught in Chesapeake tributaries will be too small to eat.

All catfish are excellent at locating bait by smell and are most effectively sought where there is a current strong enough to carry a bait's scent a long distance. Because of their great sense of smell, stinky baits are often the best bet when going for these fish. Cut menhaden and herring are old standby baits, but in recent years many anglers have discovered the value of using mass-produced "stink baits" with designer scents. They usually look and smell disgusting, but they do work. Chicken livers are another favorite bait of the cat hunters. Ready to try chasing whiskers? These tips will help.

1. When choosing a place to catch cats, look for three major details: structure, depth, and current. Catfish like to hide around structure, they like holding in holes that are deeper than the surrounding water, and current will carry the scent of the bait to the fish. If you find a deep hole with a tree laying in the bottom and good current sweeping past it, you have found a prime catfish location.

Tidewater catfish: blacken and enjoy.

2. In winter months, mass schools of channel cats will hold at mid-depth in deep creek holes. I know this sounds nuts—catfish suspending at 15' in 30' of water in a tidal creek while it's snowing—but I've seen it happen time and time again. In this situation you will usually hook these fish by accident, snagging them in the belly as you reel in your line. (Often this will happen while fishing for perch). If you happen to be fishing a tidal creek and snag a cat in this way, try jigging cut baits at mid-depth. Usually these fish are present in huge numbers and it's possible to catch dozens out of the same hole in this situation.

3. Catfish will change their local range radically depending on salinity. Some years, they will be found only up in the tributaries. Other years, they can be caught out near the Bay Bridge. It all revolves around salinity, and after a rainy spring look for a hot catfish season. After a dry spell, hunt for cats deep in the creeks and way up tributaries where there's more freshwater.

4. Bridges are always good catfish attractors. As long as the location has the necessary low salinity, casting a cut bait out near a bridge piling is usually a successful way to go. The fish will be found on both up and downcurrent sides of the piles, as well as out to the sides.

5. Keep catfish baits on bottom. Even a traditional top-and-bottom rig may keep the bait higher than you want it. Instead, rig up with short leaders and use chunks of fish that will sink (from the back and tail sections of the baitfish) not float.

6. Don't be choosy about your cut baits when going for catfish. It's not imperative to have fresh bait, and many anglers swear they do better using old, rather stinky baits that have been sitting in the refrigerator a tad too long for their own good.

7. Peeler crab is also an excellent catfish bait, one that often gets overlooked. Many anglers stick with the traditional cut fish time and time again. But peelers will boost the number of strikes you get over cut fish in some situations.

   During rainy seasons when catfish move out into the Bay proper, soft clams also will out-fish cut fish quite often. Crush the clam and thread the snout onto your hook, then run the point into the clam's body, and fish it on muddy bottoms where soft clams are commonly found.

8. Catfish are a low-yield fish. While a 3 or 4 pounder looks big, you should be aware that it will only produce a pair of quarter-pound fillets. Accordingly, cats less than 4 or 5 lb should usually be released. Otherwise, you'll find yourself doing a lot of cleaning to get a little bit of meat.

9. When handling catfish of any type be very careful—their dorsal and pectoral fins have sharp, spiky points that can deliver a nasty puncture wound. Often, such a cat cut will become infected. To avoid this problem unhook cats with a pair of pliers or cut the line and tie on a new hook after landing one.

10. Channel cats particularly like gravel bottoms. Of course, gravel bottoms are a rarity in Chesapeake tributaries. Mud and/or sand is much more common. But if you find a gravel bottom with good depth and current, there's a good chance you've just found a channel cat hot spot.

COBIA

Of all sportfish available in the Chesapeake, cobia hold the top ranking for sheer strength. These fish fight with long winded, determined runs and they usually won't give up the fight until they've been in the cooler for a good, long while. They commonly swim right through nylon mesh nets, strip the gears on spinning reels, and as often as not, swim away free while an angler curses his luck.

Cobia can be particularly frustrating because they can often be spotted on the surface, finning about near buoys, sea turtles, or other flotsam. When seen up on top, cobia are usually not in a feeding mode. Anglers might cast lure after lure to these finning fish, without generating one iota of interest.

Chumming with baits set at all levels in the water column is the most common way to score a cobia in the Chesapeake. These fish usually feed near shoals and humps that are relatively shallow, and often the best cobia fishing takes place in 15' to 20' of water. There's no mistaking a bite with cobia—usually they will suck down the bait then rip line off the reel for a solid 10 to 20 seconds before slowing down, if they ever do slow down. As a result, you'll need to up-size your gear over the Chesapeake norm to catch these fish. Gear at 30 lb is minimal, 40 lb class is appropriate, and 50 lb class gear is not out of line. Although spinning gear can be used, conventional star drag reels are much more common. When it comes to cobia, stay away from level automatic wind reels, however, as large fish will have the brawn to burn out the worm gear that drives the level winder.

When cobia fishing you should be prepared for multiple hook-ups, as these fish often travel in pairs or small pods. When one is being brought to boatside, a second rod rigged with a live bait or lure should be kept at the ready; often a fish or two will follow the hooked fish, providing the opportunity to get a hook into a second cobia.

So, just how big a cobia can you hope to hook into on the Bay? In Maryland, the largest ever caught (it was taken at the Middle Grounds) was 97 lb 12 oz. In Virginia the biggest cobia tilted the scales at 104 lb 8 oz. The IGFA, however, has recorded a fish that topped 135 lb. Want to beat that mark? These tips will help.

Cobia are some of the largest, hardest fighting fish to be caught in the Chesapeake.

1. When you spot a cobia on the surface and do not have any live baits onboard, you can sometimes get the fish to strike a bucktail dressed with a twister tail (or similar lure) by casting it between 5' and 10' in front of the fish, and allowing it to free-fall. If the cobia chases the lure as it falls, wait to feel a slight bump on the line (that's the fish sucking it into its mouth) then set the hook. Cobia on the surface will hit lures fished this way about twice as often as those cast and retrieved along the surface.

2. Once you've fought a cobia up close, it will often swim parallel to the boat just out of gaffing range. The fish will attempt to hold its position and rest. Don't let it—if you allow the fish to recover its breath, it will dart away and you'll have to start over again from ground zero. Instead, when you see the fish use this tactic tighten up on the drag and force the cobia closer to the boat. Usually, this will trigger the fish's final run.

3. Never cast beyond a cobia on the surface and bring the lure from the fish's tail towards its head. This is not how a baitfish will commonly act, and it often spooks cobia.

4. Most Bay chummers use menhaden for cobia, but it's an accepted fact that cobia prefer shellfish to finfish. Take advantage of this by going to your local seafood store, and asking if they have any "die-off" hard crabs. Usually they are happy to hand you a bag full of dead crabs; if not a few dollars should be all it takes. Smash up the crabs and mix them in with your chum flow. Setting out a half of a peeler crab as a bait is a good idea, too.

5. If a cobia comes to boatside quickly, don't attempt to land it right off the bat. Instead, pressure it one way and another, tap it on the tail with a gaff, or otherwise aggravate it so the fish fights harder and tires itself out. If you gaff and land a "green" (energetic) cobia, you are in for a big, big mess—these are powerful fish and will go absolutely crazy in the cockpit of a boat if they aren't bone-tired.

6. Cobia will attempt to roll off of a gaff hook, often with success. If you strike and the cobia rolls off the hook, try aiming for a point farther forward on the fish's body. The underside of its head and gill area are good targets. Also, strike and lift the fish into the boat in one fluid motion. This way, if the fish rolls off the gaff hook, at least there's a good chance it'll land in the cockpit.

7. Cobia love live eels. Anytime you'll be fishing for cobia or foresee the possibility of lucking into one, it's a good move to toss a few live eels into the livewell before leaving the dock.

8. Cobia don't have sharp teeth, but they do have many small abrasive ones. As a result, you should use a stiff, abrasion resistant

leader. Considering its nearly invisible nature, fluorocarbon leader is a natural choice.

9. Whether chumming or casting to finning cobia, superlines or braids are generally not the best choice for line. Remember that these fish are real bulldogs. They will put an unbelievable amount of pressure on your tackle. If you're using a superline, there's a pretty fair chance the fish will break a rod or strip the gears on your reel.

10. Cobia are one of the best and most unique eating fish in the Bay. For a real treat, try this Floridian recipe: Mix 50% blue cheese salad dressing with 50% mayonnaise. Coat the cobia steaks, and bake until the mixture turns brown on top. It sounds strange, but tastes great!

CRAPPIE

Crappie are a freshwater game fish but we'll include them because they inhabit many of the tidewater creeks and rivers feeding the Bay. This species can be further divided into black and white crappie, but fishing tactics and techniques don't vary between whites and blacks. (The easiest way to differentiate between the two is to count the dorsal spines; white crappie have six, while blacks have seven or eight dorsal spines). Although they are not among the fish usually listed as most important or most sought after, there are plenty of Chesapeake anglers who regularly chase these fish in the headwaters.

Crappie are not large fish and neither Maryland nor Virginia lists records for them in tidal water. The IGFA's record is 5.3 lb, but a crappie over a pound is a nice fish and a 2 pounder is a trophy in anyone's book. They feed mostly on small finfish—almost exclusively, in freshwater—and are most often caught with minnow. In tidewater, however, crappie also will eat shrimp, scuds, and on occasion small crabs.

Crappie have relatively thin mouths, and for this reason they must be netted and never swung onto the boat or shore, or the hook will likely rip free. When setting the hook while crappie fishing remember to be gentle, or you may rip the hook right through the fish's jaw. It's also important to note that crappie are mid-depth feeders. Unlike many fish in the Bay and its tributaries, they don't usually pick meals off the bottom or attack fish on the surface. More often, you'll locate crappie suspended in the mid-depth region of the water column. Tidewater crappie are also extremely structure-oriented fish. You will not find them out in the middle of a creek, or even (unlike crappie in freshwater lakes) over a drop or edge. Instead, they will be found next to pilings, brush piles, and fallen trees. Often, they will be within inches of the wood and won't move so much as a foot to attack a bait. If you can tempt them to eat using these ten tactics, however, a pile of crappie makes for an excellent meal.

1. When you catch a crappie in tidewater, fish the exact same spot again. Often you will find tightly-packed schools of a dozen or so fish, and repeated casts to the identical spot will result in repeated

Crappies are one of the tastiest residents upriver.

hook-ups. Even if the spot seems blank after you've caught a fish or two, work it hard before moving on.

2. Crappie holding tight to wood feed right against that wood. Often you will find a series of pilings or a bulkhead that holds fish, yet casts a foot away from the bulkhead or pilings doesn't produce strikes. For whatever reason, crappie seem to be aware of critters (and bait) that are oriented to the same structure they are hanging on. When casting and retrieving the bait, you'll only get a second or two in the target zone. To maximize your catch, fish areas like these with bobber and minnow combinations. The bobber will allow you to cast into the tiny target zone and keep your bait in it for an extended period of time.

3. Crappie like small minnow. Even larger fish are much more inclined to hit the smallest minnow in your bucket. In fact, it might be more accurate to say that crappie like tiny minnow. Scale down hooks accordingly (#6 is usually about right) and toss out the smallest bait you've got.

4. When crappie are holding tight to fallen trees, and casting in close results in snag after snag, get into the trees with them. You'll need a fairly small, narrow boat to use this tactic; poke in as close as possible and get on the bow with a three foot length of rope. Secure it to a cleat, then pull the boat as far as possible into the brush, and tie off onto one of the tree branches. Since you surely stirred up the area getting in there, relax for a few minutes and allow the spot a chance to calm down. Then pull a few feet of line off your rod, and drop your bait down vertically, right next to the boat and in the mess of branches and limbs. If no strikes come, shift to the other side of the boat. If you try all reachable holes in the brush without any strikes, double the length of your line and try them all again. Often, this is the best way to drag crappie out of heavy cover in tidewater areas.

5. Unlike most game fish, you'll find crappie on the downcurrent side of structure. Most other fish are caught around solid structure on the upcurrent side, but for whatever reason, crappie often orient the other way around. Spots where the current smacks the shore or eddies in front of it are also good for finding crappie.

6. If you don't already know where the crappie are on any given tidal creek or river, plan on moving a lot until you find them. Commonly, a given shoreline will be covered in dozens of fallen trees that look like crappie heaven. Yet all will be deserted. Then, after fishing all those great looking spots, you'll suddenly get bite after bite next to one specific tree that looks like all the others. Come

back in a week, and you'll likely find the fish in that same spot, while all the other excellent looking trees remain barren.

7. When fishing minnow under bobbers, don't set the hook on a sideways-moving bobber. Usually, this situation arises when fishing during the colder months. The fish will sometimes grab a minnow and slowly swim away, without swallowing it. When this happens, your bobber will appear to slowly move off to the side but won't go down. Resist the urge to set the hook and wait until the bobber sinks below the waters' surface—this signals that the fish has the bait all the way into its mouth and is returning to its hiding place.

8. Lily pads often hold crappie in tidewater. Whenever you see a cluster of pads and you're on the hunt for crappie, try fishing next to them for a while. Same goes for shorelines lined with lily pads.

9. Crappie are easily spooked. Dragging a tacklebox across the deck, speaking loudly, or banging the hullside of an aluminum boat are all enough to spook a school of fish. Whenever you approach a crappie spot do so slowly and quietly.

10. In discolored water, fish minnow on the hook of a marabou jig. These jigs increase the profile of the minnow, and if you match the jig color with the water color, will increase their visibility greatly. Unlike some other lures, crappie don't seem disturbed when the minnow are trailing marabou.

CROAKER

Pound for pound, it's hard to find any fish that fights with more determination and gusto than croaker. Many a Chesapeake angler has fought what they thought was a hefty striper or weakfish to the surface, only to discover it was a 3 lb croaker fighting like a fish twice its size. On top of that, croaker are great eating. And on top of that, they even talk to you—wonderful entertainment for the kids. In fact, between fighting abilities, vocal abilities, and a willingness to bite most baits at most times, croaker may hold the number one spot as the most kid-friendly fish on the Bay.

Croaker are close relatives of drum, and the croaking noise they make is similarly formed in the air bladder. Interestingly, the largest recorded croaker from Chesapeake Bay beats the IGFA all-tackle record by a wide margin, leading some to believe that there's a new world record out there, just waiting to be set. The fish was caught in the Tangier Sound, and weighed 6 lb 3 oz. Virginia's state record is 5 lb 13 oz that also beats out the "world record," which the IGFA puts at 5.8 lb.

Though fairly small in maximum size, in the Chesapeake it is often possible to locate schools of fish in the 3 lb range and load a cooler with them. But be careful—between the sharp dorsal spines, sharp gill plates and boney heads (croaker are also called hardhead) filleting croaker is no easy chore. Setting a daily catch limit of eight or ten fish per person will keep the cleaning chores reasonable, while providing plenty of table fare for the family.

A quick glimpse at a croaker's mouth is all it takes to see how they feed; with jaws pointed down towards the bottom, croaker eat worms, grass shrimp, small crustaceans, bivalves, and similar critters living in the mud or sand. They will also scavenge, and in fact you will catch croaker on just about any bait if it's set on the bottom. When targeting them directly, bloodworms, peeler or soft crabs are probably the best baits, followed by squid. Surprisingly, you'll also catch plenty of croaker bouncing jigs. This is particularly true when using scented plastics, like Powerbaits and Exude jig tails.

Although croaker are among the easiest fish to catch, many anglers target them very early in the season when their numbers are low simply because they're the first recreationally caught fish other than stripers to migrate up the

Croaker are the Bay's bottom fishing mainstay.

Bay each spring. They can be caught in Virginia waters as early as March some seasons, and certainly by April. Within two or three weeks of their initial arrival in the Bay, they will be available in the middle Bay and will continue migrating all the way up to Rock Hall or even Turkey Point, depending on salinity levels and the amount of rainfall that particular spring.

These early spring fish will be tougher to catch than they will be in May and June, simply by virtue of the fact that there aren't as many in the Bay yet. The best way to target them is to fish when croaker bite the best: at sunset and after dark. When the sun goes down you can find croaker on oyster bars, off drop-offs, and sometimes milling around over muddy bottoms. They move shallow during this time frame, and bank anglers may actually out-fish boat anglers during this early season. When you locate one, however, you usually locate an entire school of fish and every rod onboard will get bent. To get (and keep) your rods bent over under croaker power, use these tips.

1. Don't give croaker a lot of time to eat baits. Usually, by the time you feel the fish it has eaten the bait and is leaving town. Croaker aren't careful, dainty, or hesitant in the way they eat, they just suck it down and keep on going. So as soon as you feel it on the line, set the hook and bring the fish in.

2. A croaker die-hard I know has developed his own secret weapon for catching croaker that out-fishes anything else I've ever seen. Here's how to make these special croaker baits: Cut squid into inch-wide, three inch long strips and spread them on a cutting board. With an ice pick, punch numerous holes into each strip. Then put them into a plastic container, like an old margarine tub, and set it in the refrigerator. Next, place a soft crab into a cheese cloth or strainer, and smash the juices out of it. Pour the crab juice into the tub of squid strips, stir, and let it sit in the fridge for a few days before you bait your hooks with it. Yummy.

3. If you're fishing for croaker with peeler crab, rip the legs off before threading your hook through a knuckle. The legs won't make a very tempting piece of bait anyway, and croaker will grab, shake, and run with a bait; if it grabs the leg, you may lose the entire bait without getting a hook into the fish.

4. There will be times—often when flounder fishing—that croaker become a nuisance because they eat your baits so quickly you can't get them to the fish you're targeting. When this happens, bait up with the largest bullhead minnow you can find, only (no additional squid strip or crab chunk). Very large croaker will still eat the minnow, but for the most part, average fish will leave it alone.

5. When fishing for croaker in the dark don't bother with night lights. This is one occasion when they won't help you any, and there's no reason to bother with all the lights, batteries, and wires. Instead, depend on the scent of your baits to bring in the fish. Make sure your baits are fresh and replace them often.

6. Make sure you get a firm grip on a croaker's gill plates before you try to remove the hook from their mouth. Croaker have a way of flaring their gill plates, and these plates have a very sharp outer edge. If you're not careful, they will cut your hand.

7. During the day a good place to locate croaker is in cuts and creeks with three or more feet of depth and strong current. Deeper cuts, like those running behind islands, with 10' to 12' of depth, will at times be loaded with croaker.

8. Croaker tend to be a bit more scattered about late in the year, as they move out of the Bay. This migration can start as early as late August. When this period begins, don't spend a lot of time in one spot just because you've caught a fish or two. The croaker aren't schooling as they were earlier in the year, when one fish on the line usually meant a hundred below the boat.

9. Croaker may be the one kind of fish that can be reliably caught over artificial reefs planted in the Bay. While most of these reefs really don't support a heck of a lot of good fishing, they will be visited by croaker that eat the mollusks and crustaceans on the reef. So if you see those familiar "Fishing Reef" markers and it's croaker you're after, give them a try.

10. In much of the Chesapeake, you'll rarely catch croaker in open water deeper than 40'. Of course there are exceptions, but good croaker anglers will spend their time focused on depths shallower than this, and often take the bulk of their fish from 12' or 14' of water—don't be afraid to fish shallow when you're after croaker.

FLOUNDER

Flounder might not hold the number one spot as the most sought-after species on the Bay, but they are certainly in the top five. On top of that, many flounder anglers are dedicated to the fish and spend their time pounding flatties whenever possible. The middle and lower Bay offer great opportunities to catch large numbers of flounder, but not many are doormats. The largest of the species tend to stay closer to the ocean, and although more large fish will be caught in the southern reaches of the Bay, most of the really big ones don't enter Chesapeake territory. That's why the Virginia state record (17 lb 8 oz) and the Maryland state record (15 lb) both come from coastal bays. The IGFA's largest-ever doormat was weighed in at 22 lb 7 oz and was caught in New York waters.

Flatties feed mostly on small fish, which explains why the bull minnow is the number one all time flounder bait. Still, some anglers swear by squid, and the favored flounder rig along the coast is a Fluke Killer dressed with both—a squid strip/minnow combination. The minnow used are the biggest possible, and squid strips are usually cut at about two inches wide and five inches long; flounder are not afraid of large baits.

Still other dedicated flattie fans stand by bucktail/minnow/squid combos, and another sect prefers bouncing jigs. Of one thing there is no doubt: all of these techniques are effective.

Unlike most fisheries, there are a good number of constants with flounder. One is that they like clear water. In churned-up, muddy water it's not a good choice to focus on flounder. Low-light days can be productive, though less so than bluebird days, and when it's cloudy or raining it's doubly important the water be clean and clear. Flounder show a preference for sand bottoms, though you will sometimes take them on shell bottoms. Over mud, it's a rarity. Flounder are also predictable in that they like a moving bait. Motionless baits usually go untouched, and when jigging, the motion should be so fast it's almost violent. 99 times out of 100 flounder will hit lures as they fall, and you won't know it until you sweep the rod tip up to jig it. For this reason, always keep a firm hand and be ready to apply maximum pressure when you go to jig upwards. One final regularity: flounder hold tight to the bottom. If you want to hook one, you must keep your bait or lure as close as possible to dead-on at all times.

Flatties like this one create dedicated anglers.

Trolling for flounder is also popular, especially in deep water where the current is so strong it's tough to keep a bait down. At the CBBT, in particular, wire-lining for flounder is a top technique. The rig and technique is the same used when bottom bouncing for stripers, except that when wire-lining the depth should be kept constant instead of ever-changing. This particular fact holds true whatever technique you're using to catch flatties—when you catch a fish note the depth, and stick with it. The downside to wire-line trolling? Lots of weight is necessary to keep that bait down deep. Remember—if it leaves the bottom, you're not in the flounder zone.

In deep, open water, you'll usually find flounder on edges between 12' and 40' deep. You'll catch 75% of your fish in a 5' depth spread, through a tidal period. When the tide shifts expect that the flounder will too, and try to move with them.

In shallow water, jigging, casting dressed bucktails, and dragging Fluke Killers are the most effective techniques. All will work but beginners should stick to Fluke Killers and bait, which is the easiest way to catch the fish. Interestingly, a flounder takes a baited rig very differently than it hits a jig or bucktail. When it first grabs the bait the angler will feel the rod tip quiver. Set the hook now and the fish will go free. The angler has to wait until he feels a "thunk, thunk, thunk" on the end of the line. This is the time to set the hook. It could take anywhere from a second to ten seconds to go from quiver to thunk, but you must wait for the thunk to catch these fish. Conversely, jig and bucktail anglers need to set the hook immediately and solidly upon feeling the strike. Usually the lure will either hit home and set solidly in the fish's jaw, or pull free with little resistance. The stronger the hook-set, the better off you are.

During flood tides in clean water, serious flounder experts look for fish in extremely shallow water—depths of two feet or less. Anywhere riprap lines the shore you stand a fair chance of finding flatfish, and in some seasons, light tackle anglers casting to points and drops right on the shoreline will strike it rich with flounder. Cuts are another flattie hot spot. Any that drain marshes or salt ponds can be productive, even if they're just a few feet across. Cast to the mouths of cuts like these during the very beginning of the ebb tide until it's dropped about half-way, and you stand a good chance of finding fish.

Once on the line, another unusual trait of flounder is the way they fight. Large flounder often fool you into thinking you've hooked bottom—they don't move, not even an inch, when you pull on them. Then, as you apply more pressure, you'll feel the fish's head slowly lift off the bottom. The slow-but-steady pull generates a feeling similar to the sensation of hooking a large mat of weeds that holds fast to the bottom for a second or two before slowly ripping away. Once you've lifted the fish off bottom, it will suddenly come to life and pull with hard, twitching jerks. Then you'll get the slow tug again, maybe a run or two, and more of those hard jerks. The feeling is very unique, and you won't mix it up with other fish when you have a flattie on the line.

The flounders' northern range varies greatly from year to year. You'll consistently find them from Chesapeake Beach south along the Western Shore, and on the Eastern Shore, from Eastern Bay south. You'll usually also find them from the Bay Bridges south—in some years, thick between

Thomas Point and Franklin Manor—and some years they're caught all the way up to Poole's Island.

The final uniqueness of this strange, lovable, and challenging species: the meat is awesome. Many people will eat flounder over all other fish, and with good reason. The meat is white, firm, and flaky. Filleting a flounder is also a bit different than cleaning other fish. Split the fillets by slicing down along the lateral line, all the way to the backbone, then slide the knife along the top of the bones working from the center of the fish out towards the edges. You'll come away with two delicious strips of meat from each side. Prepare for the feast by filling the cooler, with these tips.

1. Flounder usually show a preference for bright colors. White, chartreuse, yellow, and red are usually best. One exception: in slightly off-colored water, purple will often be the top producer.
2. In discolored water, choose Fluke Killers, Roadrunners, or other rigs that have a spinning blade. They seem to do better than other lures in this situation, the prevailing theory being that the fish can hone in on the vibrations produced by a spinning blade.
3. Some knowledgeable fluke sages drag a weight or a length of chain as they drift. Many people believe that flounder will follow the trail of puffing, disturbed sand to the lure.
4. Save some of a flounder's white belly meat for bait. Strips of flounder belly sometimes outperform all other baits, and they are amazingly tough. Sometimes you'll catch a half-dozen fish on the same bait, and it won't be any the worse for wear.
5. Never let a flounder hang in the water while someone's going for the net. It's imperative to keep a constant tension on the line with flounder, or that jerky head-shake will rattle the hook loose. As soon as someone hooks up, someone else onboard should immediately go for the net and stand ready.
6. When choosing a plastic jig for flounder, go with the paddle-tail style. Who can say why they like them better, but flounder show a clear preference for paddle tails over twister tails of the same color, especially in the middle and upper Chesapeake.
7. When wire-lining for flounder and you get a fish on, don't slow or change the boat's speed. Again, it's that jerky head-shake thing. As soon as a flounder feels a change in the tension on the line or the least bit of slack, he'll give it that shake. So keep the boat speed steady as the fish is brought in.
8. Flounder have sharp teeth. Of course you should handle them with care, but this also means you should look for slightly thicker leaders than would be the norm for fish that top out at 20 lb. Use a line

that has good abrasion resistance and feel it for nicks and cuts after each fish you catch.

9. To hold a flounder pinch it with a couple of fingers on the top of the gill plates, just behind the eyes. Trying to grab it by the tail will only provide entertainment for your crewmates, and because of the shape of the fish, it's impossible to grab it around the middle.

10. When jigging for flounder in water over 12' or 15' use superline. Remember the need for that fast, firm hook-set? With mono, it just won't be fast or firm enough because of the stretch in the line. Fish with superline, and you'll increase the number of solid hook-ups by 25%. Similarly, choose a rod with a firm, fast-action tip.

Freshwater anglers take note—the Chesapeake has plenty to offer you too, especially largemouth bass.

LARGEMOUTH BASS

Naturally, the largemouth bass is one of the most written about and talked about sportfish in the nation. While it may be true that in Chesapeake country it plays second fiddle to saltier species, the largemouth bass still has a large and dedicated following in this region. In fact, the Chesapeake has hosted the BASS Masters Classic, among other big-dollar tournaments.

Most of the bass fishing on the Bay takes place in the northern parts of the upper Bay, but it is notably popular in the Potomac (and its tributary creeks), Nanticoke, and Wicomico watersheds as well. Maryland's state record comes from the Pocomoke, at 9 lb 1 oz, but Virginia doesn't list largemouth bass as a marine gamefish. There's not much chance of a new world record coming from any of Maryland's waters, as the old mark of 22 lb 4 oz is more than twice the size of any Bay-caught bass. In fact, most tidewater bass run between 1 and 3 lb and a 5 pounder is truly huge for those caught on and around the Bay.

As with most area, in the Chesapeake region bass are generally considered catch-and-release sportfish. It is legal to keep them in Maryland and Virginia during the proper seasons, but few anglers do. Additionally, bass populations on the Bay and its tributaries can vary greatly from year to year. Weather and especially rainfall amounts will expand and contract the largemouth's range, feeding patterns, and overall population numbers.

While tidewater bass do act essentially the same as their freshwater brethren, there are some important differences to keep in mind. Adjust the usual freshwater bassing tactics accordingly, and you can have a ball with bass in Bay country.

1. You will often be faced with off-color water when tidewater bass fishing. Chocolate, tannic, and dark water is often present in both tidal tributaries and the northern Bay. As a result, you should plan to use dark colors more often than you might when freshwater fishing for bass. Root beer, black, and creme hues will all come in handy.
2. In the marine habitat, piers and bridge pilings play a huge role in a largemouth's life. These two forms of structure probably account

for 80–90% of all the bass caught on Chesapeake waters. Pay heightened attention to them at all times.

3. Bass seem to be more inclined to schooling in brackish water than in fresh. A hole with good cover in a lake, for example, might hold a single large bass. But in tidewater, there's a better chance that the same type of hole with the same type of cover will hold a half-dozen mid-sized bass.

4. If you're a freshwater angler who's trying bassing on the Bay, make sure your reels and tackle are up to the salty challenge. Plenty of bassers have launched and fished in the Chesapeake only to discover that the next day, their prized tackle is covered in a layer of rust. Even way up north on the Chesapeake, corrosion will take a heavy toll on gear that's made for the freshwater environment.

5. Because of tidal flow and salinity, tidewater bassing allows you to extend the usual bass fishing season. When farm ponds, reservoirs, and slow-moving bodies of water are frozen solid, anglers can still get in good largemouth fishing in tidewater. Hitting the warm water releases at power plants is also a cold weather option not open to traditional bassers.

6. Unlike bass living in purely freshwater, tidal bass will change and adapt feeding patterns according to the migrations of saltwater species. When shad are in town, for example, shad-imitating lures are a good choice. When herring move into the tributaries, again, match the hatch. The downside? It is occasionally possible for bass, among other predators, to gorge themselves silly on a plentiful bait until they have no desire whatsoever to feed. If this is a potential problem, you may be able to solve the issue by moving farther up into freshwater zones, where these fish may not be present.

7. Stay away from freshwater baits in tidewater. Sure, you'll catch some fish if you toss shiners out in the Bush River. But shiners don't live there naturally, and you'll catch a lot more fish by using big bull minnow, instead of freshwater shiner. Again, this boils down to matching the hatch.

8. Small white perch make a good live bait in practically all of the water bass can live in that's attached to or feeds the Chesapeake. White perch occur naturally just about everywhere in the region, and no matter where a bass lives, if he's tidewater, he's seen a white perch at some point in his life. Make them more attractive by clipping off a pectoral fin, so the perch struggles.

9. Crayfish patterns work in tidewater. Here's the exception to the match the hatch rule. After all, there can't be very many crayfish in-

habiting tidal zones or the upper Chesapeake. Yet for whatever reason, lures with crayfish patterns work well for tidewater bassing.

10. Be careful with bassboats on the Chesapeake. All too often an angler sets out to cross the Bay in a bass boat without taking into account the different and more violent nature of the Bay waters as compared to lakes and reservoir. Simply put, the Chesapeake gets too rough for a boat with low deadrise, a fine bow, and gobs of horsepower. On top of the seaworthiness issue, many bass boats are built for freshwater use and do not have 316-grade stainless steel fittings. As a result, a single Bay trip can prove disastrous for some bass boats.

Watch out—that duckbill-like mouth of the pickerel is full of needle-sharp teeth.

PICKEREL

Topping out at less than 10 pounds—the IGFA world record pickerel is 9 lb 6 oz and the Chesapeake record is 6 lb 8 oz—the chain pickerel may not seem such a tough customer. Well, that's only true until you try to get one off of a hook for the first time. Chain pickerel may be named for the chain-like pattern on their flanks but the name could just as easily apply to the chain-saw-like mouth full of teeth they posses.

Pickerel inhabit most Bay tributaries in one area or another, usually where the salinity levels are relatively low and grass beds are plentiful. In many rivers the upper, fresher areas are consistently inhabited by pickerel. In some other rivers that have a salinity level closer to the edge of their tolerances, pickerel may be plentiful one year and absent the next. They also tend to make seasonal appearances, with a stronger showing during the late fall, winter, and early spring months. So far as Chesapeake fish go, pickerel are essentially a cold-water predator.

Pickerel have a tasty white meat but are extremely boney fish. As a result, only the largest should be kept for food. Many anglers grind pickerel meat and form it into patties or "fishburgers" to eliminate the need for careful, tedious bone removal.

These fish prefer to feed in and around grass beds, taking full advantage of their camouflage, and ambush their prey with sudden, speedy bursts of violence. They grab their prey in their duckbill-like mouth, and pierce it with multiple dagger-like teeth until it stops struggling. This unusual feeding technique calls for specific angling techniques—listed below—if you want to be successful with pickerel.

1. Pickerel have teeth sharp enough to slice right through monofilament, but they will shy away from rigs with wire leader. The most effective way around this problem is to use jigs tipped with baits when pickerel fishing. Hair-body jigs—marabou and bucktail in the three-inch range—usually provide enough distance from the minnow to the line that the pickerel won't cut you off. Note,

however, that you can only expect to catch a handful of fish on a single jig before it's shredded beyond recognition.

2. A pickerel's eyes are located far forward, close to the top of its head. This is because they like to sit deep in the grass, waiting for a minnow to pass overhead. As a result, it is possible to present your baits within a few inches of a pickerel, yet out of the fish's field of view. I've been in several situations where the pickerel were sitting two feet down in a weedbed, in three feet of water. Minnow suspended two feet down under a bobber went ignored, yet those fished just six inches higher were slaughtered. If you don't seem to be getting the strikes you think you should be getting when fishing for pickerel, try raising your bait's level in the water column.

3. Pickerel will grab a baitfish and hold it partially in its mouth, waiting for it to die before attempting to swallow it. As a result, if you set the hook when you first feel a nibble (while fishing with minnow) you will often yank the bait away from the fish. Instead, upon feeling a pickerel strike, you should freeze; don't put additional pressure on the line, nor should you slack it. Soon, you will feel a slow pump of the pickerel's tail, as it swims off. This is your cue to action, as the pickerel usually won't begin swimming away until he's sure the baitfish is dead or near dead and can't escape. When you feel that tail pumping, it's time to set the hook.

   Judging how long to wait in this scenario is a real guessing game, because the pickerel may wait anywhere between two and twenty seconds before swimming off. The length of time a fish will wait seems to vary from place to place and day to day, however, the one constant factor to pay attention to is water temperature. In 35°F water expect the pickerel to wait a good long time before swimming off, and in 45°F or warmer temperatures, it should make a move much more quickly.

4. Although the majority of the pickerel you catch will in fact be in weedbeds, there is a second place you'll often find them: laying alongside trees or poles floating or partially floating sideways in the water. Specifically, look for fallen trees or overhanging branches that have snagged logs as they floated past. Cast and retrieve your baits parallel to these logs, just under the surface, and you'll often hook up.

5. In relatively warm conditions, when water temperatures are over 45 or 50°F, pickerel are suckers for spoons and spinners. For some reason gold always seems to work better than silver. Spoons in particular are great lures to cast into water where the weedbeds reach within a foot or so of the surface, since their wobbling action

allows you to retrieve relatively slowly without sinking into the weeds. When a pickerel strikes a spoon or spinner, don't hesitate to set the hook.

6. When fishing marabou jigs tipped with minnow, consider going to a Roadrunner-style jig instead and you'll experience more strikes. As shown by their affinity for spoons and spinners, pickerel like things that flash, shine, and vibrate. Even the single, small blade of a Roadrunner makes a noticeable difference when fishing for pickerel.

7. The availability of pickerel in the upper reaches of most Chesapeake tributaries makes this a fish that will often be caught when ice fishing in or around the Bay. When pickerel are biting through the ice, however, you'll need to change your tactics significantly. Since you will usually have out tip-ups, bobber rigs, or other static lines, you won't have the ability to feel the fish take the bait, wait for it to turn, and set the hook. Instead, the pickerel will often eat the bait all the way down before triggering the indicator or tip-up, and by the time you reach the line, will often have the bait deep down in the gullet. As soon as you put tension on the line, it'll cut you off. So if you're targeting pickerel through the ice, you'll need to use a trace of leader. Instead of using the traditional wire, stick with low-vis wires like Tyger leader (multi-strand, highly flexible wire) or titanium leaders.

8. During parts of the year when weeds die off or disappear from coves or creeks where pickerel are known to be, look for them under piers and boathouses. When traditional pickerel cover disappears, these structures seem to attract the fish. Note that pickerel won't usually move under such cover in an area unless there were, during other seasons, weedbeds nearby. But when a storm or unusual currents, dredging, a cold snap, a warm snap, or other unusual conditions cause the weeds to suddenly die off, try flipping your baits under the piers and pilings and you'll quickly discover where the fish went.

9. Yellow perch patterns are also effective on pickerel. Lures with the yellow background and vertical bars will often take fish when other lures or baits don't seem to be working. For whatever reason—don't ask me why!—this seems particularly true of Rapala Fastbacks in open water and Normark Jigging Rapalas.

10. When an area of a cove, creek, or river that holds pickerel is weed-choked, make your own highway to heaven. Tie any large lure onto a heavy rod, and cast it right into the middle of the mess. Start reeling the moment it hits the water, and drag back a nice, big, fat weedball. Repeat the process a half-dozen times,

and you should have created a trough, your "highway," through the cover. Now leave—you've spooked every fish within casting distance. But don't go too far off. Within a half hour or so the fish will have calmed down, and now you have a prime strip of open water to cast through.

When entire bodies of productive pickerel water are choked off by excessive weed cover, you can spend an hour or two in the morning doing nothing but creating these slots of open water. Many will close up, particularly if you're in an area with current, but if you open up a good number of them, you'll always end up with some productive, fishable water to show for your work.

RED DRUM

Red drum, also called redfish or channel bass, are another seasonal visitor to the Bay. You can count on them making a showing in Virginia waters every season but whether or not they venture very far into Maryland is a toss-up any given year. Sometimes they don't, and sometimes they are caught as far north as the Magothy River. During the summer of 2003 there were good numbers of puppy drum (small redfish, under 5 lb or so) along the Western Shore of the Bay from Herring Bay all the way up to Ft. Smallwood, near Baltimore. This, of course, is not the norm. During an average season, don't expect to find red drum much farther north than the Potomac River.

Since they are an excellent food fish, they grow large and put up a significant fight, red drum are a highly sought-after gamefish. Just how big do they get? The top fish in Maryland is 74 lb 6 oz and Virginia's record fish just tops 85 lb. The IGFA recorded a whopping 94 lb 2 oz fish—these are serious bruisers. Big drum in this category are usually called "bulls," a somewhat ironic term as most larger drum are females. Of course, fish of this size are the exception, not the norm. Most drum caught in the Bay range between 2 and 20 lb. These are the best for eating, as larger, older fish sometimes have coarse flesh.

Red drum are easily differentiated from their black drum cousins by body shape and markings. Reds tend to have more elongated bodies, and they don't have the small whiskers present on blacks. Their body is more orange than black, with a white underbelly, and reds have a spot located on or near the tail. In some cases, they may have two or three spots. Overall and aside from sheer size they look very similar to croaker and anglers have been known to mistake horse croaker for puppy drum.

Redfish have down-turned, tough mouths that give you a clue as to their favorite foods. They like crustaceans, especially shrimp and crabs. They also feed on finfish and are commonly caught on live baits. Many anglers believe that drum have a keen sense of smell and poor vision, but studies by marine biologists have more or less debunked this theory—in fact, their eye sight is average.

One feature many Chesapeake anglers find enticing when it comes to red drum is the ability to catch these big fish in shallow water, on light tackle. Unlike most fish in this size range, the majority are hooked and landed in water

The Chesapeake is one of the northernmost areas to regularly fish for red drum.

less than 10' deep. That makes it possible to cast and retrieve jigs, live line baits, or fish cut bait with little or no weight on gear in the 10–15 lb class. For any sport angler, catching a big red on tackle this light is a triumph. Here are ten tips and tricks that will help you hook into that bull red of a lifetime.

1. For whatever reason, big reds like fish heads. Fresh mullet, menhaden, and spot heads are all exceptionally good redfish baits. Peeler crabs are also an excellent bait, and provided they are fresh, they're tough to beat. Both baits are most productive when reds are gathered in small schools around cuts, channels, and other fish-attracting features, as opposed to when they are scattered across the flats and shallows. When fishing the shallows for single redfish, it's usually important to keep moving and cover a lot of territory, which makes bait fishing more or less ineffective.

2. Puppy drum love riprap. If you want to cast light or ultralight gear to pups in the 1–10 lb range, try tossing three-inch twister tail soft plastic grubs right up to riprap jetties and bounce the jig back along the bottom. This goes for the rocks around the CBBT, too, although in this area the conditions will often require you to upsize your gear.

3. When fishing in shallow water for redfish, keep an eye out for "tailing" fish. You will occasionally see the tip of the redfish's tail just breaking the surface of the water, as the fish roots around on the bottom. When you spot a tailing fish, cast at least five feet in front of it (10' is better) and give it a slow, steady retrieve.

4. Gold spoons are a favorite of shallow water redfish. Cast and retrieved through shallows with a slow wobble, they can be deadly. Those with rattles, such as the Nemire Red Ripper, often outperform other styles.

5. Weedbeds are a favorite feeding area for red drum. Look to catch drum in the "potholes" (circular holes in the weedbeds). They tend to move into these holes during falling tides and can be caught either by cast and retrieving through them or by tossing a bait into the area of open water. If the hit doesn't come within a minute or two move on, as reds hanging in the grassbeds are usually on the feed and will bite if given the opportunity. If nothing happens, chances are there aren't any fish around that particular spot.

6. There are several areas in the Chesapeake (near Smith Island in the Tangier, Pungoteague Flats and east of Robin Hood are a few) where you can find long weedbed edges, usually at or adjacent to drops from 2' or 3' to 4' or 5'. An effective way to pry reds out of these weedbeds is to troll alongside of them with un-weighted gold spoons, screwtail jigs, and Sluggo-style lures. Keep your boat just

far enough out that you don't drive through the weedbeds, and keep it at idle speed. If you have several people onboard it's a good idea to post one on the foredeck armed with a spinning rod and a lure; when he spots depressions or nearby potholes in the weeds, he can take a shot at them.

7. Popping with a cork, a Floridian technique for catching bull reds, can be used just as effectively here in the Chesapeake as it is down south. The rig is amazingly simple: just tie a couple feet of 30 lb leader to your main line and attach a hook on the end. Then secure a large bobber with a concave surface—the cork—to your line just above the leader, so it sits about three feet above the bait. Add a couple of split shot just above the hook to keep your bait down. Cast this rig into any place that looks like a winner for redfish, and let it sit for a few seconds. Then jerk the line quickly and violently, so the bobber makes a popping noise. Wait 15 to 20 seconds, and pop it again. Reds seem attracted to the commotion, and with a little luck, when they come to investigate they'll find your bait.

8. During years when rays are thick in the Bay, you're usually best off fishing for reds with lures. Many of the areas you'll find redfish also have a lot of rays, and usually, they will find your bait before the fish do. If you catch a ray or two when bait fishing, consider switching to lures before you find yourself inundated with these large, flat anti-fish.

9. Reds respond well to noise makers and vibration producers. Add chuggers, rattling lures, and lures with vibrating blades to your list of red-friendly lures. If you're casting bucktails tipped with bait, add to their attraction by clipping a rattler tube onto the hook (available at Outdoor World for a dollar or two, these small plastic rattle-filled chambers snap onto the shank of your hook.)

10. In off-color, stained, or muddy water, try lures that are root beer colored. For some reason reds seem to have an easier time spotting root beer in discolored water. Remember to slow down your presentation, and you'll sometimes catch just as many reds in dirty water as you will in gin-clear conditions.

SPADEFISH

Spadefish are less prolific than most of the other fish found in the Bay and will rarely be caught north of the lower Chesapeake as they don't have much tolerance for brackish water. Fortunately, they do pack in tight where they are found. Schools of adult spades usually number 500 or more and are usually oriented to wrecks or other significant structure, so if you catch one, you're probably in for many more.

Spadefish are unusually tough to hook because they have tiny mouths. A number four hook is the largest you'll want to use, and sixes are better. Strangely, unlike most other fish in the Bay, spadefish prefer to bite on a slack or dying tide. This makes them an excellent option when other fish you've been targeting shut down after feeding on a strong tide.

Although spadefish look like some type of tropical angelfish, they are quite good on the grill. The meat of a spadefish is firm and white, but has an unusual taste. While unique it is considered excellent by most, and spades are a desirable food fish. That angelfish-like look has another consequence: spadefish can turn their wide, flat bodies into the water, and put a lot of pressure on the line. The Virginia state record is 13 lb (Maryland doesn't even list one, as few spades are caught north of the state line) and the IGFA record is 14 lb (ironically, it comes from Virginia waters, but is not listed as the state record) and most spadefish you catch will be in the 3–5 lb range. Yet a 5 pounder can feel like a 20 lb fish on the end of the line.

Most anglers will pursue these fish with relatively light spinning gear in the 15–20 lb class. Heavier gear is useless, because you can't catch spadefish using leaders heavier than 20 or 25 lb, since anything larger is simply too thick to tie on those tiny hooks. If you've never caught spadefish, you should definitely give it a try. You'll be successful, too, if you put these tips to work.

1. Chumming clams over wrecks or structure like the CBBT islands (the third and fourth rank at the top) is unquestionably the best way to catch spadefish. Most anglers will smash a dozen or so large cherrystones together, then hang them off the transom in a wire mesh basket or a cloth chum bag. Give the bag a shake now and

Fishing for spadefish has grown wildly in popularity for about a decade.

again to make sure plenty of clam tidbits are entering the water, and add a fresh clam or two as necessary. Baits should be thin strips—not chunks—of the clam.

2. When attracted to a boat by chum, spadefish will often hold about 10' below the water's surface. Accordingly, use one or two ounces of weight to get your bait into this zone when there's a current. When the tide is dead-slack, it's usually more effective to ditch the weight and allow your bait to drift back naturally in the chum slick.

3. Never cast a spadefish bait away from the boat. Spadefish will usually stick tight to that chum line and baits a mere five or ten feet out off to the sides will often go untouched.

4. When the tide goes completely slack, spadefish will sometimes hover right under the surface. Whenever you are targeting spadefish, keep an eye out for a thin stick-like dorsal fin just breaking the water's surface. If you see them, try to drift your bait back close by and you should get a strike.

5. Spadefish are seasonal visitors to the Bay and will only be caught when the water is warm. July and August are the best months to target them, although in some years they will show up in June and in others they will stick around until September.

6. Don't set out lines, stick the rods in the holders, and expect spadefish to attack. They don't usually like static lines and want a bait that appears to be drifting naturally. The most effective way to get a bite is to fish with an open bail, letting line fall out slack as the current carries it away from the boat. Watch the line loosely, and when you see it jump, close the bail and reel it in tight.

7. Spadefishing has grown in popularity in the past few years, and as a result, many of the best locations will often have a small but tightly-packed crowd around them. To get away from this crowd—but still get in on good spadefish action—on calm days, run out into the ocean. Any of the wrecks laying just outside the mouth of the Bay can produce spadefish, but they will receive a lot less pressure than those spots in and around the CBBT.

8. Keep the clam bits flowing steadily and in good supply. Once spadefish arrive in your chum slick, they will usually hang around until the clams stop flowing. The key here is—just like with stripers—to keep the flow of chum steady.

9. When a spadefish takes a clam bit, allow it a three-count before setting the hook. They will sometimes grasp the strip of meat and turn before sucking it all the way into their mouth, and if you strike right away, may pull the hook and bait away from the fish.

10. Since spadefish require fairly specific rigs (particularly, the tiny hooks) and you're likely to encounter a wide variety of other gamefish in the same areas they frequent, whenever you go spade-fishing it's a good idea to keep rods rigged with standard chumming rigs ready to use in extra rodholders or hard top rocket launchers. If you start experiencing sudden, jolting strikes or break-offs, place a larger bait on the bigger hook and rig and lower away.

SPANISH MACKEREL

Spanish mackerel are another seasonal visitor to the Bay. Unfortunately, these hard fighting fish have a pretty limited time frame during which they stay in the Chesapeake. Usually they will first appear at or near the mouth of the Bay during July, and work their way northward as far as the Bay Bridges by August. The first cool nights of September, however, send them swimming back toward the ocean. Often, by the second week of September they are all but gone from the Bay.

Spanish mackerel are good eating fish, but their soft meat must be treated gently and quickly drops in food value if frozen. In fact, many anglers eat them fresh or not at all. Although a 13 lb Spanish holds top world-record honors, the Maryland record is a far cry from this size, at 6 lb 8 oz. Virginia's record is significantly larger at nearly 10 lb. Like many other ocean-oriented species, fishing for Spanish becomes better number-wise, as well as size-wise, the farther down the Bay you go.

These fish are good fighters that jump more often than stripers but less often than blues. Most are relatively small, hence the hectic fight comes from their speed not their bulk. On light gear they provide an exceptional battle, zipping back and forth as quickly as any fish in the Bay can. Many anglers like to target Spanish macks when they're schooled and mixed with blues feeding under birds, where it's possible to throw light lures on gear in the 8–10 lb class—the perfect recipe for an epic light tackle battle.

Spanish mackerel eat mostly fin fish and usually feed at or near the surface. As you might expect this has a lot of influence on fishing methods, and usually Spanish mackerel must be specifically targeted to produce decent catches. You may pick up an oddball fish once or twice a season while chumming or bottom fishing, but to be consistently successful with mackerel you'll have to concentrate on them.

1. For whatever reason, more often than not Spanish mackerel prefer gold over silver. The standard methods of catching these fish—trolling or casting spoons to breaking fish—works best when lure color is gold.

Spanish mackerel: fast, feisty, and fun.

2. Bump it up to catch Spanish mack. Striper trolling speeds of four to five mph won't produce any mackerel. Bluefish speeds of six or seven mph will produce some, but an eight-mph troll is better for these speedsters. Naturally, this means that you would need a ton of weight (and the heavy gear to support it) if you wanted to run your trolling lines anywhere but right on the surface. Luckily, right at the surface is where these fish usually feed. Use just enough weight to keep your spoons from flipping out of the water and skipping across the surface.

3. When casting spoons to breaking fish, you'll do best on Spanish if you rip the spoon across the surface as quickly as you can. Don't be afraid to crank the reel at maximum velocity—that's how these fish like it.

4. One other effective method of taking these fish is with live baits. Peanut bunker and finger mullet will both work. They can be drifted and live lined anywhere Spanish mackerel are present, but most of the time, bluefish will be mixed in with mackerel—and will chew the majority of your baits to pieces.

5. You may be able to find breaking fish and working birds, but that doesn't mean there are Spanish mackerel in attendance. They are usually mixed in with blues, and just as often, you'll locate a school and catch bluefish, only. Finding out if there are Spanish

mackerel around is easier than you might think, however. Simply watch the feeding fish. If there are mackerel around, you will see them jump clear out of the water, often in small groups of twos and threes. They will jump in an arc, and often "greyhound," or perform several of these jumps in a row. Bluefish will absolutely, positively, never exhibit this behavior, so if you see the arcing fish in greyhounding mode, you know Spanish mackerel are around.

6. Spanish mackerel have teeth that are fairly sharp, though they don't match those of a bluefish. They are sharp enough, however, to cut through monofilament leaders. Save your gear and land more fish by tying a 6" trace of wire leader ahead of your lures.

7. Whether casting or trolling, any time you fish for Spanish mackerel with spoons you stand a good chance of encountering massive line twist. Trolling spoons at high speed is the worst case scenario when it comes to twist, and ten minutes is sometimes enough to trash a spool of line. Accordingly, whenever you troll for these fish make sure you use high-quality ball-bearing swivels between your main line and leader.

8. When breaking fish aren't visible, try trolling along tidal breaks and scum lines. Often, Spanish mackerel will orient along changes in the water and any tide line or color change is a good bet for trollers.

9. When Spanish macks are in the area but are not feeding on top or around color changes, it's time to try trolling deeper. Most anglers commonly keep just an ounce or two of weight in front of their spoons to keep the lure in the water. But you can up that to three or four ounces that will take the spoon down a couple of feet. This, of course, is still not very deep—but some oddball days this contradictory tactic makes all the difference in the world. Bottom line: when you're not catching fish, give the abnormal a try.

   Other days, a few ounces of lead simply won't make enough of a difference. If this is the case you'll have to get those spoons down farther and lots of weight is not the best way to go, since that requires upsizing your tackle. Remember, most of the Spanish you'll catch are just a few pounds, and it's really not much fun trolling for them with heavy tackle and a pound of lead. Instead, try pulling planers. A #1 or #2 planer is usually all it takes to get a small spoon 20' below the surface.

10. On slick calm days, try increasing your trolling speed even more than usual. Conversely, in rough seas drop it back a bit. You'll find you get just as many strikes. For whatever reason, the mackerel seem to have a tougher time catching the lure when the water is riled, yet they show less interest when it's glassy out.

When it comes to light tackle, shallow water fishing, speckled seatrout are often the fish of choice.

SPECKLED SEATROUT

Speckled seatrout—specs, as they're often called—are very similar to weakfish in body shape, possess the same delicate flesh, and have the same set of vicious looking teeth. But when it comes to catching them, the differences are much greater than the similarities. Specs are shallow water feeders and provide Chesapeake anglers from the Choptank south with a great light tackle alternative.

Speckled seatrout average 1–3 lb in the Bay and its tributaries, but occasionally gators in the 10 lb range are caught. The largest recorded catch on the Maryland portion of the Bay is 13 lb even, and in Virginia, 16 lb, but the largest ever taken on hook and line was over 17 lb. Specs are very popular gamefish in Florida and along most of the Gulf Coast, especially in Texas. They are also called winter trout, salmon trout, and spotted weakfish, in some areas. Their favored diet consists of shrimp, crabs, other crustaceans, and small baitfish. Some anglers have tried importing fresh gulf shrimp for use as bait in the Chesapeake with some limited success (frozen shrimp doesn't work well in most cases), but generally speaking specs in the Bay and its tributaries are caught on soft or peeler crab, or artificial lures.

Specs hit a lure with vigor, and they may be caught at different levels of the water column. That's part of what makes fishing for them so interesting—during different tidal cycles, you may catch them up near the surface, then at mid-depth, then down near the bottom. They're rarely caught in water over 20' deep, most are caught in 10' or less water, and many are caught in 2' deep shallows near points, creek mouths, and tidal rips.

Speckled seatrout will establish patterns in their feeding techniques that may hold for a week, month, or even a season at a time. This pattern can usually be identified after fishing through a full tidal cycle a couple of times, and if you can figure it out, you'll catch a lot more fish. Let's say you find that at the flood tide they're feeding near the surface, and on a dropping tide, they feed near bottom. The next time you go fishing, note the current tidal cycle and stick to fishing according to the pattern you saw the previous trip—if the tide is dropping, cast and retrieve near bottom, and if it's flooding, try retrieving near the surface. More often than not, you'll find that the pattern holds, at least until the next major shift in weather patterns or forage availability. Here are ten tips that are sure to help you catch more trout.

1. Specs usually like a vigorous, moving bait. Instead of slow and steady retrieves, stick with erratic, faster retrieves. When hopping jigs along the bottom, pop them up vigorously. Constantly vary the retrieve and keep that lure moving at all times.

2. When casting lures to speckled trout in the Bay, it's tough to beat a 4" curly tail jig, either chartreuse, pink, or white in color. Rig it on a 1 oz jig head, and you can use it for all ranges through the water column in the areas you're likely to locate trout.

3. Never stop the retrieve short of the boat. Specs will often follow a lure right up to the surface. If you stop reeling when the lure is five or six feet away, you will end up missing some fish that would have charged and struck in the final seconds.

4. Moving water is key for locating speckled seatrout in the shallows of the Chesapeake. Anywhere the current creates a rip or is visibly moving, you're likely to find these fish. Points, cuts, and rips near islands in the Tangier Sound are prime speckled trout territory and offers some of the best spec fishing in the entire Bay. They make an early showing here in April, remain through June, then reappear in late September or October.

5. Don't be afraid to search out cuts barely big enough to get your boat into. You'll find the largest speckled seatrout inhabiting five foot wide, two foot deep cuts at times. When patrolling a shoreline or marsh in search of specs, cast as far up into those little cuts as you possibly can. Remember that most of them will have slightly deeper patches of water on the inside of a bend, and the edges of these holes is often where you'll locate the best fish.

6. Multiple specs will congregate in the same spot, even if the productive water is only a few feet across. Often, you'll find a point or bar that creates a tidal rip, which attracts specs. You'll find that you must pinpoint cast to the very tip of the rip, or the very base of the rip, to get a strike—anywhere else, and your bait gets ignored. Yet if you cast to that spot over and over again, you'll catch fish after fish. So don't move on simply because you've already caught a fish from a very small hot spot; keep working it until you're sure there aren't any other hungry trout around.

7. Bang the shoreline with your lures. Especially in areas where there's a sharp drop-off, speckled trout will often be feeding within inches of the marsh grass. Make your casts as close to the shoreline as possible, and whenever you can, cast parallel to shore and retrieve along it.

8. Shortly after the specs arrive in the shallows, the rays arrive. There's usually a ten day to two week period between the specs' and rays' arrival, which provides you with the opportunity to bait fish for specs with peeler or soft crab. It's often tough if not impossible to get fresh softies at this time of year, but if you can and if you cast it into two to three feet of water on bars and points very close to those rips and strong currents you're usually casting lures at, you'll score big. Once the rays arrive it gets tough to fish bait, as they will snap up most of your offerings before the trout can get to them.

9. Specs are strong fighters, and pound for pound, will out-fight weakfish. However, they have that same weak jaw that's easily ripped. So it's even more important that you fish with a loose drag when you're after specs. Don't over pressure the fish and allow them to run as much as they like. Also as with weakfish, make sure you have a net ready before the fish is sighted, and get that net under the fish well before you lift its head out of the water.

10. If you're fishing plastic tail jigs, make sure you have plenty of extra tails onboard. As with bluefish, specs will often short-strike and "tail" the jig (eat the last ½" off of the jig). When this happens immediately swap out the tail. It may look like it will still work, but that last half-inch provides some critical motion. Fish with it and you'll eventually realize that the fish will not strike it half as much as they will hit a fresh one, with a whole tail.

The undisputed champion of the Chesapeake, the striper.

STRIPERS

Without any doubt, the striped bass is the most popular gamefish in the Chesapeake. They're good fighting, good eating, and after a decade-long moratorium and one of the few success stories in fisheries management, available in good numbers. Before the moratorium went into effect, stripers had become rare in many areas of the Bay. During the '80s, for example, to catch more than one or two keepers in a day was quite unusual. When the fishery was shut down bluefish in the 2–8 lb range had almost entirely replaced the Bay's striper population. Then the moratorium went into effect. Five years into it, we began to hear rumors of people catching good numbers of stripers by accident, while fishing for blues. A few years later, most Bay anglers started picking up one here and one there, purely by chance. And when they reopened the season it seemed like keeper-sized stripers were packed gillplate-to-gillplate in just about every good fishing spot in the Bay. Of course, the fishery has had ups and downs even in the decade since then. But barring any natural disaster or legislative stupidity, stripers are back in force for the foreseeable future.

The striped bass is commonly called rockfish in Maryland and Virginia. Striper and linesider are a couple of other nicknames you'll hear. They average 1–5 lb in the Bay, but 10 and 15 lb fish are relatively common. Much larger fish—up to 60 lb and above—are present in the spring when they migrate into the Bay tributaries to spawn. During trophy season, 30 and 40 pounders are not uncommon. By some estimates, up to 50% of all the stripers along the Atlantic seaboard are born in the Chesapeake and return to it to spawn. Maryland's state record rockfish is 67 lb 8 oz, and Virginia's is 61 lb 12 oz. The world record striper was a hair over 78 lb, but catches nearing 100 lb have been claimed by commercial netters. After spawning, most of the large spawning stripers in the Chesapeake migrate back to the ocean and travel up the coast to feed in bait-rich northern waters of New Jersey, New York, and Massachusetts.

Stripers have sandpaper-like teeth, which makes handling them by the jaw relatively easy. Note to catch-and-release anglers: hoisting large stripers by the jaw and holding them vertically can do internal damage to the fish; they should be supported with a second hand (wet it first, so you don't remove the fish's protective coat of slime) behind the anal fin. They feed not by biting into and cutting their prey, but by sucking it in and grabbing it; most meals are swallowed whole. Some favorites of the striped bass include: eels, soft or peeler crabs, menhaden, spot, bloodworms, manoes clams, and herring.

Stripers can be taken with dozens of different methods, many of which are discussed in this book. Whichever you choose to use, remember these striped bass tips—they're applicable to all methods and modes of angling.

1. In most conditions, stripers feed like clockwork, in relation to the tides. Commonly the change of tide is the best, from one hour or so before the slack tide to a half hour or so after.

2. Striped bass are light-sensitive fish. On bright, bluebird days, look for the fish in deeper water and on cloudy low-light days, look for them in shallow water or close to the surface over deep water.

3. Stripers are schooling fish, and they often school by size. When you're catching 14" fish one after the other, consider changing your game plan entirely or move to a different location. Otherwise, you're likely to catch throw-backs all day.

4. Bursts of feeding activity are based on tidal cycles, but sunrise and sunset provide two other opportunities for striped bass to feed. From the first hint of light until the sun breaks the horizon, and from the moment it dips out of sight at the end of the day until it becomes completely dark, striped bass will often feed heavily.

5. A rockfish's metabolism changes with the water temperature, so adjust your lure retrieve speeds, jigging techniques and trolling speeds accordingly. In the hot summer months provide lots of action and speed, but early and late in the year, keep it slow and lethargic.

6. Even the largest fish of this species will sometimes take a bait with a gentle nibble. Particularly when chumming for trophies early in the spring, treat each and every tiny little bite as if it's the real thing.

7. Stripers like to grab their prey, and squeeze the life out of it. This means that they often will grab a baitfish and swim with it clenched tightly in their jaws for several seconds, before sucking it all the way in. As a result, whenever in doubt, give the fish a five or even a ten second count from the time you feel it pick up a bait to the time you set the hook.

8. When fishing in a menhaden chum slick, stick with menhaden baits. Stripers seem to become focused on the type of fish or chum that attracts them, as they peruse the baits offered to them.

9. When trolling or jigging for stripers in the Chesapeake, remember this old Bay adage: "If it ain't chartreuse, it ain't no use."

White is the next most commonly effective color, followed by yellow and on occasion (particularly in cloudy or stained water) pink, purple, and red.

10. Stripers are slow, steady fighters that do not burn themselves out on single, spectacular runs. When catching large ones on light gear, give them their head. Do not attempt to muscle or push the fish, which often leads to break-offs. Instead be patient; the fish will eventually wear down.

Deep water jiggers often target weakfish.

WEAKFISH

Although weakfish take a backseat to stripers and blues in the hearts and minds of many Bay anglers, these fish top the list in several other areas of the country. Their popularity in some areas is unparalleled by all but redfish, and weakfish are a mainstay of anglers from the Carolinas to the Keys.

These fish are known as weakfish because of their tender, easily-ripped mouths. Some also call them yellow-fin seatrout, gray seatrout, or simply seatrout. The are very similar in body shape and appearance to speckled seatrout, but they feed in different ways and are usually not found together. Both species are easily identified as members of the trout family by their "canine" teeth—two long, sharp fangs centered on the top jaw, and two slightly smaller fangs on the lower jaw. While these teeth can cause injury to unwary anglers, on the whole they don't hold a candle to bluefish when it comes to making anglers bleed.

One other important feature shared by both weakfish and specs: Their meat is incredibly good eating when cared for properly, but turns to mush when cared for improperly. Time and time again, you'll hear people say trout are not good eating. Ask them how the fish were chilled after they were caught. Most of the time, the answer is that they were placed in a wooden or fiberglass fishbox with a block of ice, or a bag of ice shoved in there somewhere. For seatrout, this kind of treatment just does not cut it. Two key factors must be addressed if you want your trout to taste good. The first is temperature; being in a box with ice is not good enough. The bottom of the fishbox must have a layer of ice, and no more than an hour or so after being put into the box the fish should have chipped or shaved ice placed on top of it. The second is pressure; stack large fish, ice blocks, or large chunks of ice, soda cans, or bottles on top of a trout, and its meat will turn to mush. To keep your trout in prime shape, here's what you do: first dump a bag of ice into the cooler, to provide a bottom layer. Then keep a second bag of ice in the cooler, but don't open it. After you catch a few trout, rip a hole in the second bag and put a thin layer of the ice over the fish—after dropping the bag on the deck a few times, to make sure that it's broken up and no large chunks remain. You'll find that the meat is so sweet, you'll be tempted to fish for trout every time you go out.

One more trout meat tip—if you place trout fillets skin down in the oven and spread crab imperial over them, the meat will take on the taste of the crab.

Trout don't get as large as some of the other important sportfish in the Bay. A 10 lb or larger fish—called a "gator" trout—is extremely rare these days (they were more numerous several decades ago, but followed the usual pattern of an over-harvested species). The Maryland state record is 16 lb 8 oz, and the Virginia record is 19 lb even. On average, trout in the Bay run between a ½ lb and 3 lb. The IGFA recorded a 19 lb 2 oz fish caught in Delaware Bay, as the largest recreationally caught weakfish ever. These fish will feed on most small baitfish including bay anchovies, peanut bunker, and small spot, but their favorite meals are soft or peeler crab.

Trout aren't as tolerant of low salinity as some other species are, and as a result, during years with a lot of runoff, the fishery can be poor for middle and upper Bay anglers, especially. In fact, in some years there's no real fishery at all north of the Choptank. On the flip side, in years of drought they can be caught in decent numbers as far north as Baltimore Harbor.

Because of the trout's weak mouth membranes, you'll have to take special measures in the way you hook, fight, and land these fish. For starters, remember that if you hook trout, you will lose some. Don't take it personally. At times, usually when jigging in deep water, you'll have five hits for each solid hook-up. Since their mouths tear so easily, you need to make sure you're fishing with a light drag. Don't over-pressure a weakfish or the hook will pull every time. Similarly, don't try to slam it home when you set the hook; just use a smooth, authoritative motion. Once the fish is on don't jerk the rod tip, and prepare a net well before it reaches the surface. Don't even bother trying to lift a trout out of the water and swing it onto the boat; you may as well just shake your rod until the fish falls off the hook.

If you get the fish to the surface and for whatever reason a net isn't ready, you're in trouble. Let the line go slack, and the fish will fall off the hook. Lift its head out of the water, and the fish will fall off the hook. The best way to handle this situation is to swing your rod tip fore or aft and force the fish to swim back and forth at the surface, maintaining tension, until it can be landed. Of course, in order for this to be a problem, you'll have to hook up with some weakfish, first. Use these tips to get them on the end of your line.

1. Trout like holding in deep water, more so than any other Chesapeake Bay sportfish. Often, you'll locate schools of fish holding in 60', 80' or even 100' of water. This makes jigging for them tough, but you can make it easier by rigging up at least one of your jigging rods with a superline. The lack of stretch and better water-cutting properties allow you to use half as much weight to get down deep, and stay there. Berkley Fireline is my favorite for

deep water jigging, but there are a half-dozen reputable brands out there you can try.

2. Trout are just about the only fish on the Bay that sometimes prefer a nonmoving bait. Dead-sticking—dropping your jig or lure into the strike zone, putting your rod into a holder, and leaving it there until a fish is on—can be deadly on trout. This isn't the norm, but it happens often enough that you should try dead-sticking whenever there are trout around but they don't seem to be eating your baits.

3. Trout school seasonally. Early in the year much of the Bay will see a spring run of seatrout, and they will be traveling in small pods. This is when you try to catch one or two, then move on and try to relocate the pod, or hunt for another pod. In the summer, large numbers of these fish will scatter out into the tributaries and locating schools can become very difficult, if not impossible. This is when you either have to peck them out one at a time, or focus on night fishing. In the fall the trout will stack up again, but not in pods—these fish will form huge schools. This is when you can park on top of 'em, and load up.

4. Trout are ambitious eaters and will try to eat a bait half their size. If you're over a big mass of trout but keep catching undersized fish, don't be afraid to swap up to a lure that seems ridiculously large. A 6" long, 6 oz jigging spoon, for example, is not out of the question when catching barely legal trout.

5. Match the hatch. Weakfish will show a strong, sometimes overwhelming nature to eat only the lures or bait that imitates their prey du jour. When they are feeding on three inch bay anchovies, for example, that big spoon will often go untouched. Switch to a three inch feather jig, however, and you might just load the cooler.

6. Look for caterpillar-like markings right against the bottom on your fishfinder. For some reason, maybe the way that trout form schools or their body density, they appear on most quality fishfinders as caterpillars crawling across the bottom. Often, the caterpillar will be connected or partially connected to the bottom. A caterpillar-like shape that extends 5–10 ft off the bottom indicates a nice solid mass of trout.

7. During the summer and early in the fall, you'll often find trout on the fishfinder but they won't touch a bait or lure, regardless of the tidal period. When this happens, return to the very same spot after dark and set up to night fish. During this time period, the weakfish will often feed exclusively or nearly exclusively after dark.

8. In the early spring when trout first make a showing in the Bay, they'll be organized in fairly small, tight pods. Don't spend a lot of

time drifting along, or focusing on an edge or hump. Instead, spend your time milling around with a close eye on the fishfinder. Drop only when you're sure your baits are going to fall right on top of the fish. You'll spend more time hunting and less fishing, but in the long run, you'll catch more fish.

9. When you're catching a lot of undersized fish from water over 35' deep, switch tactics or locations. From depths this great, most of the fish you pull up won't have time to pressurize, and their belly will be popping out of their mouth. Scientists tell us that some of these fish will survive, but many don't. Instead of throwing a lot of soon-to-be dead fish over the side, make a change.

10. Be very gentle when handling trout you plan on releasing. Their bodies are as delicate as their mouths are, and if you squeeze them slightly when removing the hook, it's pretty certain the fish will have some kind of internal damage.

YELLOW PERCH, WHITE PERCH, AND SPOT

While yellow "neds," which are also called ring perch, may not be the most glamorous fish in the Chesapeake, they certainly rank among the tastiest. Unfortunately, they are also rather vulnerable to pollution caused by runoff, and in some cases, have been wiped out of entire watersheds. During the construction of I-97 between Baltimore and Annapolis, for example, when great amounts of runoff entered the Magothy, Severn and South Rivers, the yellow perch populations there took a nose-dive. It wasn't until the late '90s that they began to bounce back, and even today, their numbers are so depressed that the state has seen fit to enforce a ban on keeping those caught from these rivers. Luckily, there are still plenty of perch around in other watersheds and hopefully, they'll be back in good numbers in those tributaries they have fared poorly in.

Yellow perch are one of the most abundant and popular recreationally caught fish in the United States. They range through all 50 states and well into Canada, and can be caught during all seasons, in all temperature ranges. In fact, these fish are one of the better bets for ice fishermen, as well as springtime shoreline anglers. The vast majority of the perch caught in the Chesapeake region, however, are taken during the spawning run. From early March through April (the exact duration of the spawn depends on weather conditions) perch swarm up the tributaries into small feeder creeks and streams, where they densely populate holes and river bends. This is when it's possible to catch bucket-loads of yellow neds.

What many Bay area anglers do not realize is that yellow perch can be located staging just downstream of these spawning areas, bunched in tight schools, from early or mid-January through the spawn. During the winter months when fishing pressure is low and the perch stick tight to specific pre-spawn spots, it's possible to experience non-stop action. Locating the pre-spawn staging area in any given creek or river is not too tough. The key is to find the transition zone between open river water and marshland creek. Anywhere that a 25' or 30' across creek with some freshwater flow into it

Perch keep Chesapeake anglers busy during the winter months.

meets with an open river, you'll be able to find such spots. Once you locate the junction of creek and river, look for major bends in the creek. The outside of each bend is usually scoured by the current and will have a hole in it significantly deeper than the surrounding water. The first bend in any given creek is usually, though not always, the best. Any hole between 10 and 30' deep might hold pre-spawn perch, but the ideal is in the 18' to 22' range. The holes on each bend are usually deeper closer to the mouth of the creek and become smaller and smaller as you work your way upriver. These creek holes are where the yellow perch will lay in wait much of the winter before moving up for the spring spawning run. One of the best, most easily recognizable examples of such an area is Watts Creek, off the Choptank River (see MER 13, 14.) Find this type of spot, and you'll find winter yellow perch.

Most yellow perch range between 6" and 12", but occasionally, fish over a pound are caught. The Maryland record is 2 lb 3 oz, and I have seen my wife catch and release heavier perch; there's a new state record out there, somewhere. If you want to beat the IGFA's best, however, you'll have to top 4 lb 3 oz. Usually, the fat, heavy fish are females laden with roe. When fishing for yellow perch during the spawning run, it's best to let these fatties go and keep the long, slender males for food.

The white perch is a very popular, good eating panfish. Unlike yellow perch, however, white perch are actually a member of the bass family. Observant anglers will note that although it is shorter, stockier, and lacks stripes, the white perch is notably similar to striped bass in body shape and taste.

According to state records the largest white perch ever pulled from the Chesapeake was a hair under 3 lb, but the IGFA lists one just over 3 lb. Most perch caught in the Bay region range between 6" and 12", and any perch over a pound is a fish to be proud of. Unlike yellow perch, whites tend to have a diet that is more varied and depends less on tiny finfish. Grass shrimp, scuds, worms, and small shellfish are some white perch favorites.

The white perch has a spawning run similar in nature to the yellow perch, with a few important differences. First, it usually occurs a few weeks later than the peak of the yellow perch run. Most years there are a couple of weeks during which the tail end of the yellow run and the beginning of the white run overlap, after which, the white perch run peaks. Secondly, males always seem to arrive in large numbers before the females. Prior to the overlapping weeks most of the white perch caught in the headwaters will be smallish males.

One of the nice things about white perch is that they are not nearly as tidal-sensitive as yellows. Generally speaking, if they are in the area you're fishing, you will catch them. This makes white perch a great fish to target when you're fishing with kids, since it almost always ensures fast action. Turn them on to perch-jerking with these tips.

1. Yellow perch are very tidal-sensitive. You can sit in the exact same spot for hours on end without a nibble, and without changing baits, then suddenly as the tide shifts, load the boat. When you believe you have located fish in good numbers but aren't getting any bites, it's best to wait for a change in the tide before giving up on the spot. Or, you may want to mark the spot and return to it later in the day, after a tide change. White perch, however, usually bite throughout the tidal ranges.

2. Yellow perch can be caught on dozens of different baits and lures. Grubs, spinners, grass shrimp, night crawlers, peeler crab, the list goes on and on practically forever. But when it comes to catching perch in relatively deep holes and cuts 18' and over, nothing beats a bullhead minnow hooked through the lips on a simple old top-and-bottom rig. It seems strange, but after years of experimenting I always come back to this simple combination, and it always outproduces all the other options.

3. Look to find the best perch action in holes and channels during a falling or low tide. Also, expect these fish to be active at or near the

bottom. But when a flood or rising tide comes, shift tactics and try fishing the shallows. Often, yellow perch will move from deep holes up onto mud flats just a couple of feet deep during the flood.

In this situation, tiny ½" long mud crabs are usually the best bait (grass shrimp also work well during this period). Of course, mud crabs can't be purchased at the bait shop. But during the low tide you can often scoop them up along muddy shorelines, by turning over rocks and shells in a few inches of water. Sometimes, you'll even see these little crabs scampering along the shoreline. Or, after catching a fish or two in the shallows, gut one and empty its stomach; often, you'll find a half-dozen mud crabs inside.

4. Post-spawn, during much of the summer, and late in the fall, both yellow and white perch can often be located in the same areas as you catch pickerel; over weedbeds in coves and creeks off the major rivers. It will take different tactics, however, to catch them in these conditions. Small lures excel in this situation. Two and three-inch grub tails, shad darts dressed with Power Wigglers, spinners, and Beetle spins are good producers.

When fishing small lures during these times of year, don't go for the slow and steady approach. Perch like fast, erratic retrieves and will strike like they mean it. Jerk your rod tip strongly and often and keep that lure darting all over the place.

5. Never underestimate the ability of a yellow perch to eat a large bait. Giant bull minnow five inches long will be eaten by yellow perch barely six or seven inches with regularity, especially during the pre-spawn months. In fact, when fishing in the holes during January and February, bait up with the largest bullhead you can find in the bucket each and every time. Interestingly, this trait carries through to freshwater during cold weather, as well. Fishing large shiner on the bottom for stripers or walleye in Deep Creek, Liberty, Lock Raven, or Piney Run will inevitably produce a perch or two, even though the baits look too big for a perch to handle.

6. Watch the dorsal fins when taking perch off the hook. They are like a series of small daggers, and if you simply grab the fish, you'll end up bleeding. But that's not the only weapon these little fish pack. Their gill plates are also incredibly sharp, and if your hand moves across them from the tail to head direction, they will cut you.

7. When bait fishing for perch, it's best to set the hook fairly quickly. Perch tend to suck a bait right down, and if you give it a three or five-count before setting the hook, many of the fish you catch will be gut-hooked. Since a large proportion of the perch caught are usually throw-backs, this can result in a lot of dead fish.

8. On a slack tide, look for perch to hold on structure. Specifically, sunken trees or other wood obstructions will be holding the fish. Once the tide is moving again, they often won't stick too close to the timber.

   Undercut banks with fallen timber is one of the best places to locate yellow perch on a dead tide. These are tough areas to fish—bottom rigs will snag instantly, and bobbers will usually float right into branches if you've casted them close enough to get a bite. In this situation, a small jig tipped with a minnow is usually the best bet. Cast and retrieve it, however, and you're still in for a lot of snags. Instead, control your drift so your boat moves along the edges of the branches, just two or three feet away. Then strip eight or nine feet of line out, hold your rod tip up high, and swing your minnow/jig combo out over the branches. Drop it in between the thick cover and hold it there for as long as possible. When you move enough that you think you may be in danger of snagging the branches—or when you feel a fish on the end of the line—pull it out and re-position your boat for another shot.

9. If you're ice fishing on a Bay tributary in the hopes of catching a perch, try tying a fly about a foot up from your lure or bait. Perch under the ice can become finicky, and in this case they will often move up close to investigate a bait without eating it. Often, however, they'll decide to inhale a tiny fly.

10. Tidewater yellow perch sometimes have worm-like parasites living in the meat. Don't worry too much about these. They are easily spotted and cut out of the fillets and can't live in humans anyway. Try breading and frying yellow perch fillets, and you won't be disappointed.

You'll catch spot in many of the same places with many of the same baits as white perch, during the warm months of the year. One of the smallest gamefish in the Bay, spot are also one of the most underrated. Pound for pound nothing fights harder than spot, they make both excellent food and excellent bait for almost any predator that swims in the Bay, and they usually travel in schools large enough that you can enjoy hand-over-fist action.

The smallest record in the books belongs to spot, at 2 lb 6 oz, and the world record stands at just 1 lb. (Up until a few years ago, no one had bothered to submit a record for spot to the IGFA. Since then, no one's bothered to top it!) Yet these little bottom feeders feel twice their size on the end of the line. They are more and more plentiful as you move south along the Bay, but in some years, are present in large numbers all the way up to the Pool's Island area.

Spot are an extremely cyclical fish, due to their relatively short lifespan. They seem to run in three year cycles, with their numbers going from thick to mild to thin then back to thick again. Every five to six years the Bay will see a run of "jumbo spot" in the 2 lb range, which are excellent eating fish. Here are a few tips to help you catch more of these little gamesters.

1. When it comes to spot, the bait to use is bloodworms, bloodworms, and bloodworms. Spot can smell out small bits with no problem, and a couple of bloodworms is all you need to load up on them. Use number six or eight hooks and cut the worm into one-inch segments, then thread them onto your hooks.

2. Looking at a spot you can clearly see the down-turned nature of its mouth. The shape of their mouth assists spot in bottom feeding, and it is rare to catch one with your bait more than a foot or two off the bottom. When fishing with a top-and-bottom rig, in fact, you will catch spot on the bottom hook three or four to one over the top hook. Accordingly, thread your best baits onto the bottom hook.

3. When live-baiting with spot, consider hooking them through the back, just behind the dorsal fin, regardless of where you are placing the bait in the water column (remember, lip-hooked fish will swim into the current while back-hooked fish are forced to swim down.) For some reason, spot seem to live much longer when hooked this way.

4. Spot have a very distinctive strike that feels like a jackhammer on the end of your line. When you feel this type of strike set the hook right away, as spot usually eat a bait quickly and without hesitation.

5. If you run out of bloodworms, spot gut is an excellent spot bait. Gross, but true: behead and gut a fresh caught spot, and take out the entrails. Locate the intestines, and cut them free. Run them between your fingers to squeeze out the goo inside, then thread the intestine on your hook just as you would a bloodworm.

6. If you're pier fishing, you can bring in the spot by pseudo-chumming. Here's the drill: get a landing net, boat hook, or other strong item on a long handle. Walk up and down the pier, to each piling, and rub the end of your device against the barnacles growing on the piling. Smash as many as possible and allow them to fall to the bottom. In about half an hour, you'll often find the area loaded with spot that have moved in to feed on the barnacle bits.

ABOUT THE AUTHOR

L enny Rudow is Senior Technical Editor and Fishing Editor for *Boating Magazine,* the world's largest power boating magazine, and is a regular contributor to fishing magazines nationwide including *The Fisherman, Texas Fish & Game,* and *Sport Fishing.* His first cast was made at age three in Stony Creek, and Rudow has fished the Chesapeake avidly ever since.

*More Chesapeake books from
Cornell Maritime Press and
Tidewater Publishers*

Birds & Marshes of the Chesapeake Bay Country
Brooke Meanley
ISBN 10: 0-87033-207-4   ISBN 13: 978-0-87033-207-4

Boater's Medical Companion
Robert S. Gould, M.D.
ISBN 10: 0-87033-402-6   ISBN 13: 978-0-87033-402-3

Boater's Weather Guide
Margaret Williams
ISBN 10: 0-87033-417-4   ISBN 13: 978-0-87033-417-7

Chesapeake Almanac: Following the Bay through the Seasons
John Page Williams, Jr.
ISBN 10: 0-87033-449-2   ISBN 13: 978-0-87033-449-8

Chesapeake Bay: Nature of the Estuary, A Field Guide
Christopher P. White
ISBN 10: 0-87033-351-8   ISBN 13: 978-0-87033-351-4

Chesapeake Wildlife: Stories of Survival and Loss
Pat Vojtech
ISBN 10: 0-87033-536-7   ISBN 13: 978-0-87033-536-5

Exploring the Chesapeake in Small Boats
John Page Williams, Jr.
ISBN 10: 0-87033-429-8   ISBN 13: 978-0-87033-429-0

Fiberglass Repair: Polyester or Epoxy
David and Zora Aiken
ISBN 10: 0-87033-567-7   ISBN 13: 978-0-87033-567-9

Gunning for Sea Ducks
George Howard Gillelan
ISBN 10: 0-87033-386-0   ISBN 13: 978-0-87033-386-6

Harvesting the Chesapeake
Larry S. Chowning
ISBN 10: 0-87033-469-7   ISBN 13: 978-0-87033-469-6

Lighting the Bay: Tales of Chesapeake Lighthouses
Pat Vojtech
ISBN 10: 0-87033-466-2   ISBN 978-0-87033-466-5

Naturalist on the Nanticoke: The Natural History of a River on Maryland's Eastern Shore
Robert A. Hedeen
ISBN 10: 0-87033-467-0   ISBN 13: 978-0-87033-467-2

Nautical Etiquette and Customs
Lindsay Lord
ISBN 10: 0-87033-356-9   ISBN 13: 978-0-87033-356-9

Nautical Rules of the Road
B. A. Farnsworth and Larry C. Young
ISBN 10: 0-87033-408-5   ISBN 13: 978-0-87033-408-5

Outlaw Gunner, The
Harry M. Walsh
ISBN 10: 0-87033-162-0   ISBN 13: 978-0-87033-162-6

Patapsco, The
Paul J. Travers
ISBN 10: 0-87033-400-X   ISBN 13: 978-0-87033-400-9

Rivers of the Eastern Shore: Seventeen Maryland Rivers
Hulbert Footner
ISBN 10: 0-87033-092-6   ISBN 13: 978-0-87033-092-6

Shorebirds
John M. Levinson, Somers G. Headley
ISBN 10: 0-87033-424-7   ISBN 13: 978-0-87033-424-5

Watermen of the Chesapeake Bay, The
John Hurt Whitehead III
ISBN 10: 0-87033-374-7   ISBN 13: 978-0-87033-374-3